CHRISTOPHER CATHER
and Fellow of the Royal Historical Society. With degrees in
History from Oxford and Cambridge universities, and a PhD
in Middle Eastern History from the University of East Anglia,
he is currently a freelance lecturer at Cambridge University
and the University of Richmond, Virginia, where he has
taught courses on Middle Eastern History. He also teaches
History at the Cambridge-based INSTEP course, an affiliated
overseas programme of American institutions. His books
include *Winston's Folly*, which was followed by articles in the
Sunday Times on Iraq, and television and radio appearances in
the UK and USA. He divides his time between Cambridge,
England, and Richmond, Virginia.

Other titles in the series

A BRIEF HISTORY OF

THE
MIDDLE EAST

CHRISTOPHER CATHERWOOD

RUNNING PRESS
PHILADELPHIA · LONDON

ROBINSON

First published in the UK by Robinson,
an imprint of Constable & Robinson, 2006

This revised edition published in the UK by Robinson, 2011

3 5 7 9 10 8 6 4 2

A CIP catalogue record for this book
is available from the British Library.

ISBN 978-1-84901-508-0

Robinson
An imprint of
Little, Brown Book Group
Carmelite House
50 Victoria Embankment
London EC4Y 0DZ

An Hachette UK Company

www.hachette.co.uk
www.littlebrown.co.uk

First Published in the United States in 2011 by Running Press Book Publishers
A member of the Perseus Books Group

Books published by Running Press are available at special discounts for bulk purchases
in the United States by corporations, institutions and other organizations. For more
information, please contact the Special Markets Department at the Perseus Books Group,
2300 Chestnut Street, Suite 200, Philadelphia, PA 19103, or call
(800) 810-4145, ext. 5000, or email special.markets@perseusbooks.com.

US Library of Congress Control number: 2010928998
US ISBN: 978-0-7624-4102-0

10 9 8 7 6 5 4 3 2 1

Digit on the right indicates the number of this printing

Running Press Book Publishers
2300 Chestnut Street
Philadelphia, PA 19103-4371

Visit us on the web!
www.runningpress.com

Typeset by Saxon Graphics Ltd, Derby
Printed and bound in Great Britain by CPI Group (UK) Ltd., Croydon CR0 4YY

Papers used by Robinson are from well-managed forests and other responsible sources

MIX
Paper from
responsible sources
FSC® C104740

To god-daughters Becca,
Charlotte and Rosie, Alicia, and Amalie.
And to the world's best godmother,
my wonderful wife Paulette.

CONTENTS

PREFACE TO THE SECOND EDITION

The Middle East is never out of the news. Since I wrote the first edition of this book in 2005, there has been an invasion of Lebanon by Israel, followed by a similar incursion by Israeli defence forces into Gaza. The Iranian regime has held an election whose legitimacy has been questioned, and Iranian security forces have killed protesting civilians in the streets in a way that echoes the murder of demonstrators under the Shah back in 1978–9. Iran has also ratcheted up the stakes on the issue of nuclear weapons, and the possibility of a nuclear arms race in the Middle East has now become a reality.

As I write the new edition in mid-2010, Israeli commandos are intercepting six ships carrying aid to the blockaded Palestinians in Gaza. Several people in the flotilla died: Israel accuses them of being extremist-linked Muslims out for martyrdom, whereas their defenders describe them as innocent humanitarians murdered by trigger-happy soldiers. Either way, commentators in British and American journals and news-papers suggest Israel has lost out in terms of publicity and cred-ibility, and Iran has gained mightily in prestige throughout the Muslim world and in the Middle East in particular. To others, though, Israel is the besieged nation, a beacon of democracy surrounded by dictatorships, with the hard-line persecuting Ayatollahs of Iran becoming an increasing threat to world peace.

In other words, not only do events unfold in the region by the day, but the decisions and actions of the key players remain as deeply controversial and divisive as ever. Since so much of what happens is linked to how people in the second decade of the twenty-first century see the past – from the Holocaust in the 1940s to events and battles dating back in the seventh century, nearly 1,400 years ago but like yesterday to millions in the Middle East – an understanding of history is as vital to comprehending today's news headlines as it has ever been. The task of this book continues.

Before we even begin a history of the Middle East, we ought first to define our terms.

The very expression 'Middle East' is, as commentators rightly point out, a Eurocentric or certainly a Western term. The original term was Near East, but even that does not help us very much. For, if we look at a map, the area is only in the east if you look at it from Europe or the USA. Seen from China, for instance, it is in the west. (The Chinese, for example, call themselves the Middle Kingdom, which might be an accurate reflection of how the Chinese have seen themselves historically, but does not provide geographic accuracy.) Strictly speaking, therefore, it might be better to call it something like south-west Asia.

Historically other terms existed before Near East or Middle East. These have included the Levant (as the sun rises there), the Orient or, if we look just at the region of Iraq where much of the Hebrew Scriptures are situated, the Fertile Crescent.

This does not take us much further, however. The Islamic conquests in the seventh century initiated the Golden Age of the Caliphates – roughly the seventh to the thirteenth centuries – and placed a vast swathe of territory under the control of the new Muslim Caliphs stretching from Spain and Morocco on the Atlantic eastwards to the borders of the Hindu Kush in what is now Pakistan. Anatolia also faced increasing Muslim inroads as Byzantine power waned. This entire region was profoundly and permanently altered by Islamic culture, and remains strongly Muslim to this day. Ethnic Arabs live in the northern part of Africa as well as the ancient Fertile Crescent and the Arabian Peninsula, and, for over seven centuries, they ruled over an Empire that included parts of Spain. Similarly the Turks, whose origins are in Central Asia, conquered not only the Arab heartland but much of south-eastern Europe as well, holding sway over these areas for over 500 years.

As a consequence, to use the newer, and geographically more precise term, south-west Asia, would be considerably to curtail what we can look at in this book. For one can argue, historically, that large areas of both Spain and the Balkans, to take but two examples, were at times politically and culturally very much an integral part of a broad Islamic civilization that stretched for thousands of miles beyond the traditional confines of the term 'Middle East'.

This therefore begs the original question – what exactly comprises the Middle East? In this book I have adopted a pragmatic approach, starting off with the region that we think of as the Middle East today, since that is the region where most of the action I will describe took place, but stretching well beyond those borders when necessity dictates a change of geographic emphasis. Therefore I include Egypt; what we now call Israel, Palestine, Syria, Lebanon, Iraq and Iran; the countries of the Arabian Peninsula, including those of the Persian Gulf; and Turkey, even though that did not become mainly Islamic until the Middle Ages. But I am leaving out the Caucasus (traditionally for some reason thought of as part of Europe); the Sudan (although the northern part of that is Muslim); Northern Africa beyond Egypt; and Islamic Central Asia, though I will refer both to these and the peripheral lands – Spain, the Maghreb, the Balkans – when historically necessary.

In ancient times, the empires within the central Middle East region were centred on the Fertile Crescent and Egypt, and expanded at their peaks westwards to Greece and eastwards to Afghanistan. In Roman times, that empire controlled northern Africa and much of the Middle East, including Anatolia, but not the territory ruled by the Seleucid, Parthian and then Sassanid Empires in what is roughly today's Iran.

The extent of Islamic rule in the Golden Age of the Caliphates has already been mentioned above, while the Ottoman Turks for their part controlled what we call the geographical Middle East, much of northern Africa and large swathes of South-East Europe, as far as Hungary. But they were never able to conquer what we now call Iran, although they did rule the Crimea for a long while.

Historically, the Middle East has also been lumped together, with the rest of Asia, and called the Orient. This nomenclature has become controversial, especially since the late Palestinian Christian-American writer Edward Said wrote a book called

Orientalism. In this he rightly attacked the condescending way in which many in the West have looked down upon the peoples living in this vast area, especially its central, Middle Eastern, component. While perhaps unfair on some of his critics, the book and Said's subsequent strictures did draw attention to the need to avoid writing biased history, and the expression 'Orient', which is surely far too broad, has thankfully gone out of favour. Thanks to television, we no longer regard the region as mysterious or exotic, filled with snake charmers and harems.

We do, however, as the eminent Pakistani social anthropologist and peace campaigner Akbar Ahmed reminds us in *Islam Under Siege*, still tend to regard the area's main religion, Islam, as being innately violent, a myth that will be disproved throughout the course of this book.

(In any case, only a very small percentage of the world's Muslims live in the region, with the biggest Muslim-inhabited nations being India, Indonesia and Pakistan, none of which is either Arabic or in the Middle East.)

So while some misconceptions and stereotypes are thankfully behind us, others have reared their ugly heads, especially after the attacks on the USA in 2001 and those in Europe in the years following.

As we will see in the Introduction, it is difficult, when looking at the entire history of the region, over thousands of years, to consider everything. Much of Assyrian, Babylonian and Egyptian culture is fascinating. Anyone who has been to the Middle East, or seen the astonishing artefacts in museums in cities such as Berlin, London or New York (where there is an entire temple to visit), will understand the lasting appeal of these ancient civilizations.

However, in order to draw a line, I have considered them mainly in the light of what affects us now and, in particular, the rise of the three great, and still very extant, Middle Eastern monotheistic religions: Judaism, Christianity and Islam. No one worships Ra or Mithras today. However, Zoroastrianism is regarded by many as having influenced the existing mono-theistic faiths, and so where the past does impinge upon the present, I have given such faiths full due. Those wanting to know more about Abu Simbel or the Hanging Gardens of Babylon, to take just two of the justly famous relics of the past, will need to read elsewhere, and I have given due details in the bibliography.

Events in the Middle East are changing all the time. They will probably have changed by the time that you read this. But that all goes to show what a vitally important part of the world it remains, and why it is so fascinating to study. Furthermore, since my main aim is to show how we in the West owe so much to the region, that basic truth still holds, however much might have changed politically in the area now. We remain as much the intellectual and cultural descendants of the great discoveries of the Middle East as we have always been.

ORTHOGRAPHIC NOTE AND NOTE FOR SPECIALISTS

Is it Usama bin Ladin or Osama bin Laden? Muhammad or Mahommed? (Or even Mehmet?) Qur'an? Koran? Quran? Or perhaps Coran?

Spelling Arabic words is an orthographer's nightmare, since there is no fixed system of transliteration. Arabic words are consonants only, with the vowels as diacritical marks. So each book, newspaper or journal has its own way of spelling.

In this book I have tried to follow one consistent spelling throughout. It may or may not be the one with which you are familiar. But whatever the spelling, the people described are the same.

Secondly, this is a book for the general reader with an interest in the Middle East. It is therefore an overview and cannot be exhaustive, for reasons given in the Preface. I hope that specialists will understand.

Sometimes, too, for example, I have quoted from or been inspired by a single author more than once in the same chapter. As this book has no footnotes, I have not always been able to show, for instance, that the insights of Professors X or Y have been useful twice, or even three times in formulating my own views. Readers would probably find endless references in the text along the lines of 'as Bernard Lewis reminds us' rather repetitious.

DATES

BC and AD are used in this book, as they will be more familiar to most readers than the more neutral BCE and CE, which stand for the more religiously neutral terms Before Common Era and Common Era respectively.

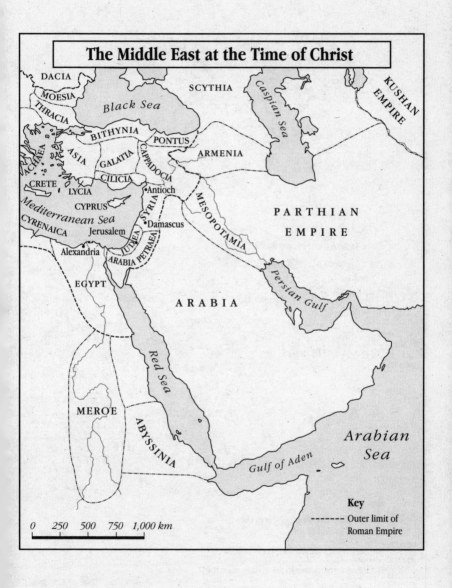

The Middle East at the Time of Christ

DACIA
MOESIA
THRACIA
Black Sea
SCYTHIA
Caspian Sea
KUSHAN EMPIRE

ACHAEA
BITHYNIA
ASIA
GALATIA
PONTUS
CAPPADOCIA
ARMENIA

CRETE
LYCIA
CILICIA
CYPRUS
Antioch
SYRIA
MESOPOTAMIA
PARTHIAN EMPIRE

Mediterranean Sea
CYRENAICA
Jerusalem
Damascus
JUDEA
ARABIA PETRAEA

Alexandria

EGYPT
ARABIA
Persian Gulf

Red Sea

MEROE
ABYSSINIA
Gulf of Aden
Arabian Sea

0   250   500   750   1,000 km

Key
- - - - - Outer limit of Roman Empire

The Height of the Abbasid and Fatimid Caliphates, AD 800–1000

KHAZAR EMPIRE

•Kashgar

R. Syr Darya

Aral Sea

QARAKHANIDS

TRANSOXIANA

KASHMIR

KHWARIZM

Samarkand

Bukhara

Urgench

Balkh

R. Amu Darya

Hindu Kush Mountains

Lahore

PUNJAB

•Itil

•Kabul

•Multan

Caspian Sea

Merv

Ghazni

GHAZNAVIDS

Caucasus Mountains

Derbent

Baku

AFGHANISTAN

R. Indus

Tiflis

Ardabil

•Tus

•Herat

SEISTAN

SIND

Trebizond

Tabriz

Nishapur

Zaranj•

Daybul

KHURASAN

A

•Rai

AZERBAIJAN

PERSIA

Amid

R. Tigris

Nisibin

Mosul

Hamadan

•Isfahan

Tiz

Aleppo

JEZIRA

IRAQ

Yazd

Ormuz

Antioch

R. Euphrates

Baghdad

•Shiraz

atakia

SYRIA

Basra

Persian Gulf

Muscat

Tripoli

Homs

Kufa

OMAN

Beirut

•Damascus

BAHRAIN

Acre

PALESTINE

•Jerusalem

A R A B I A

airo

HEJAZ

Asyut

•Medina

EGYPT

Red Sea

•Jeddah

•Mecca

Aydhab

Sana

YEMEN

Hodeida

Zabid

R. Nile

Taizz

Aden

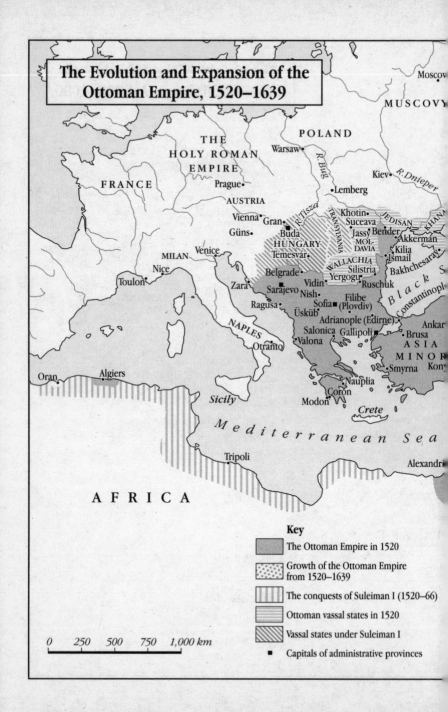

The Evolution and Expansion of the Ottoman Empire, 1520–1639

Moscow

MUSCOVY

THE HOLY ROMAN EMPIRE

FRANCE

POLAND

Warsaw

Prague

Kiev

R. Dnieper

R. Bug

Lemberg

AUSTRIA

Vienna • Gran

Khotin

Suceava

TRANSYLVANIA

JEDISAN

Bender

Güns

Buda

HUNGARY

Temesvár

R. Tisza

Jassy

MOLDAVIA

Akkerman

Kilia

MILAN

Venice

Nice

WALLACHIA

Silistria

Ismail

Bakhchesaray

Toulon

Zara

Belgrade

Vidin

Yergogu

Ruschuk

Black S

Sarajevo

Nish

Sofia

Filibe (Plovdiv)

Constantinopl

Ragusa

Üsküb

Adrianople (Edirne)

NAPLES

Salonica

Gallipoli

Ankar

Otranto

Valona

Brusa

ASIA MINOR

Algiers

Oran

Nauplia

Smyrna

Kon

Sicily

Coron

Modon

Crete

M e d i t e r r a n e a n   S e a

Tripoli

Alexandri

AFRICA

Key

The Ottoman Empire in 1520

Growth of the Ottoman Empire from 1520–1639

The conquests of Suleiman I (1520–66)

Ottoman vassal states in 1520

Vassal states under Suleiman I

■ Capitals of administrative provinces

0   250   500   750   1,000 km

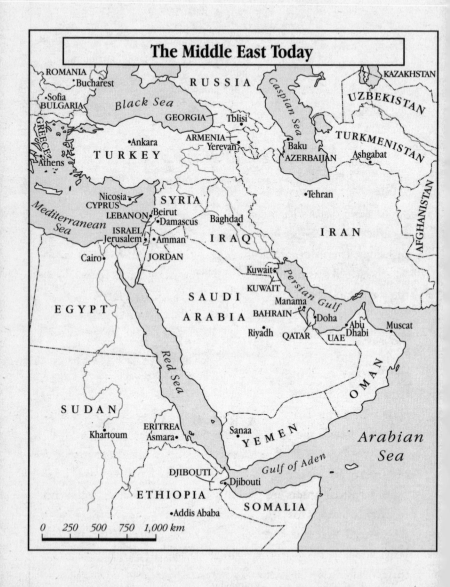

The Middle East Today

ROMANIA
•Bucharest
RUSSIA
KAZAKHSTAN
•Sofia
BULGARIA
Black Sea
Caspian Sea
UZBEKISTAN
GEORGIA
•Tblisi
GREECE
•Athens
Ankara
ARMENIA
Yerevan
Baku
AZERBAIJAN
TURKMENISTAN
•Ashgabat
TURKEY
Mediterranean Sea
Nicosia
CYPRUS
SYRIA
•Tehran
IRAN
AFGHANISTAN
LEBANON•
Beirut
•Damascus
Baghdad
ISRAEL
Jerusalem•
•Amman
IRAQ
Cairo•
JORDAN
Kuwait
KUWAIT
Persian Gulf
EGYPT
SAUDI
ARABIA
Manama
BAHRAIN
Doha
QATAR
UAE
Abu
Dhabi
Muscat
Riyadh
Red Sea
OMAN
SUDAN
ERITREA
Asmara•
Sanaa
YEMEN
Arabian
Sea
Khartoum•
DJIBOUTI
Djibouti•
Gulf of Aden
ETHIOPIA
•Addis Ababa
SOMALIA

0   250   500   750   1,000 km

INTRODUCTION

A famous history, *The Middle East* by Bernard Lewis, begins in a typical Near Eastern cafe. Although the work and erudition of Lewis, the internationally acknowledged elder statesman of Islamic studies, is incomparable, I am going to start somewhere different, and perhaps surprising. I will commence not in an Arab- or Turkish-speaking country, but where I am writing this: Cambridge, England.

Let's eavesdrop on a class in the Mathematics Faculty. The students are studying algebra, the form of mathematical calculation made famous by outstanding Arabic scholars centuries ago, when my British ancestors were living in wattle huts, wearing woad, and probably unable to read or write.

Down the road is one of the most illustrious astronomical observatories in the world, where Nobel prizes have been won. Its astronomers are studying the star Aldebaran, following in the footsteps of the illustrious Arab astronomers who discovered that star and countless others, again, hundreds of years ago. Nearby are the numerous high-technology laboratories that make up what locals jocularly describe as 'Silicon

Fen', the European end of the better-known Silicon Valley in California, and a technology cluster in which Bill Gates and Microsoft have invested millions. For all the complex machines to work, each one needs algorithms, another mathematical term which, like the others, is firmly Arabic in origin.

On Sundays, well over 1,000, from countries all over the world – Britain, China, Nigeria, Singapore, Uganda, Brazil, the USA – are to be found in church worshipping Jesus Christ, born in the Middle East around 2,000 years ago. Cambridge also has a Jewish Society, together with a synagogue for followers of a faith that began in the Middle East many centuries earlier and is the first great surviving monotheistic religion anywhere in the world, as well as an Islamic Society – not all of whose members have Middle Eastern or South Asian ancestry, since there are now increasing converts from people of European origin – and a mosque. These Muslims are followers of the third major monotheistic religion to arise from the Middle East, Islam.

Mathematics, stellar astronomy, computer technology, Christianity and Judaism, and then Islam – all have their origins in the Middle East.

Read a book on the history of the Middle East today and the odds are that you will be reading about the decline of a once great region that has been rapidly overtaken by the West. Historically, there is a powerful case for this argument. Ever since the Ottoman Empire failed to capture Vienna in 1683 the world of Islam has grown less powerful, militarily, politically and economically, than the West. In the twentieth century the Ottoman Empire, the one remaining Islamic superpower, was defeated, and large swathes of the Middle

East were placed under direct Western rule. The glory of the Orient has long since departed.

But against this misleading way of looking at Middle Eastern history I want to contend something different. From mathematics to the predominant Western religion, Christianity, we live in a truly global civilization that was created by people living in the Middle East; Abraham, the Pharaohs, Jesus Christ, Avicenna and Averröes all come from this area. Thus rather than looking at a triumphant West, and a stagnant, fallen Middle East, today's twenty-first-century Western world owes everything to its intellectual origins in the Middle East.

Although much of the content that follows should be historically obvious, Middle Eastern history is filled with minefields, not because of what actually happened in the past, but because of how people read back the present into the past. We will see this more frequently as we get nearer our own time, especially when we consider the fall of the great Muslim superpower, the Ottoman Empire, in 1918. We still live with the consequences of that defeat, even in the twenty-first century. Feelings run more than deep, and history becomes not so much an objective study but a political football, designed to legitimate current feelings and wrongs. Did the British betray their Arab allies? Did the Jewish people have a legitimate right to return to the Middle East, and in such numbers?

The furore engendered by these controversies is obvious, but makes writing a history of the Middle East very difficult. To take one example: some may find my decision to look at the other two Abrahamic faiths – Judaism and Christianity – rather than what most other works do and concentrate on Islam only, puzzling. But when one remembers that Islam proclaims itself a fulfilment of Judaism and Christianity, then the relevance of seeing how monotheism arose becomes clear.

As a result of my interaction both as a historian and as a concerned lay person with Christians, Jews and Muslims, I have had the enormous privilege of being asked to be involved, albeit in a small way, in a very courageous three-faith dialogue. This was established after 2001 in the USA, by the Muslim Akbar Ahmed, the distinguished Islamic scholar and the Jewish Judaea Pearl, the father of murdered Jewish *Wall Street Journal* writer Daniel Pearl.

I hope that further understanding of Middle Eastern history causes peace rather than strife, and that knowledge brings with it reconciliation rather than division. If this book succeeds in that, at least for most of its readers – there will always be some people for whom you can never win – then it will all have been worthwhile.

Finally, as with any work of this kind, I have had to rely heavily on the works of others regarding periods outside my own area of expertise. This is therefore a secondary work, based upon synthesizing published sources.

So vast is the history that I have covered that difficult decisions had to be made about what to include and exclude, and in this I am grateful for the advice of my editorial team. This book is aimed particularly at the general reader and the mature adult students I teach in both Britain and the USA who take continuing education courses. The bibliography is intended to be a source of general knowledge, so that those who want to follow up on subjects I have passed over briefly – such as the history of the arts, for example – can find where they can discover what I have omitted.

With those caveats in mind, I hope that readers will enjoy the book.

I

ANCIENT EMPIRES

Having defined the Middle East historically and geographically, we will start with two areas within it: the Fertile Crescent – roughly today's Iraq – and then Egypt. For these two civilizations are pivotal to the beginnings not just of the Middle East but to life as we know it in the West.

One of this book's main points is that our world is also Middle Eastern in origin, and that unless we understand, for example, ancient societies such as the Sumerians and the Egyptians, our grasp of what made our civilization will be incomplete. Our globe was a much more connected place than we have given it credit for in the past, and the dawn of our part of it, the West, began long before Greece and Rome, and in a place well beyond the confines of Europe.

The Sumerians: the earliest known Middle Eastern civilization

The Sumerian civilization is one of the very oldest on earth, with clear signs of human activity as early as around 5000 BC. It is thought that they came from what is now Turkey and Iran. This, however, is one of the many interpretations, and here I agree with Colin Renfrew in his popular 1980s work *Archaeology and Language* and in his more academic contribution in 2002 to *Examining the Farming/Language Dispersal Hypothesis*. Renfrew's basic thesis is that the spread of language and civilization goes together with the spread of agriculture. But he states that there is still no scholarly consensus on the issue – that there remains 'an acute sense of problem' even though work on DNA has made migration easier to follow. He argues, surely correctly, that new groups coming into an area and spreading their genes and language successfully must have the economic means to enable a population increase to happen. They do this through agriculture, and in terms of the Indo-Europeans from whom the present-day inhabitants of Europe and Iran descend, this all began with ancestors who settled in Anatolia and west Asia around 8,000 years ago. Ethnically speaking, DNA research has shown that these last three groups are closely related – the linguistic links between, for example, ancient Greek, Celtic, Iranian and Hindi having been proved as long ago as the eighteenth century.

By around 3500 BC Sumerians were settled in cities in the Fertile Crescent, that strip of land bordered by the Tigris and Euphrates rivers, in which it was possible to live, in an otherwise arid desert climate. It was from one of these cities, Ur, that a nomad called Abram, later known as Abraham, ventured out to become the reputed ancestor of many of today's Semitic races (see p. 7). Ur was inhabited from around 5000 to 300 BC, and is best known for the spectacular royal tombs that date to around 2500 BC, many of whose artefacts have managed to survive in the museums of

Baghdad, including the looting in 2003. Ur was excavated from 1922 to 1924 by the British archaeologist Sir Leonard Woolley.

As well as inventing bureaucracy, their most famous discovery, again around 3500 BC, was the wheel. This was a vital tool that we take all too much for granted. But, for example, it was unknown to highly advanced contemporary American civilizations such as the Olmec and Maya. The Sumerians were known for their stepped pyramidal structures, or ziggurats, and to them we also owe the sixty-minute hour, the 360 degrees that form a circle, and also faience, which some believe to be the world's first ever synthetic material. The Sumerians also developed an early form of alphabet, cuneiform, and along with Chinese, which developed separately, and a long distance away, the Sumerian script is the oldest known written language.

(Semitic is a term used in two senses. Ethnically, it applies to present-day Jews and Arabs and in the past also applied to groups such as the Babylonians and Assyrians. Linguistically it is part of the large Hamito-Semitic family of languages, encompassing northern Africa and south-west Asia, including not just Hebrew and Arabic, but many interrelated languages, such as those of the Tuareg peoples of Africa, the Ethiopian Amharic language and several others.)

The Hittites: an Indo-European Empire

Another important group in ancient times was the Hittites, an Indo-European group (see below) based on the Anatolian plateau, where present Turkey is situated. They have been credited with introducing the Iron Age, using iron weapons instead of those of bronze and copper. Some think they may be ancestors of the Kurds, who are also Indo-European, but this is now difficult to prove.

The Hittite Empire lasted some 600 years. It began around 1800 BC – two centuries after the Hittites arrived in the region – reached its zenith in terms of power and size, around 1380–1350 BC, and was finally destroyed by a group known to history as the Sea Peoples, thought to be from around present-day Libya and other parts of Northern Africa in around 1200 BC.

(Indo-European is now used as a language term, to include languages as far apart geographically as English, Greek, Latin, Persian and Hindi. While its origins remain disputed, the proto-Indo-European ancestral language is thought by most to have originated in what is now southern Russia, and to have existed as a single language until between 3000 and 2000 BC – the wide range here perhaps indicating that there is no real consensus. But in the early twentieth century German philologists all agreed, and experts have continued so to agree, that Hittite is an Indo-European language, as, for example, is Tocharic, a branch of the linguistic family as far away as Central Asia.)

The Phoenicians: a great trading nation

The Phoenicians – a Semitic people – began their rise to prominence in what is now Lebanon around 3000 BC. (They should not be confused with the quite separate Mediterranean-bordering race, the Philistines.)

Among the ancient world's greatest traders, they managed to explore beyond the Pillars of Hercules at the end of the Mediterranean as far as Britain. They founded the Carthaginian colony in North Africa, which produced the Romans' enemy Hannibal, and also settled in Sicily and in southern Spain. Their god Baal was a source of constant temptation to the Jewish peoples, as, alas, was their belief in child sacrifice. Their main claim today, however, is the fact that they invented the first ever phonetic alphabet, from which all others derive.

Assyrians and Babylonians

3000 BC, or thereabouts, saw the dawn of another famous ancient civilization, the Assyrians, the successor to that of the Sumerians. Their first major empire was conquered by the Babylonians, who had begun to emerge around 2000 BC. One of the most notable Babylonian rulers, Hammurabi, was famed as a law-giver; his legal codes established principles of equivalence in punishment and retribution (such as taking just one eye for one eye) that still exist today. The memory of the Babylonians has been kept alive as a source of pride in the region down to modern times, with the former Iraqi dictator, Saddam Hussein, active in rebuilding Babylon not far from the current capital, Baghdad. He also had a Hammurabi Division in his army.

For a while, no particular group held predominance. But then around 1200 BC the Assyrians discovered iron, possibly from the Hittites. This gave them an advantage over still-Bronze Age tribes, and the Assyrian Empire began slowly to rebuild.

In 745 BC their new king, Tiglath-Pileser III – known to
generations of irreverent Victorian and Edwardian schoolboys as
It Tickleth Me Fancy – began another series of conquests which
included the Jewish northern kingdom of Israel, at which we
will look later. It was the Assyrian King Sennacherib (d. 681 BC)
who moved the capital to Nineveh, which was situated on the
Tigris opposite the present-day city of Mosul. (Nineveh's
famous Ishtar Gate can be seen today in the Pergamum Museum
in Berlin). Eventually the Assyrian Empire stretched from
Turkey to the Persian Gulf and across to Egypt. But then it
began to implode, and was taken over by a neo-Babylonian
grouping we know as the Chaldeans.

This meant a return to Babylon as the capital, under the reign
of King Nebuchadnezzar II, in 605 BC. In 586 the Chaldeans
captured the remaining Jewish kingdom, Judea, and took the
Jews into exile. The so-called Hanging Gardens of Babylon
have stayed in the memory as one of the Seven Wonders of the
Ancient World, along with the pyramids of Egypt.

The Chaldeans also left an important linguistic legacy – the
Aramaic language. Much of the Book of Daniel in the Hebrew
Scriptures is written in this language and it is also the one that
Jesus himself spoke. While it only exists today in the liturgical
language of Syriac, its close relative, Arabic, is spoken worldwide, both by Arabs as their own language, and by Muslims of
all nationalities as the official language of the Islamic faith,
usually, in the latter case, in the classical version in which the
Quran is written.

But as we see dramatically in Rembrandt's famous picture
of Belshazzar's Feast, even this mighty dynasty did not last for
ever. In 539 BC Babylon fell to Cyrus the Great, the first

member of the Persian Achaemenid dynasty, whose ancestors had ruled over the kingdom of Elam in what is now south-western Iran. Cyrus had begun his imperial journey by subduing the Mede kingdom in the north-west of modern Iran and founded an empire that was to last until it was overcome by Alexander the Great in 331 BC, over 200 years after its foundation. As a result of these conquests the empire Cyrus established is sometimes known as that of the Medes and Persians, and he would be especially revered by his new Jewish subjects for allowing them to return to their homeland in 516 after seventy years in exile.

The Persian Empire used Aramaic as its official language, and introduced the idea of hierarchical rule, since considerable power was devolved from the centre to local commanders, or satraps. They also employed the Phoenician alphabet as their script, thereby getting rid of the ancient cuneiform of the Sumerians.

Semitic civilizations: a remarkable linguistic continuity

Linguistically, there are links between the languages of these ancient civilizations – for example that of the main Fertile Civilization groups, the Akkadians, and successor languages, such as the one spoken by Jesus – and those used in our own times. (Akkadian is a term for the proto-Babylonian and proto-Aramaic languages, as well as for the earlier rulers of Sumer, the most powerful of whom was Sargon, who ruled over the area in around 2350 BC.) Because we do not learn such ancient languages in the West even if we increasingly learn Arabic, we forget that there is a remarkable degree of linguistic continuity between what we think of as distant times, and the ordinary languages spoken in the region in our own day. We thus miss a fascinating thread linking, for example, modern Iraq to Nineveh and the languages of the Bible.

While we might have problems, for example, in understanding someone from Chaucer's time, we can usually understand Shakespeare, or the King James (Authorized) Version of the Bible. It is the same with present-day Arabic speakers and the ancient language of Aramaic, which was spoken not just by Jesus in the first century, but was the official lingua franca of the Medo-Persian Empire several centuries before.

Take, for example, the words for the numbers one to ten, spoken in three ancient languages. These are Akkadian from around the twenty-third to sixth centuries BC; Aramaic, of the sixth century BC to around the sixth century AD; and present-day twenty-first-century Arabic, taken from *Empires of the Word: A Language History of the World* by Nicholas Ostler.

Number	Akkadian	Aramaic	Arabic
one	isten	had	wahid
two	sina	tren	ithnayn
three	salas	talata	thalatha
four	erba	arbaa	arbaa
five	hamis	hamisa	xamsa
six	sess	sitta	sitta
seven	sebe	saba	saba
eight	samane	tamaniya	thamaniya
nine	tise	tisa	tisa
ten	eser	asra	asra

As Nick Ostler notes, counting from one to ten has not really changed over 4,000 years – the degree of linguistic continuity is remarkable. Whether the ancient Akkadian rulers, the prophet Daniel (who spoke Aramaic), Jesus, Muhammad and a modern Arab could all understand each other easily is debatable. But they could certainly have grasped a good deal of what the other was saying. An interesting modern parallel would be the similarity between the Flemish spoken in Belgium, the Dutch of the Netherlands and the Frisian of north Holland and adjacent parts of Germany and Denmark.

Ancient Egypt

While it is accepted intellectually that ancient Egypt is in the Middle East, there is still a tendency somehow to dissociate it with the region, as we perceive it today. Since this is a tendency that extremist Muslims also share because the Egypt of the Pharaohs is pre-Islamic, it is important to combat such perceptions as we look at the unfolding story of the Middle East, from ancient times to the present.

Egyptian civilization also developed from around 3500 BC. (It is important to remember that Lower Egypt is in the north, and Upper Egypt in the south.) In approximately 3100 BC came the first ruler, or Pharaoh, of a united Upper and Lower Egypt, known to us as Menes.

The Egyptians themselves, certainly so far as their language goes, were (and are) clearly a Hamito-Semitic group, with both Semitic and Hamitic in their language. Archaeology now takes their roots far back to Palaeolithic times, with strong evidence of African as well as Mediterranean elements. We know the ancient Egyptians mainly for their extraordinary skill at building the pyramids. But they were also skilled agriculturalists, with most inhabitants living not too far from the river Nile, which has been the lifeblood of the region for millennia. Egyptians were also traders and eager astronomers, and, for much of the history of Pharaonic Egypt, they were a major regional power, frequently ruling well beyond their natural borders, to the south in Nubia and to the east in parts of Palestine.

Their language was not known or decipherable until the decoding of the Rosetta Stone in the 1820s by a young French scholar, Champollion. This object can be seen today in the British Museum, having originally been discovered by French soldiers invading Egypt in 1798. It had a decree in the original Egyptian hieroglyphs, in a later form of the language called Demotic, and also in ancient Greek, a language well known to the stone's European discoverers.

Egyptian hieroglyphics appear to us as pictures, but are in fact symbols representing sounds, and so are, like Chinese characters today, an alphabet. The language itself has been called Hamito-Semitic, so is related to many of the other contemporary ancient tongues. Today's Coptic, still spoken in the liturgy of the Coptic Orthodox Church, is its direct descendant.

Ancient Egypt also had a very stylized form of portraiture that did not change much over thousands of years. By around 2800 BC they began to write using papyrus, an aquatic plant found in Egypt, from which a paper-like substance could be made. Because of the dryness of the climate, these materials have survived to the present day in unusually high numbers for manuscripts that are so old. One example, the *Harris Papyrus*, is over 30cm long and dates to around 1160 BC.

Religion and its numerous gods and goddesses, many with animal shapes, lay at the heart of Egyptian life and society. The ancient Egyptians believed strongly in the afterlife, one of the key doctrines of their religion that affected the way in which they behaved, as the enormous monuments to the dead attest. The Pharaoh himself (there were a few female Pharaohs such as Hatshepsut, but they were rare) was regarded as divine. Numerous dynasties ruled over the millennia, mostly Egyptian, but some, such as the Semitic Hyksos, and the ethnically Greek Ptolemies, were from other races. Some, notably in the book *Black Athena*, have suggested African origins for some parts of Egyptian civilization, but this is not a majority view.

What happened when in Egypt: a bird's-eye view

Egyptian chronology is now in dispute outside mainstream archaeological circles. But here, by way of introduction, is the majority view, well enunciated for years by the distinguished British Egyptologist and doyen in the UK and USA of its current archaeology, Kenneth Kitchen.

Prehistoric Egypt lasts to around 3100 BC, and is then followed by what we call the Archaic Period, of roughly 3100 to 2680 BC, the first two dynasties of a succession of ruling families that reigned over Egypt until 30 BC.

Then we have the Old Kingdom, from roughly 2680 to 2180 BC, what Kitchen describes as the first flowering of

Egyptian culture, much of which has now been excavated. These are the Pharaohs of dynasties three to six. They include the earliest of the pyramids, the Step Pyramid of Pharaoh Djoser, the earliest cut-stone building still surviving anywhere in the world. Dynasty four saw the creation of the Great Pyramid of Pharaoh Kheops, about which much astrological and other similar nonsense has been written, and which, in reality, was simply an enormous tomb. During this time the Egyptians also managed to get as far down south as Nubia, in today's Sudan.

Next we have the first of what Egyptologists describe as an 'Intermediate Period', one in which the power of the Pharaohs diminished, and no one single ruler was truly in control. The First Intermediate Period, dynasties seven to eleven, takes us down to 2040 BC.

The Middle Kingdom, dynasties eleven and twelve, is the second major period of Egyptian civilization. Here power of the Pharaohs extended as far as Syria and they seem to have invented the short story as a form of literature. Amun-Re emerged as a synthesis of various pre-existing gods as a major deity in the Egyptian pantheon, with Osiris as a significant god for the afterlife.

Next comes another gap, the Second Intermediate Period, of dynasties thirteen to seventeen, lasting from about 1786 to 1540 BC. The Pharaohs in this period include those from the Hyksos, a group of non-Egyptian Semitic-Asiatic interlopers – the term literally means 'foreign people' – whose leaders constituted the fifteenth dynasty and were overlords to the sixteenth. The fact that these foreigners were able to subdue Egypt shows how weak that power had temporarily become.

It has been suggested that the Biblical Joseph lived in Egypt in the Hyksos period, since his Semitic origins would not have been a problem to the equally non-Egyptian Hyksos rulers. This is if the Kitchen chronology is right, which revisionists dispute.

Finally, after this interval of chaos comes the last great period of Egyptian independence and international power, the New Kingdom: dynasties eighteen to twenty, lasting from around 1552 to 1069 BC. This is the time of the greatest of all Pharaohs, Rameses II, and also of the Exodus, as described so vividly in the Hebrew Scriptures (or Old Testament). The Exodus, the central motif of the Jews, was a political act – the dawn of a new power – as well as an event of profound religious significance. Dating this epochal adventure is very hard, as there is little consensus even among those who take a fairly conservative view of when most of the events in ancient Middle Eastern and Mediterranean history happened. One date that appears to have much credence is circa 1280 BC, though even that is open to question. Nevertheless, the escape from slavery and the slow invasion of new territory was a defining time in the history of the Jewish people.

This is also the period of the one supposedly monotheistic Pharaoh, known to history as Akhenaten, who will be considered in the next chapter. But in no time the Egyptians were worshipping the old gods again and the brief theological experiment, if that is what it was, was over.

So too, soon, was the power of ancient Egypt itself as an independent entity. While we might, justifiably, be awed by the treasures of the boy ruler, Tutankhamun, already the power of Egyptian-born Pharaohs was on the wane. Kenneth

Kitchen describes Pharaoh Rameses III of the twentieth dynasty (he came to power in around 1190 BC) as the last of the great local rulers.

We therefore come to the Third Intermediate Period, one that mainstream Egyptologists believe lasted from 1069 to 332 BC, that of dynasties twenty-one to thirty-one. It is a period of sharp decline, with what Kitchen calls occasional but brief periods of recovery. By 332 the area had been conquered several times by foreign armies, including those of the Persians and in 332 the first of the Greek-born Ptolemaic dynasty came to power. This inaugurated a period of Hellenistic rule that lasted down to 30 BC, when Egypt became a province of the Roman Empire. Not until Colonel Nasser and his revolutionaries assumed power in a coup in 1952 were Egyptians again ruled by their own people.

The children of Israel: a brief history in context

Of all those living in the Middle East in ancient times, one group was to make a permanent difference to global history, and to our own world as well. This was the Israelites, the ancestors of today's Jews. Since their main and lasting contribution was religious, we shall consider them in more depth in the next chapter. Here an overview of their history will serve to place their faith into its historical context.

After many years of growth and then of struggle, the Children of Israel were to occupy what they regarded as the Promised Land. As the Hebrew Scriptures – the Bible – show this took some time and much fighting, including against tribes that practised gruesome rituals forbidden to the Jews, such as child sacrifice and temple prostitution. Archaeologists do not agree upon exactly how long or when the conquest occurred. The date many give for the period of the 'Judges' – that part of Jewish history between the Exodus and the establishment of the first kingdom – is roughly 1240–1050 BC. Therefore the conquest, which the consensus seems to think began in around 1220 BC, did not take place overnight. But whenever it did take place, the process of gaining a new land left its permanent mark upon the psyche of the conquerors – it remains an immensely significant issue in the twenty-first century for those Israelis who want the borders of a Greater Israel to be shared with those conquered by Joshua, the Jewish leader who succeeded Moses and launched the invasion of the new homeland. Such a state would comprise modern Israel, together with territory currently in Syria, Jordan and the Palestinian Authority-controlled areas. This shows how the events of thousands of years ago continue to resonate power-fully today; for the rest of us this is just ancient history, but for the inhabitants of the Middle East it could have happened last week.

Initially, the new state in which the different tribes settled was a kind of theocratic republic. The people were ruled by prophets speaking on behalf of the one God, a being who the Jews realized was not just a tribal deity, or even simply *their* tribal deity, but the one and only God who existed. This was the era the Hebrew Bible describes as the time of the Judges. But, very approximately, some time before 1000 BC the Jewish people decided that, like all the nations around them, they too had to have a king. Their first attempt, Saul, proved a failure, their second, David, a success.

David, who some think reigned around 1010 to 970 BC, is a character known in scripture, but not necessarily to archaeologists. Even within Israel, theologically conservative specialists agree with his existence, those of a more sceptical bent do not. Billions around the world do, however, and a book such as the *IVP Bible Dictionary* (InterVarsity Press) gives helpful archaeological details for those for whom the traditional view is convincing.

It was under King David that the Jews first occupied their new capital, Jerusalem, literally the City of Peace, in roughly 1000 BC. Previous to this the city had been the headquarters of another tribe, the Jebusites, and Jerusalem had been occupied, for certain, as far back as 1800 BC. After David's conquest, it functioned as the Jewish capital until the exile in 586 BC, and then again after the return seventy years later, until the Romans turned it into a pagan city in AD 135. Yet whether ruled by the Jews or not, Jerusalem has traditionally been regarded as the capital of both the Jews and Judaism.

David also expanded the borders of the Jewish kingdom, and it is his boundaries that are still deemed to be the natural frontiers of any Jewish state by religious Jews today. In that sense, what David was able to conquer three thousand years ago remains a major issue for our own time.

David, not only a warrior, was also a poet, and numerous of the Psalms in the Hebrew Scriptures are attributed to him. As well as being high poetry, they are also wonderfully human, as the psalmist wrestles with many of life's complexities, which we still, as fallible human beings, find hard to resolve. It is not surprising that people in the twenty-first century sing them with as much fervour as they were first chanted thousands of years ago.

It was David's son Solomon who built the first large-scale temple. He too protected the infant state's borders, but also, the Bible records, allowed a major degree of syncretism – the absorption of elements of local religions or cults – to enter the country. Solomon's son Rehoboam proved to be a tyrant, and the ten northern tribes rebelled, splitting the original kingdom permanently into two in 931 BC. Only the two southern tribes – Judah and Benjamin – remained under the Davidic dynasty based in Jerusalem that continued to rule down to 586 BC. Israel was to have a shorter existence; conquered in 722 BC by the Assyrians it lasted well over a century less as an independent state than its southern neighbour. Many groups around the world claim a descent from the 'lost' ten northern tribes, but only the tiny extant remnants of the Samaritans – the mixed-race descendants of the Jews of the northern kingdom of Israel who had inter-married with the local inhabitants, also Semitic but not regarded as Jewish – have a genetically proven claim.

A godly people: from the Kingdom of Judah to the USA

If one reads the Hebrew Scriptures, the history of Judah is one of continual struggle to keep to the original Jewish faith, and to avoid following the local gods, with their practice of child sacrifice and similar gory beliefs. By and large, from what the scriptural account tells us, Judah was slightly more successful at this than Israel, though as the author of Chronicles makes clear, standards in the southern kingdom were often lacking as well.

Some kings succumbed; others, such as Josiah, resisted. Their actions are relevant to us in the West because their behaviour was often used as a historical role model, especially after the Reformation. England's Edward VI was likened to Josiah by his enthusiasts, for example, as explored in more detail by Oxford church historian Diarmaid MacCulloch in his book *Tudor Church Militant*.

The notion of a godly kingdom also applied to many of the Puritans who founded colonies in the United States and derived, in their instance, from their understanding of the Old Testament. They believed profoundly that the New World was a later equivalent of the Jewish Promised Land. As well as this, they saw themselves as pioneers in a new territory which they believed God had given to them in the same way that God had bestowed the original Promised Land on the Jews, the first chosen people.

The Americans derived much of this thinking from the English Puritans, who felt similarly about the Commonwealth and Protectorate period in Britain from 1649 to 1660. During Cromwell's rule, England was likened to the Kingdom of Israel under David and Solomon (i.e. before its division) and thereafter to Judah by many of his supporters, and by writers and soldiers on what we would now describe as the radical left of the Parliamentary movement. The cultural and religious influence of the Judaic kings therefore lasted for thousands of years, down to our own time.

American exceptionalism, as it is now often called, therefore has roots going back to the New England Puritans. It is a recurring theme in American history, and several books, including the University of Pennsylvania historian Walter

McDougall's work *Promised Land, Crusader State* examine this motif in America's self-image from 1776 to the present day.

Adrian Hastings explored this theme in more detail in his influential work *The Construction of Nationhood: Ethnicity, Religion and Nationalism*. Significantly, the lectures upon which the book was based were given in Northern Ireland. There the hard-line Protestants, led by the Rev. Ian Paisley, harbour similar sentiments to those of the Scottish (and thus mainly Protestant) settlers in seventeenth-century Ulster. They too, the legend goes, were God's people creating a new land for God. Since many of the subsequent settlers in the New World – such as the Scotch Irish in the Valley of Virginia – were of Protestant Ulster origin, the myth of a divinely led people creating a new frontier land for God was perpetuated.

This excursus into present-day national myths and troubles is relevant, because history is permanently being rewritten and reinterpreted. Ultimately, it can be argued that it is a matter of opinion whether or not the 'three centuries of darkness' did or did not happen. (See discussion of Peter James' book for details.) But how America sees itself globally in the twenty-first century is important, and the theological underpinning of such a world view, even if we do now live in more secular times, does matter.

Likewise, strife in Northern Ireland, and the continuing, far worse, conflict in Palestine, all harks back to how people *today* interpret what a brave band of Jewish exiles from Egypt did *then*, even if it was thousands of years ago. We are never fully free from the effects of history, however much we would like to be.

Judah: the survival of a people

Judah was in the unenviable position of being sandwiched between two major rival powers, that of Egypt to its west and south, and whoever controlled Babylonia to its east and north. While the kingdom lasted longer than that of Israel, it proved unable to preserve its independence, and eventually the Jews were taken to exile in Babylon.

(Many Jews remained in the region until 1948, when they were expelled from Iraq – a British survey of Baghdad in the 1920s revealed that the biggest single ethnic group in that city was Jewish. For example, today's Saatchi and Sassoon families are of Iraqi Jewish descent.)

According to the Hebrew Scriptures, the main exile lasted for seventy years. Some scholars, such as Bernard Lewis in *The Middle East*, ascribe enormous importance theologically to this period of exile, and in particular the realization that there is a Devil who opposes God and his people.

There is no archaeological evidence to show how it is that Jews of that time began to believe which particular doctrines. Conservative scholars tend to give older dates to Biblical doctrines, and those of a more liberal persuasion usually ascribe later dates and give greater credence to outside influences, such as those of the Zoroastrians. However, it is true to say that unlike the contemporary Zoroastrian religion, in which the good and bad gods are effectively co-equal until the end of time when Ahura Mazda wins, in Judaism Satan is less powerful, although the cosmic struggle is very real.

Since the struggle between good and evil carries forward into both Christianity and Islam, it has proved to be a vital doctrine, however or whenever it arose. Even in today's post-religious age, it remains a powerful concept, both in popular belief and even in fiction like *Harry Potter*. It is also a key component of what the writer Paul Johnson, in his *A History of the Jews*, calls 'ethical monotheism', which he considers one of the greatest contributions of the Jewish people to the rest of us in the millennia that have followed.

Our modern system of ethics is becoming increasingly post-religious, as people, at least in the European part of the West, have less faith than their forbears. Even so, one could argue that our basic ethical system is the grandchild of that of the ancient Jews, via Christianity, and that our conceptual frameworks go back perhaps to the Jewish flight from Egypt (taking a conservative view). If other interpretations are correct, such ethical monotheism derives from later Kings of Judah such as Josiah, and the ruminations of exiles in Babylon, wrestling with the problem of why it all went so wrong, because God's chosen people had been defeated and exiled by a pagan army.

Eventually the remnants of the Judaic exiles were able to return by the remit of the Persian ruler Cyrus who, as Bernard Lewis reminds us, is afforded a degree of praise given to no other pagan ruler in the Bible. But once back, the Jews were no longer independent, and were under the authority of whoever controlled the bulk of the Middle East. For just under 200 years (536 to 331 BC), this remained the great Persian Empire, which, at its peak, stretched from present-day Egypt to the Hindu Kush.

Some talk of Alexander: from Greeks to Romans

Then around 331 BC Alexander, a warrior prince from the hitherto backwater kingdom of Macedonia, founded a huge new empire, destroying that of the Achamaenid kings. His moniker 'the Great' reflects the scale of his conquests, which stretched from Greece to Afghanistan.

Alexander's empire split after his early death aged thirty-three in 323 BC, but the successor dynasties were Greek – the Seleucids in the former Persian domains, and the Ptolemies (down to Cleopatra) in Egypt – and the Greek language, Greek culture and Hellenic civilization (Hellenic after *Hellas* for Greece) remained highly influential in the Middle East for over two thousand years. Greek now became the international lingua franca of regions either directly under Greek rule, or strongly influenced by it culturally. In Bactria, in present-day Central Asia, Greek artistic and cultural influence combined with Buddhism to form a unique blend that influenced regional iconography for millennia afterwards.

While most ordinary people continued life unchanged, the effect of Greek thought made a powerful impact on the collaborator classes needed to make Greek rule work and on the intellectuals. The Greeks themselves set up new cities, many named Alexandria after Alexander himself. As we shall see, the influence of all this on the Jews was to be considerable and long lasting.

Some writers, especially in the United States, have referred to the contest between what they call Jerusalem vs. Athens in terms of trying to see which tradition, Jewish religious or secular Greek, has had the most influence on the West. This is surely a false dichotomy, since the two are not always as separate as some people think, nor are they necessarily so opposed. Jewish ethical monotheism has been highly influential in quite different arenas as, for example, Greek mathematics and geometry. In addition, Hellenism, the Greek way of thinking, especially in disciplines such as philosophy, had an enormous influence on the post-exilic Jewish people as well.

It is significant, for example, that the early Christian gospels were all written in Greek – or, strictly speaking, its popular or *koine* version – as this was the common language that could be understood by literate people across a radius of thousands of miles.

Hellenic can be used, therefore, instead of the ethnically more restricted word Greek. As E. A. Judge has pointed out, in this period 'Hellenist' effectively meant 'civilized' and did not apply just to those of Greek ancestry. There were places of actual Greek settlement – the Decapolis in the Holy Land, for example, and cities as far away as those in the Hindu Kush, whose descendants still have strong European features to this day as explorers down to Michael Palin have discovered. But there did not need to be actual ethnic Greeks present for Hellenism to flourish, and it remained influential long after much of the once enormous Greek Empire had been conquered by the Romans and further east by many different local tribal kingdoms.

As Judge also points out, the intellectual centres of Hellenic thought were not limited to the Greek ethnic homeland. Towns such as Pergamum, in today's Turkey, along with Alexandria (now in Egypt) and similar cities came to wield enormous influence on the lives of the different peoples around them. (Visitors to Berlin can see the remains of much of

Pergamum in the Pergamon Museum.) Jews, as we shall soon see, also fell under Greek influence, following the Greek translation in the Hellenistic city of Alexandria of the Hebrew Scriptures we call the *Septuagint*.

The Roman–Jewish world of Jesus

The region we now refer to as Israel and Palestine itself remained under Seleucid rule until around 165 BC, when a new and Semitic dynasty called the Hasmoneans was able to re-establish semi-independence. Then in 63 BC, the great Roman general, Pompey (later a rival of Julius Caesar) conquered much of the Middle East, and the Hasmoneans were forced into the role of vassal kings.

The Hasmoneans were not descendants of King David, however, and so lacked religious legitimacy in the eyes of many strict Jews. Temple worship had already begun again, and the Hasmoneans were able to rebuild Solomon's temple to yet greater magnificence. The most famous Hasmonean was King Herod, familiar to many a singer of Christmas carols. He was the ruler who organized the massacre of the innocent children, killed on his orders when he heard about the birth of a child who some were already describing as the legitimate Jewish Messiah, or liberator.

At this same time, various sects arose in the Jewish world, each with their own interpretations of the Hebrew Scriptures. The Zealots were highly political, and there were several rebellions against outside rule, culminating in a major revolt from AD 66–70, and the mass Jewish suicide at the fortress of Masada in AD 73.

The Sadducees were the official establishment, controlling the Temple and many of the key religious posts on the Sanhedrin, the official Jewish religious body that decided all religious issues. They were also collaborators, and had close links with whichever secular power was in office – the Romans by the time that Jesus came. They believed in what we call the Old Testament, but not in what they thought were extraneous beliefs, which in their case included, for example, resurrection from the dead and an afterlife.

The Pharisees were equally religious, and believed in a parallel, oral tradition of rabbinical teachings that had evolved over the centuries addition to the Scriptures called the Torah, in the same way that the Roman Catholic Church – unlike the Protestants – would argue that the tradition of the Church is of equal weight theologically to the Bible itself. Becoming a Pharisee was open to people of all social backgrounds, unlike the often high-born Sadducees. By the time of Jesus the Pharisees were very proud of their extensive religious knowledge but, as the New Testament argues, they had perhaps become almost too proud of it, and become sadly enmeshed in the letter rather than the spirit of the law.

Finally there were small, often remote, groups such as the Essenes, who lived separate from the rest of society in special communities, rather like the monks in Christian and Buddhist traditions. The Essenes were ascetics, who rejected the Hasmonean monarchy, and have become famous today because of the discovery of the Dead Sea Scrolls in the twentieth century, which has preserved their teaching.

Then, from the despised, culturally backward province of Galilee, came a Jewish teacher who was a member of none of the above groups. This rabbi was, to use a phrase employed of his early disciples, to turn the world upside down. He was to change not only the Middle East, in which he was born, but the West as well, since Western civilization today lives in the shadow of his birth religion and the one that he founded. I am describing Judaeo-Christian civilization and its founder, Jesus Christ.

2

THE DAWN OF MONOTHEISM

Perhaps the greatest contribution of the Middle East to global civilization, and the biggest way in which it changed our world for ever is monotheism, the worship of just one god. Nowadays we take this for granted, even though we still have many polytheistic faiths, such as Hinduism and the many animistic religions. But when, in the Middle East, the Jewish people insisted that there was just one god, they were, without realizing it, creating an intellectual and spiritual revolution that reverberates down to our own time. For Christianity and Islam, the two global monotheistic faiths today, both make the claim to be uniquely and universally true, in what one Muslim writer, Bassam Tibi, has described as the 'clash of universalisms'.

Monotheistic precursors: Akhenaten and Zoroastrianism

Akhenaten, the fourteenth-century Pharaoh, is sometimes credited with the origins of monotheism. Beginning his reign as

Amenhotep IV, he rejected the traditional religion of Egypt in favour of the worship of the disk of the sun, the Aten. But as Susan Tower Hollis points out (in reviewing Erik Hornung's book *Akhenhaten and the Religion of Light*), this was a faith with 'no revelation, the god did not speak, and there was no book or scripture'.

Hornung, Hollis points out, 'skirts a definitive statement' on whether the worship of the Aten was the first monotheistic faith or not. If experts disagree, it is difficult to know how best to interpret the evidence. Many, such as the psychologist Sigmund Freud, have linked Jewish monotheism to the influence Akhenaten had on Moses, but without any tangible evidence, this is impossible to prove. It has even been suggested that he was the first atheist! His subjects were not allowed to worship other gods, which might point to monotheism, but that is the only tantalizing clue that we have.

He is perhaps most famous now as the husband of Nefertiti, whose portrait can be seen in Berlin. My own view is that he used his role as the interpreter of the Aten to consolidate his own power as Pharaoh – worship my god, obey me. However, the new religion did not outlast his reign. In no time the Egyptians were worshipping the old gods again and the brief theological experiment, if that is what it was, was over.

While the worship of the Aten cannot be properly described as the beginnings of monotheism, the ancient Persian religion of Zoroastrianism, even though it had two forces in perpetual combat with each other, comes closer to what we now think of as a long-term religion. For while the LSE sociologist Anthony Smith has observed that no one now worships Zeus or Venus, Zoroastrianism through the Parsees of India has a shadowy descent to our own time.

It was the Medo-Persian Empire that introduced the teachings of Zoroaster, a semi-mythical figure, as a national religion. This was, in essence, a dualistic faith, with a good God, Ahura Mazda, pitted in a cosmic struggle against a demonic figure, Ahriman, or Angra Mainyu. Some argue that Ahura Mazda was the first monotheistic god, but since these two beings were, in essence, equal, despite Ahriman's eventual predicted doom, it is perhaps fairer to call it dualist theism rather than a strictly monotheistic faith.

But although Zoroastrianism is virtually dead, except among the tiny Parsee community, the concept of a struggle between good and evil has become a very strong one, even among those today of no religious faith. Furthermore, Iranians today, while Muslim, believe in a divergent form of Islam, Shiism, and that perhaps is a legacy of their own pre-Islamic faith.

Abraham, father of three faiths

The ancient Sumerian civilization may seem a very long time ago. But there is one way in which it profoundly influences us even now. This is through its most famous inhabitant, Abraham, from the Sumerian city of Ur in today's Iraq.

Right up to and including our own century, Abraham, the Patriarch, and founder of Judaism, has been revered by millions around the world. Sadly, though, many of his current followers dispute his legacy, often violently. For Abraham, as we will discover later, is as highly regarded by Muslims as he is by Jews and Christians.

We see this in the twenty-first century in the Intifada, the ongoing struggle between Jews and predominantly Muslim

Palestinians. Both sides equally reverence the identical spot in Jerusalem, the Temple Mount, which is closely associated with a key event in Abraham's life – his decision to sacrifice his son, until enabled by God to choose an alternative sacrifice. Both the Jewish temple and the present-day Al-Aqsa Mosque commemorate the place where believers in all the three Abrahamic faiths hold that the event took place.

(Here Jews and Christians on the one hand and Muslims on the other differ. In the Hebrew Scripture account, the son in question is Isaac, and in the Quran, it is his other son, Ishmael.)

Consequently, for both Jews and Muslims, the site of the sacrifice is holy, and each side claims Abraham as one of their own. A figure born thousands of years ago thus unites and divides people in our present day. He is the founding Patriarch for the Jews, and an early prophet or forerunner of Muhammad himself for the Muslims. Jews claim descent from his son Isaac, and Arabs from his other son Ishmael.

On the other hand, the peace lovers in the three great modern monotheistic faiths see him not as a source of strife but as a focus of reconciliation and unity. We have a new expression to cover Judaism, Christianity and Islam – the 'Abrahamic faiths'. This term, used even more after 11 September 2001, is designed to foster unity between the three faiths, and to remind us what we have in common. Jews, Christians and Muslims can all claim, if not physical, certainly spiritual descent from a common ancestor.

Who then was this ancient desert nomad, whose wanderings thousands of years ago still affect us today? Here the answer is not so simple.

Abraham, or Abram of Ur, to give his original name, is someone believed in despite any direct historical evidence for his existence outside the scriptures of these three faiths. However, archaeological finds certainly confirm events contemporary to Abraham, and tie in with the accounts in the Hebrew Scriptures.

Here, as with the similar cases of Jesus and Muhammad, all depends on whether or not you yourself have religious beliefs. Those who are religious have no problems, whereas those whose scepticism leads them to need independent corroboration tend to regard ancient scriptures – Jewish, Christian, Muslim, Hindu, Buddhist or whatever – as no more than fairy tales.

However, as regards the founders of all three monotheistic religions, enough evidence now exists to convince those of all faiths or none that the actual people themselves existed, even if non-believers inevitably resist the divine elements of their respective stories.

But Abraham is important, both as a literal figure – a single individual whom God called out of the ancient Middle Eastern city of Ur, as Jews, Christians and Muslims have taught down the millennia – and as a potent symbol of ethnic and religious origins when he, or people like him, in an amazing and religiously innovative Semitic tribe came up with a wholly original view of looking at the world, as non-religious historians would prefer us to think. Either way, the result is remarkable; God's call to Abraham, real or mythic, changed the nature of religion and the societies that religion helped to create for ever.

Salvation faiths: religions for the long term

Anthony Smith is surely right to say that the three Abrahamic faiths are clearly distinguishable from others. He calls them 'salvation religions', and ascribes to this element of salvation the fact that, unlike many other religions, they still exist as potent forces today, each one based upon a unique God reaching out to humanity through a chosen individual – Abraham, Jesus, and Muhammad respectively.

While other religions – notably Buddhism and Hinduism – have existed from ancient times, they are different in nature from these three. For although Buddhism spread beyond its Indian origins to the rest of Asia and Hinduism likewise, the two successor faiths to Judaism both make claims to be universally true and genuinely cross-cultural and global in a way that is not so true of other world religions.

(Localism would be very true of Hinduism, for example, especially as seen by its more zealous present-day Indian followers such as the nationalistic movement, the RSS, and their compatriots in its political wing, the BJP.)

The Jews, Abraham's descendants, and ethnically speaking from the Semitic group around them – Phoenicians and Assyrians and then the Arabs of today – did not evangelize much beyond their own ethnic boundaries. The only notable exceptions are key characters such as Ruth the Moabitess and Naaman the Syrian, since they were not born Jewish but chose freely to follow the Jewish faith which they, like all Jews, believed to be uniquely true. Christianity and then Islam took this much further, in rapidly crossing national and ethnic boundaries from the beginning – Christianity even more so, since there is no equivalent to a special religious language such as Arabic in Islam.

The three Abrahamic faiths are together believed in by billions globally, and both Christianity and Islam are still expanding, probably more so now than ever before. Africa, Asia and, in the twenty-first century, Europe, are all witnessing a growing confrontation between the two global successor faiths. This does not just refer to inter-religious violence, such as 9/11 or Christian/Muslim riots in Nigeria and Indonesia, but also in peaceful terms to millions of people actively converting to them and thereby rejecting their ancestral poly-theistic faiths.

The faith of the Jews: the dawn of a monotheistic people

Abraham had a son, Isaac, who in turn had two sons, Esau and Jacob. The Hebrew Scriptures do not try to hide people's mistakes; Abraham lied to protect himself (on one occasion telling an Egyptian ruler that Sarah was his sister, not his wife, in case the ruler wanted to kill him to get her), so too did his grandson Jacob, similarly to get out of trouble. But these same scriptures, or *Tanakh*, to give its Hebrew name, shows that God loves repentant sinners.

Jacob in turn had twelve sons, branches of which later became the Twelve Tribes of Israel. The youngest but one, Joseph, who was born according to some around 1900 BC, was rejected by his brothers and ended up in a powerful position in Egypt as a principal adviser to the Pharaoh.

The Pharaoh whom Joseph served is not named, and some think it possible that since he was so sympathetic to a visitor of Semitic race, the relevant Pharaoh could have been one of the Hyksos, a non-Egyptian dynasty from Canaan. But such a date and an overlap with the Hyksos would seem impossible since most people date that dynasty as existing 300 years later. But chronology is often either unclear or controversial – some mainstream Egyptologists are unhappy with the received chronology, as well as those who attribute strange powers to the pyramids – and so such a conjecture is pure speculation.

Either way, Joseph is said to have saved Egypt from famine, and his family came to live in the country, in which they remained for centuries. Some speculate that there were now two groups of Jews – one in Egypt and one in what became their historic heartland of Palestine – but the traditional belief is that all the Jews were now in a single place, in Egypt.

By the time we get to Moses, who some think was born in approximately 1520 BC, the now much larger Jewish population of Egypt was in a far worse position – most of them were slaves living in the Nile Delta. (One expert has said that dates for Moses vary by a full 300 years either way.) The resulting plea of Moses to Pharaoh, 'Let my people go,' has resonated for millennia with all oppressed peoples, and Moses himself has become an iconic figure whether he is literally believed in or not, as shown by Melanie Wright's book *Moses in America: The Cultural Uses of Biblical Narrative*.

Films such as *Moses Prince of Egypt* are, like so much of Hollywood, pure speculation. But it is interesting that the great Jewish law-giver was someone well versed in Egyptian knowledge. There has been much scholarly speculation that it was the Jewish people who were influenced into their historic monotheism by the Egyptians. So it is important to note that Akhenaten, the supposedly monotheistic Pharaoh whom we looked at earlier, did live, according to the accepted mainstream chronology, until around 1350 BC. This would, according to such dating, be around 170 years *after* the birth of Moses and therefore long after the Children of Israel had left Egypt. You cannot influence someone before you are born.

Needless to say, not all historians agree on chronology, especially if Moses was contemporaneous with Rameses II, who reigned around 1273 BC, therefore *after* Akhenaten. But theories on what happened when regarding contentious issues like this often depend on prior religious belief. So if the dates suggested by Egyptologist and Middle East specialist Jacob Fellure are correct, then Moses preceded Akhenaten.

Yet if non-crank archaeologists such as David Rohl in *Test of Time* and Peter James in *Centuries of Darkness* are right, then we have all got our chronology seriously wrong! Both books show that if Egyptian chronology is realigned, then the whole timescale of the Hebrew Scriptures (or Old Testament) suddenly falls into line with a very different set of Egyptian Pharaohs, a revision that enhances the credibility of the Old Testament record.

One of the reasons that mainstream Egyptologists such as Kenneth Kitchen dismiss Rohl and James is because there are plenty of cranks out there, while fully recognizing that neither scholar is in that unfortunate category.

The last person to suggest a change in ancient Egyptian dating was a writer called Immanuel Velikovsky, who also seriously suggested that Venus was from outside the Solar

System, and had entered it only a few thousand years ago. Needless to say, the overwhelming majority of serious scientists laughed such nonsense to scorn.

However, both Peter James and David Rohl are mainstream archaeologists, and neither of them is linked to any particular religious need to interpret ancient events in a special way. Their New Chronology ideas should at least be taken seriously, as if their chronology is correct, it is certainly good news for those who take the Bible seriously.

If we stick for safety's sake to a more mainstream chronology, archaeologists suggest around 1420 BC for the exodus of the Jewish people out of Egypt. There are verifiable documents of forty years later by Canaanite tribes asking for Egyptian help against an invading tribe called the *Habiru*. According to the Hebrew Scriptures, the Israelites spent forty years in the wilderness in between leaving Egypt and invading what we now call Palestine.

One theologically traditionalist scholar, Norman Geisler, thinks that as the Bible gives no name for the Pharaoh of the Book of Exodus, the answer was probably Pharaoh Amenhotep II. This is a view I have not seen even in conservative commentaries, such as those published by the theologically conservative university-orientated publisher, InterVarsity Press. Finally, as an article in *Time* magazine in 1998 comments, an absence of evidence does not necessarily mean anything either way!

While I tend to be convinced by the Rohl/James hypothesis that says it was definitely not Rameses II, it probably does not matter who the actual Pharaoh was. The main thing is that the Children of Israel were now out of

Egypt, and, after a period of wandering, now about to embark on setting up a country of their own.

The main task of Moses and his brother Aaron (known to Muslims as Musa and Harun) had been to escape Egypt. The Children of Israel were able to do just this. If one takes a traditional view of religious inspiration, Moses was the leader who gave to the Children of Israel the law code described in the Pentateuch, the first five books of both the Hebrew and Christian scriptures. (Many have noted similarities to the much earlier law code of Hammurabi, which as we saw dates to around 1700 BC.) Either way, the Jewish law code is quite remarkable, especially the ethics of the Ten Commandments, and is still followed by billions of people, Jewish and Christian, and admired by many who reject any kind of religious belief.

God the law-giver: the origins of our moral code

Let us look briefly at the Ten Commandments.

Here I am using the latest English translation, the *English Standard Version*. I am starting from the beginning, since it is important to see what follows in the context of the ethical monotheism – to use Paul Johnson's phrase – that is the great discovery of the Jews. Here I am quoting from Exodus, chapter twenty; the Commandments are reiterated in Deuteronomy, chapter five.

I am the Lord your God, who brought you out of the land of Egypt, out of the house of slavery.
You shall have no other God before me.

You shall not make for yourself a carved image, or any likeness of anything that is in the heaven above, or that is in the earth beneath, or that is in the water under the earth. You shall not bow down to them or serve them, for I the Lord your God am a jealous God, visiting the iniquity of the fathers on the children to the third and fourth generation of them that hate me, but showing steadfast love to thousands of those who love me and keep my commandments.

You shall not take the name of the Lord your God in vain, for the Lord will not hold him guiltless who takes his name in vain.

Remember the Sabbath day to keep it holy. Six days you shall labour, and do all your work, but the seventh day is a Sabbath to the Lord your God. On it you shall not do any work, you, or your son, or your daughter, your male servant or your female servant, or your livestock, or the sojourner who is within your gates. For in six days the Lord made heaven and earth, the sea, and all that is in them and rested the seventh day. Therefore the Lord blessed the Sabbath day and made it holy.

Honour your father and your mother, that your days may be long in the land that the Lord is giving to you.

You shall not murder.

You shall not commit adultery.

You shall not steal.

You shall not bear false witness against your neighbour.

You shall not covet your neighbour's house, you shall not covet your neighbour's wife, or his male servant, or his female servant, or his ox, or his donkey, or anything that is your neighbour's.

While neighbours no longer may have oxen to covet, the foundational principles of loving your neighbour as yourself, of not stealing or murdering, remain at the core of ethics systems everywhere, a code first recognized by a small Semitic people fleeing for their lives from an angry Pharaoh. A look too at the dietary and medical laws shows a remarkable prescience of what is safe to eat in a desert society, and the stipulation against bloodletting is something forgotten by Western medicine until comparatively recent times.

The spirit of the Ten Commandments is still with us today, in the twenty-first century. For most people, the theological underpinning at the beginning – of loving God above all else – no longer applies. But nearly everyone would agree that, for example, theft is wrong, murder is abominable, and perjury undermines the entire legal system. Now through Christianity and Islam the law code of the Jews has become effectively universal, at least so far as the basis of morality is concerned. The faith part may have gone, but the ethics of the Hebrew Scriptures have remained.

Take for example another quotation, which appears slightly later in the book of Exodus:

> You shall not pervert the justice due to your poor in his lawsuit. Keep far from a false charge, and do not kill the innocent and righteous, for I will not acquit the wicked. And you shall take no bribe, for a bribe blinds the clear-sighted and subverts the cause of those who are in the right. You shall not oppress a sojourner. You know the heart of a sojourner, for you were sojourners in the land of Egypt.

How often countless victims of injustice down the millennia must have wished for judges who could not be bribed, and did not favour the rich over the poor! Likewise, many an immigrant must have wished that she or he were not oppressed, as, alas, is the case of countless immigrants down to our own time.

Those who have not read the Hebrew Scriptures have a tendency to contrast what they think of the God of the Old Testament with the seemingly more benign God they encounter in the New Testament. But this is to misinterpret the Hebrew Scriptures altogether. For example, take this quotation:

> You shall not mistreat any widow or fatherless child. If you do mistreat them and they cry out to me, I will surely hear their cry, and my wrath will burn and I shall kill you with the sword and your wives shall become widows and your children fatherless.

This is powerful language. But it is used in defence of the widows and fatherless, two of the most vulnerable categories both then and now. The teaching of the Hebrew Scriptures on such ethical issues remains strong throughout, down to the strictures of the Prophet Amos, whose denunciations of social and economic oppression are surely as powerful in the twenty-first century as they were nearly three thousand years ago when he first proclaimed them.

In terms of economic justice, radical Christians from Latin America to Britain and the USA are also trying to update the teaching of a Hebrew book we seldom read today, that of Leviticus. Much of it remains obscure, since the temple system and detailed commands on the nature of the lamp-stands are hard for us to comprehend. But today politically progressive Christians base much of their doctrine on what has sometimes been called the 'bias to the poor' on this very book. In particular, they use chapter twenty-five, and the teaching on *Jubilee*. According to this principle, everything sold within a forty-nine-year period had to be sold back to the original owner in the fiftieth year, so that capital accumulation – largely landholdings in these ancient times – would be impossible to go beyond a certain point.

Economic oppression was also outlawed:

> If your brother becomes poor and cannot maintain himself with you, you shall support him as though he were a stranger and a sojourner, and he shall live with you. Take no interest from him or profit, but fear your God, that your brother may live beside you. You shall not lend him your money at interest, nor give him your food for profit . . . If your brother becomes poor beside you and sells himself to you, you shall not make him as a slave: he shall be with you as a hired servant and as a sojourner. He shall serve with you until the year of the jubilee.

Again, the ethical implications of this are clear, and are surely still relevant in the modern, industrial times in which we live today.

In terms of present-day applications, it is significant that the group founded in Washington DC by the radical Christian Jim Wallis was at first called Sojourners, which is also the title of their journal. Now Wallis is known in both the USA and Britain for his book *God's Politics*. He is supported in America by many Democrats and in the United Kingdom by Gordon Brown. But the theological basis for his work – and that of the similar Jubilee Centre in Britain – is all taken from the teaching of the millennia-old book of Leviticus.

This is not to say that the Jewish people always kept to such norms – far from it, as a reading of any of the later prophets makes abundantly clear. But they did at least have a firm moral basis for the kind of society that they were trying to create out there in the wilderness, and then in the Promised Land itself.

The story of the Exodus, and of the slow conquest of the Promised Land, is one of the most exciting in world literature and remains an equal source of religious inspiration to the Jews of today, with regular feasts to commemorate different parts of the story. But despite the close genetic kinship of the Jews with their Semitic neighbours, it was now that they started to be radically different from them in a way that has distinguished them right up until the present. The story is in fact one of the most remarkable in history, since the whole legacy of the West owes its intellectual, moral and religious origins to the Jews every bit as much as to the civilizations of Greece and Rome, or to the Celts. There is a sense in which when the Jews made their successful dash for freedom into the Wilderness, the story of Western civilization also began.

3

FROM CHRIST TO CHRISTENDOM

Jesus of Nazareth: man and message

Jesus, whose Jewish name would have been Yeshua ben Joseph, the founder of the world's first universal monotheistic faith, Christianity, was born in the Middle East, around 4 BC, just before the Hasmonean King Herod the Great died. (BC and AD were invented many years later, and depended on guesstimates of when Jesus was born that we now know to be inaccurate.)

As we saw with Abraham, the founder of Judaism, and will see with Muhammad and the origins of Islam, nothing significant has been written about any of the originators of the three major monotheistic faiths outside of their own scriptures. If for believers this does not present a problem, non-believing writers lack outside confirmation for the three lives in question. Much depends, therefore, on what you *already* think, so one should always be sceptical of people who say they are being more objective one way or the other. As with Abraham, this would include secular historians as much as religious writers, since atheists or agnostics are by definition as partisan as believers.

Expert writers such as the scholar R. T. France estimate that Jesus was born four years ahead of his 'official' birth. Raised in what we today would call a skilled working-class home, he spent the early part of his life in obscurity, working as a carpenter. But when he turned thirty in approximately AD 26–28, he began a three-year public ministry. The core of this is recorded in the four Gospels of the Christian New Testament: Matthew, Mark, Luke (the three 'synoptic' or straight narrative accounts), and John, whose Gospel is more thematically written than the others. This means that the traditional date for his crucifixion – AD 33 – is probably late, though some people have argued it is correct.

Nearly all Jesus' active ministry, which reached its climax in Jerusalem, took place in what was then called Canaan, with most concentrated in an even smaller area, Galilee. Mainstream Jewish thought had passed Galilee by, which explains why Jesus' disciples were rather looked down upon by the more sophisticated intellectuals and bureaucrats of the time.

Jesus was born under Roman rule – as we saw in the last chapter, the Romans had occupied the entire area for over sixty years already, through the Hasmonean dynasty of loyal client kings. Some of the region was governed directly, but other parts, rather like the former British Raj in India, were controlled via the indirect rule of local monarchs, of whom Herod the Great was the most famous. This was also similar to the client king protectorates in southern Africa, such as Swaziland or Lesotho, and present-day Botswana, now familiar through the novels of Alexander McCall Smith.

During the ministry of Jesus, Herod Antipas reigned over Galilee, but his brother Archelaus was so inefficient that Judea and Samaria were directly under a Roman Prefect, who in turn was under the Roman Governor of Syria. At the time of Jesus' death, the Prefect was Pontius Pilate.

Jesus taught that he was the Messiah, the promised one of God. The Jews had waited a very long time for such a figure to appear, especially after their centuries of foreign rule. But Jesus was the Messiah predicted by the Hebrew Scriptures – notably the Suffering Servant, the title given by the prophet Isaiah to the future deliverer of the Jewish people – rather than the warrior on horseback who would vanquish the Romans. As a result, after one of the disciples, Judas Iscariot, betrayed Jesus to the Jewish hierarchy, known as the Sanhedrin, this body took an essentially political view about who the awaited Jewish saviour, or Messiah, would be. Since Jesus' spiritual idea of his mission and the political longings of the Sanhedrin were different, the leadership did not hesitate to solve their problem – that of Jesus being a rival source of religious authority – through handing him over to their political enemies, the Romans. Jesus thus died under imperial rule.

It is important to remember, in relation to how anti-Semites would misinterpret all this, that all those involved in the arrest of Jesus were Jews, including Jesus and his disciples. Where they differed was over the interpretation of what kind of person the Messiah was and what he was coming to do. Was he an anti-colonial freedom fighter, or a spiritual saviour whose message would apply not just to Jews but to Gentiles as well?

In the light of current debate, this is not just an issue for Christians and Jews. The very fact that Jesus came for spiritual and not political reasons is a major distinction between

Christianity and Islam, a religion in which the two are inexorably fused. The fact that in the fourth century Christian leaders forgot this in their deal with the Emperor Constantine should not take away from the important point that Jesus refused to be the political Messiah that many clearly and mistakenly hoped he would be.

However, it is vital to remember, especially in the light of twentieth-century history, that Jesus and all his early disciples were themselves Jewish. Strictly speaking, therefore, to say that the Jews per se rejected Jesus is historically inaccurate. While the Establishment did so, many ordinary Jews did not. The so-called 'Blood Libel' of generations of anti-Semites, including later Christians, is therefore a calumny, as well as simply wrong. It is interesting that Jesus – or Christ, to use a Greek variant of his name – his twelve disciples (to match the Twelve Tribes of Israel) and most of the early church being Jews embarrassed Nazis from Protestant backgrounds (Catholics tended to favour the Nazis less), and Christianity's Jewish origins were thus strongly played down, or even abolished altogether.

Jesus' essential method therefore was spiritual rather than political, unlike that of the religious establishment of his time. He made it clear from the beginning that his kingdom was not of this world. His message was one of peace, and particularly peace and reconciliation with God through faith in Jesus himself. While the doctrine of the Trinity took some while to be formulated officially, it is strongly implicit in the Gospels – Jesus referred to God as his father, and promised the disciples the Holy Spirit once he was gone.

At the heart of Christianity is the message of salvation – reconciliation between sinners and God the Father through the actions of Jesus, who is God the Son. As Jesus told a puzzled Pharisee, Nicodemus, unless you are born again in a spiritual sense, you cannot enter the Kingdom of God. Furthermore, Christianity is an exclusive faith – only through Christ is reconciliation with God possible. (Strictly speaking, therefore, the description 'born-again Christian', which became well-known in the 1970s, is a tautology, since Jesus taught that a Christian is someone who *has* been born again, in this spiritual sense.)

However, Jesus also made it evident that his message would eventually be for everyone who heard it and not just for the Jewish race alone. Christians believe that after the crucifixion, Jesus rose from the dead on the third day and, after a brief period with his disciples, ascended back into heaven from whence he had originally come. While Christians celebrate Christmas – the birth of Christ – as the main festival, it would be more accurate to say that it is Easter, the death and resurrection of Jesus, which is at the heart of the Christian message.

It was Jesus crucified and risen whom the early disciples preached from the very beginning. Christianity is not just a law code of ethics, but a restored relationship, through Christ, with God. Not only that, but ordinary believers can get to know God personally, something that differentiates Christianity from all other religions. Christianity is also unique among the monotheistic faiths in that its founder proclaimed himself to be divine, something not true of either Abraham or Muhammad. Jews do not worship Abraham, or Muslims Muhammad, but Christians do believe that Jesus is God. Islam, a monotheistic faith, has no equivalent of the Christian Eucharist for example, since it is the message of Muhammad that is at the core of Islam not the Prophet himself, however revered he might be.

Followers of Islam are Muslims – those in submission to God – and emphatically not Muhammadans, as the West has misnamed them in the past.

But Christianity is centred as much around the divine person of Jesus as it is his message. This therefore meant that Christians could not worship the Emperor. The Divine Cult of the Emperor was not so much religious as political; you would not rebel against someone in whose divinity you believed. But Christianity, being an exclusive faith, rendered Emperor worship impossible, even though, as per the teaching in the New Testament, Christians believed in being good citizens.

One of the best descriptions of who Jesus is and what he came to do is from an unlikely source – the Irish rock star and poverty-relief activist Bono of U2. In a book-length interview with him called *Bono in Conversation*, conducted by a non-Christian journalist, Bono replied to the issue of whether Jesus was a madman or the Messiah, an issue that had also been raised by writer and apologist C. S. Lewis.

> Look, the secular response to the Christ story always goes like this: He was a great prophet, obviously a very interesting guy, had a lot to say along the lines of other great prophets, be they Elijah, Muhammad, Buddha, or Confucius. But actually Christ doesn't allow you that. He doesn't let you off that hook. Christ says, 'No. I'm not saying I'm a teacher, don't call me teacher. I'm not saying I'm a prophet. I'm saying: "I'm the Messiah." I'm saying: "I am God incarnate."' . . . So what you're left with is either Christ was who He said He was – the Messiah – or a complete nutcase . . . The idea that the entire course of civilization for over half of the globe could have its fate changed and turned upside down by a nutcase, for me that's farfetched.

One of the best known of Jesus' teachings is summarized in what we call the Sermon on the Mount, an event that took place early in his ministry, and was preached to a large crowd. (Once more, I am quoting from the *English Standard Version* and from their translation of the Gospel of Matthew, chapter five.)

Blessed are the poor in spirit, for theirs is the kingdom of heaven.
Blessed are those who mourn, for they shall be comforted.
Blessed are the meek, for they shall inherit the earth.
Blessed are those who hunger and thirst for righteousness, for they shall be satisfied.
Blessed are the merciful, for they shall receive mercy.
Blessed are the poor in heart, for they shall see God.
Blessed are the peacemakers, for they shall be called the sons of God.
Blessed are those who are persecuted for righteousness' sake, for theirs is the kingdom of heaven.
Blessed are you when others revile you and persecute you and utter all kinds of evil against you falsely on my account. Rejoice and be glad, for your reward is great in heaven, for so they persecuted the prophets who were before you.

Reading this, it is easy to see both the inheritance of Christianity from Judaism – the parallels with the Ten Commandments are strong – and also the very different approach of Christianity to many issues. Contemporary religions, as well as being polytheistic, also lacked the strong ethical basis so clearly apparent here. Jupiter or Apollo did not insist upon ethical standards, and if the legends about them are anything to go by, morality was not at a premium on Mount Olympus. This had not been the case with Judaism, and was not the case with Christianity (or with Islam, when it arrived). The clear enunciation of objective moral standards was thus of major appeal to people who believed that such things were vital to life, and consequentially significant in the spread of Christianity in its early centuries.

We shall look at Islam later, and here it is important to say that Muslims regard Isa, as they call Jesus, as one of their prophets. Yet, even taking into account the different organization of the Quran – according to the size of the sura (groups of verses), with the biggest first and the shortest last, not according to the subject matter or flow of the narrative – it is hard to find in that work any direct parallel to the Beatitudes above. Individual suras might give similar ethical impressions, but not through the blocks of teaching that pervades both the Hebrew Scriptures and the New Testament.

Much of the ethic of Jesus is to turn the natural standards of society upside down. For example, he taught (again using the *ESV*), using the ancient scriptures as his base:

> You have heard that it was said an eye for an eye and a tooth for a tooth. But I say to you, do not resist the one who is evil. But if anyone slaps you on the right cheek, turn to him the other also. And if anyone would sue you and take your tunic, let him have your cloak as well …

Such statements explain why the author John Stott titles his book on the Sermon on the Mount *The Christian Counter-Culture*, since our natural reaction to such circumstances is to fight back and take the other person's tunic in retaliation for losing our own. Thus in our post-Christian secular culture many, like Gandhi, were able to admire the ethical teaching of Jesus while rejecting his spiritual claims. However, it can be argued that this is not intellectually valid for two reasons. First, Jesus said that he came for principally spiritual, rather than just ethical reasons, although ethics were an essential part of his teaching. Those who admire his ethics, like Gandhi did, therefore reject the exclusive/spiritual side of his message, and thus the religious distinctiveness of Christianity, while keeping its non-religious ethics. Furthermore, as the following quotation shows, Jesus included our thoughts as well as what we actually do as an integral part of his moral code. We may never have murdered anyone, but we have surely often thought negative things, even about those closest to us.

The ethical standards of Jesus were exceptionally high. Later in the same passage from which the quotation on the previous page is taken, he showed, for example, that:

> You have heard that it was said to those of old, you shall not murder; and whoever murders will be liable to judgment. But I say to you that everyone who is angry with his brother will be liable to judgment; whoever insults his brother will be liable to the Council [the Jewish Council, or Sanhedrin]; and whoever says 'you fool!' will be liable to the hell of fire.

This in effect says that righteousness is humanly impossible to attain. While we may never — one trusts — have committed murder, we have all been angry with people in our time, and yet anger, which we think of as a natural reaction, is given the severest judgment possible. To Jesus, and thus to Christianity historically understood, humanity is ultimately in spiritual need, since the fulfilment of the ethical law is impossible.

Jesus told his disciples after the Resurrection to go into the whole of the world and increase their number. There were probably around 120 of them – possibly a few more – on the day of Pentecost, when the Bible records the Holy Spirit as coming down on the first Christians, who then began the task of global evangelism. As the Gospels hint, for example in the Parable of the Good Samaritan, this was no longer to be a faith for Jews alone.

The early church

Historians and sociologists seem never to have achieved a consensus on why Christianity spread so rapidly, especially in the first century. Church historians have attributed the astonishingly rapid growth to God the Holy Spirit, and, needless to say, that is not something that convinces secular (if not actually atheist) sociologists of religion.

However, recent historians writing from religious perspectives have tried to find causes that would appeal both to fellow believers and to secular academics alike. Most notable among these has been the British ecclesiologist and expert in missions Andrew Walls, in works such as *The Cross-Cultural Process in Christian History*, and in his critiques of the famous historian K. S. Latourette, whose epic multi-volume history of the church was published during and after the Second World War.

The first reason that Walls provides is that the Mediterranean world in which Christianity began was relatively culturally homogenous. Most of the region was under the stable rule of the Roman Empire, and linguistically Greek was widely understood, if only as a lingua franca.

Second, the Christian church from very early on was radical in its social inclusiveness once it became open to those of non-Jewish origin. This made it highly unusual in that it insisted that issues such as social class or race were of no relevance within the body of believers.

Third, as the eminent Baptist mission historian Brian Stanley of Cambridge has also emphasized, is a point that follows on naturally from this – namely that, unlike the Jewish faith which distinguished between those born Jewish and those who became Jews (namely proselytes), early Christianity made no such distinction. This enabled the new faith to be seen as something altogether different, something that Greeks, for example, could join as full members.

Finally, Christianity offered a quality of communal life that the existing divinity cults could not match, or, in the case of the more elite sects, did not even try and imitate.

A point also made by the archaeologist, Bruce Winter, is that the cult of the divine emperor failed to deliver the spiritual goods to the ordinary people, something that was not true of the early Christian church.

Thus, as the Book of Acts shows, Christianity became a genuinely multi-racial, multi-ethnic international faith from very early on; it has always seen itself as such, and increasingly so since the global spread of Christianity in the nineteenth century onwards. One of our Western misconceptions is to see Christianity as a predominantly Western faith. This has long since ceased to be the case. Today, the vast majority of prac-tising Christians now live in the Third World with, for example, Africa being far more Christian than Western Europe (and, to make another example, around sixteen times as many active Anglican Protestants in Nigeria as in England). In fact it is mainly only Western Europe that is predominantly secular, with the rest of the world, including the USA, still actively religious. In the twenty-first century, Christianity has returned to its roots.

Christianity, as we shall see, soon became illegal under the Romans. It spread, therefore, by word of mouth, or, in the words of a phrase used early on, 'gossiping the Gospel'.

By roughly AD 40, the centre of the new faith had become Antioch, on the borders of what is now Syria and Turkey, and which is also where the followers of 'The Way', to use their own description, were first known as Christians. By this stage, too, there were several thousand members of the Church, spreading all over the Roman Empire.

As with the Hebrew Scriptures, which never disguise the failings of otherwise deeply admired heroes such as Abraham, Moses and David, the New Testament is very honest about the human frailties and mistakes of God's people – there is no attempt at covering up mistakes or disagreements. Not all the disciples understood the international nature of the faith, and some took quite a while to realize that things had changed.

The Apostle Peter is a classic example. He is recorded as having problems with evangelizing a Roman centurion, or eating non-kosher food. In the Gospels, he frequently gets over-excited, and says things which he later regrets. Above all, just before the crucifixion, he denies knowing Jesus altogether, and flees in shame when he is rumbled as being one of the disciples.

One person who helped the most in making the spiritual and psychological leap started out persecuting the new religion, and then became transformed into one of its leading converts. This was Saul of Tarsus, whom we know today as the Apostle Paul. He was the author of much of the New Testament in the form of his Epistles to different churches around the Gentile, Roman Empire, which he had established himself. One of his important messages was to underline the universality of Christianity: in Christ, he wrote, there was neither male nor female, Jew or Greek, slave or free person.

Modern critical scholarship tends to give an earlier date to Paul's Epistles than to the Gospel narratives. Here I think much depends on your prior point of view. Those of a theologically liberal disposition see Paul as the effective re-founder of Christianity, a view popular in many university-based Divinity Schools. Theologically more conservative scholars, such as N. T. Wright, the recent Bishop of Durham, reject this approach as being inaccurate historically and spiritually.

One thing is perhaps important to say here, as it has become a major cause of misunderstanding: while a combination of conservative politics and theology is a normal mix in much of the USA, it is by no means the same outside of that country. Not only that, as the theologically Evangelical and politically progressive former US President Jimmy Carter shows in his book *Our Endangered Values*, it is not always the case in America either. (Writer Jim Wallis' book *God's Politics*, cited earlier, proves the same.) In most countries, especially in the Global South, it is not possible to judge someone's politics by their theology.

Christianity spread rapidly around the Roman Empire, and beyond, into some parts of Asia and Africa outside the imperial borders. However, the Roman authorities quickly realized that it was not just a variant of Judaism, but a religion in its own right. This meant that Christians were not exempt from Emperor Worship, unlike the Jews, who had been granted a special exemption from this because of the monotheistic nature of their faith. Since Christians, as monotheists, worshipped only God, the Romans savagely persecuted them from very early on – the later Epistles in the New Testament were already referring to persecution, and how to cope with it. As the saying soon went, the blood of the martyrs is the seed of the Church.

To Christians, even a nominal amount of incense on an altar to Caesar was to break the command to worship God only. For the Romans, this was a test of political allegiance, which the Christians failed, and it was for this that the infant church was so violently persecuted.

Ironically, Christianity and Judaism, the two monotheistic faiths, are the two remnants in the region from this distant time. Because the Romans took an essentially relaxed attitude to other faiths, as their adherents had no theological problem with Emperor Worship, the Roman religion per se had little long-term influence on the Middle East. If anything, it was the other way around, since several of the later pagan Roman Emperors such as Heliogabulus were from the region, and brought their local cults with them to Rome.

At this time, the heartland of Christianity remained in the Middle East, even though much of Roman-ruled Europe saw many conversions to the new faith. (Other parts were not converted for many centuries.)

The key difference between early Christianity and Islam that came 600 years later is that for the first 300 years the

Christian religion was an underground, persecuted faith, spread by conversion and not linked in any way to the formal centres of power. This is quite unlike Islam, in which political and military authority and the faith itself were merged from the outset. In the Beatitudes, Jesus expected his followers to be persecuted, and the Epistles, especially those attributed to Peter, emphasize this very strongly. This gave Christianity enormous resilience as it enabled it to be wholly independent of outside circumstances.

Among the leaders of the infant church was James, the half-brother of Jesus (being, according to Protestants, the son of Mary by her later marriage to Joseph, and to Catholics, the son of Joseph before he married Mary). But the Jewish uprising against Roman rule in AD 66, which ended with the destruction of the Temple in AD 70, resulted in the death of large numbers of Jews, most notably in the fortress of Masada, where the Jewish defenders killed themselves rather than succumb to continued Roman tyranny. These events brought about a Diaspora not just for the Jews as they fled Israel but for the young Christian church as well, thereby international-izing the movement yet further. Persecution also grew worse; many of the Jewish–Christian leaders were thrown to the lions in the circus, or burned to death – just two among the gruesome methods employed. In AD 135 a final Jewish revolt led by Simon bar Kochba, who claimed to be the Messiah, pushed the Romans to even more drastic measures, with Jerusalem being sacked and turned into an entirely pagan city. The Jewish relationship with the land was increasingly severed, with the majority of Jews now living outside the confines of the original kingdoms.

Jews did not return in large numbers to the Holy Land until the twentieth century. They now became a people without a land, with Jewish communities stretching from present-day Spain in the West to what is now Iran in the East. Nostalgia for Jerusalem never went away. But the contribution of Diaspora Jews to the countries in which they now found themselves was enormous, intellectually, culturally, medically and in many other fields. Come the advent of Islam, in which Jews were given special status as one of the two Peoples of the Book (along with their fellow monotheists, the Christians), the ability of Jewish exiles to make a positive contribution rose further still. Not only that, but because of their distinct religion, they managed to remain a discrete group, and did not, unlike, say, the Samaritans, become absorbed into the peoples around them. Their survival as a distinct group despite being exiled from their homeland is remarkable, and a considerable tribute to them as a unique people.

Not only that, the increasing scale of the Jewish Diaspora was of enormous help to the early Christians, since the synagogues were often the jumping-off point for many of the first evangelists, large numbers of whom it should be remembered were themselves Jewish.

One notable achievement of the early church was to formulate the Bible as we know it today, having worked out which books were and were not canonical. Protestants and Catholics do not entirely agree on this – the Catholic Church adding some books that Protestants reject – but the basis canon was agreed very early on in Christian history.

Slowly but surely more formal structures arose within the infant church as the numbers of converts grew exponentially and geographically throughout the Empire and beyond. Here the history of the church becomes more difficult, since different Christian denominations interpret what evolved in divergent ways, some feeling that the rise of a hierarchy was correct, while others regret it. Either way, the structure of the church became more familiar to what we know today, with a separate priesthood and leaders called Bishops, some of whom enjoyed more authority and greater prestige than others. The Church was still underground, however, being persecuted by the Emperor Diocletian, for example, as late as AD 303.

Many of the early Church martyrs have been forgotten, but others have come down to us, one of them, Polycarp (c. AD 69–155) being a good example. A copious writer of post-biblical Epistles, he dealt with many of the thorny doctrinal issues with which the early Church was wrestling. He was also one of the key leaders in the generation after those such as St Clement, who, while they did not know Jesus themselves, knew people who did. Polycarp came from Smyrna – now Izmir – in Anatolia, a town that was then Greek.

Smyrna continued as a predominantly Greek city throughout the Ottoman Empire until its seizure by the Turks in 1922. We must remember that the ethnic map of the Middle East was very different until that date from what it is now. Anatolia, for example, with its Greeks, Armenians, Kurds and later on, Turks, was a patchwork of nationalities until the formation of an overwhelmingly Turkish state – although with a Kurdish minority – in 1922 made the Anatolian Peninsula essentially the home of one race. Therefore for most of the period covered in this book, people in the region were part of larger, multi-racial, empires, with different races living cheek by jowl, either in neighbouring villages, or side by side in the same town.

Mark Mazower's book on Thessaloniki – then called Salonica – is a fascinating example of how Turks, Jews, Greeks and other groups all lived peaceably together for centuries in the multi-ethnic empires that existed until recent times. People of the three Abrahamic faiths, Muslim, Jewish and Christian, have often lived in harmony for centuries.)

To revert to the main narrative, one can see with Polycarp why persecution failed. On being asked by the Roman consular official, reluctant to see such an old man die violently, whether or not he wanted to renounce his faith or be eaten by lions, Polycarp refused, despite being eighty-six years old! By the time he was supposed to be fed to them, the animals had apparently gone, so he was burned alive instead.

Polycarp and others like him are known as the Church Fathers, and many of them are especially revered in both the Catholic and Orthodox wings of Christianity. In these two branches of the faith, their writings take a second place to Scripture itself, and while Protestants do not hold them in quite the same light, early Christian leaders, such as, for example, the fourth-century writer, St Augustine of Hippo, are held in high esteem. St Augustine came from northern Africa and was a Berber, a people now almost entirely Muslim; we forget that until the seventh century much of the present-day Islamic world was overwhelmingly Christian.

Christianity established

In AD 306 an Emperor arose for whom Christianity was a faith worth supporting, rather than a rival one to persecute. Emperor Constantine made Christianity formally tolerated in the Edict of Milan in 312, and from that it emerged as the official religion of the Roman Empire under Constantine's successors in 381. By this time the Empire, which stretched from Britain in the west to the disputed Persian border in the east, was getting rather unwieldy, so Constantine also split it administratively into sections, with a new capital at Constantinople being founded in 330.

One of the great issues discussed now for over 1,700 years is whether or not Constantine ever truly became a Christian himself, or whether he simply took up Christianity as a means of effective social control over his new domains. Since we do not have hard evidence either way of his inner thought-processes, the case is still open. But my suspicion is that the latter is true.

Either way, while the cessation of persecution was from almost all points of view wonderful news – who wants to be persecuted, after all – the advent of Constantine was a disaster for the church from which, it could be argued, it never wholly recovered. (I have examined this at much greater length in another book, *A Crash Course on Church History*.)

For our purposes, the key point is that the decision allowed outside imperial interference in the internal affairs of the Christian church. As the leaders of the Donatist group in northern Africa pointed out with some justice, 'What has the Emperor to do with the church?' Since Christ emphatically split church and state, one could argue that from a spiritual viewpoint the church was allowing itself to be hijacked by those whose prime motives were political rather than religious.

Not only that, but from the standpoint of the Middle East the result was soon to be very bad news indeed, with results that are still being felt in the twenty-first century.

Up until Constantine, Christianity was seen as a faith in its own right without links to worldly power. In our own times, it is surely no coincidence that Christianity has seen a massive increase in the Third World *after* the colonial powers have left. The average Christian today is a Nigerian or Chinese, not a white Westerner. But the deal that the Church agreed with Constantine meant – as American sociologist Robert L. Montgomery points out in his unusually titled book *The Lopsided Spread of Christianity: Towards an Understanding of the Diffusion of Religions* – that Christianity was increasingly, and unfortunately, linked to Roman power. Then, after the fall of Rome it was seen as closely involved with that of the surviving Byzantine Empire.

Furthermore the new arrangement soon saw one group of Christians persecuting another, all with the blessing of the secular power, the Emperor. While the negative effects on Christianity per se do not concern us here, this intra-Christian persecution soon radically changed the Middle East. For as we shall soon see, when the Muslims became one group of Christians was no different from any other, and all of them, whatever their particular idiosyncrasies of belief, were protected Peoples of the Book. This meant that some Christians would actually avoid persecution by being under Islamic rule, and would continue to suffer if Byzantine rule survived. The Constantinian deal would cost the church in the Middle East very dear indeed.

Following the fall of the Western Empire in 476, the Eastern Roman Empire lasted another thousand years, until it was conquered by the Ottomans in 1453. The Eastern or Byzantine Empire, which split from the West in 395, always regarded itself as fully Roman, even though it soon became principally Greek- rather than Latin-speaking.

To the Muslim world it was Rome, and its territory was often called *Roumeli* or, to use a Turkish word, *Rum*. There is a real sense in which the later Ottomans, who finally seized Constantinople in 1453, saw themselves as the successors of the Roman Emperors, albeit not in a spiritual sense, and in terms of geography, one can argue convincingly for a strong degree of continuity between the two. Right up until the nineteenth century, much of the Balkans was referred to as Roumelia, and the Greeks would refer to themselves as *Romioi*, as readers of Patrick Leigh Fermor's many travel books on Greece will know.

Because of Christianity's change in status, Constantine and his successors (excluding the pagan convert, Julian the Apostate, AD 331–363) started to interfere in the internal affairs of the Church and in its doctrine in particular. Here again, depending on one's point of view, this was either a good thing or a disaster. Now that Christianity was official, Constantine wanted the whole Church to agree to the same doctrines. He convened a Council at Nicaea, near his new capital, in 325, and this was to be the first of many Councils of the Church, to which, depending on how many are deemed canonical, Catholic and Orthodox Christians still look back today.

(For what was decided at Nicaea, see writers such as Ben Witherington and Sharan Newman. Witherington comes from the Methodist tradition of Christianity, so is an impartial witness in relation to the Catholic Church.)

But from the Church's point of view, this was something of a Faustian pact. It is possible, therefore, to agree fully with the traditional interpretation of Nicaea in terms of mainstream Christianity, and at the same time, if one takes a strong separation of Church and State view, as I would, at the same time to regret the political ramifications of the decisions taken.

For while the Church was no longer persecuted, it was the secular authorities who now determined Christian doctrine, albeit initially in consensus with leading members and officials of the Church. Soon, variants of Christianity not in accord with the official view were persecuted themselves, a move which was to prove fatal for Christianity when the Islamic invasions began in the seventh century. Dissident groups were to welcome the invaders, since the Muslims could not care less what particular doctrines individual Christians believed. It was better to live in freedom under Islam than to be persecuted under a Byzantine Emperor.

State control became known as Caesaropapism, with the Emperor having authority over the church. This existed in the Byzantine Empire until 1453, and even in the twenty-first century in some countries, including Britain, the state retains authority over the doctrines of the established religion. It took until into the seventeenth century for genuine toleration of dissenting theological views to emerge in the West. This was as a result of the split in Western Christianity in the Reformation in the sixteenth century. Catholics and Protestants went their separate ways, often with warfare and considerable violence in the process.

In the United Kingdom, non-Anglican Protestants lacked rights until 1689 and the Act of Toleration, and Roman Catholics did not have the vote in Britain until 1828. All this is, I would argue, because of a false link between Church and State that was unknown to the founders of Christianity, and took nearly 1,400 years to be rediscovered by the Christian Church.

Now most Christian churches have no state connection, and the pact with Constantine is a thing of the past. But in the part of the Middle East that was Christian, official orthodoxy was state enforced after 381, with dissident groups, such as the Nestorians, fleeing to the lands of the Zoroastrian Sassanid Empire to avoid persecution by fellow Christians.

Parallel to all this, the ongoing war between the Byzantines and the Sassanids continued. War raged from AD 337 to 350, and again from 359 to 361. Peace was finally signed in 384, and this time it actually lasted a long time, until 503, when another century of on-off wars began again. Only in 628 was a truce called, and by then it was too late: a hitherto unknown merchant in Arabia had founded a new faith, whose followers would, after his death, transform not just the Middle East but the world itself. The third monotheistic faith, Islam, was born.

4

MUHAMMAD AND THE DAWN
OF ISLAM

Arabia and the life of the prophet

Muhammad, the founder of the third and youngest of the great three monotheistic faiths and by profession a merchant, was born in what is now the Hijaz province of Saudi Arabia in around 570 AD. Although the Arabian Peninsula was not the centre of any major civilization, as much of it is desert in which large-scale living has been impossible until recent times, it was a major trading region, visited by merchants and others from all around the region and beyond. Goods would have come from Europe, Africa, South Asia, and possibly from as far afield as East Asia.

However, a number of the early Arab civilizations, especially those not too distant from the sea, were not without significance. Many peoples, especially the Ethiopians, have claimed links to the Queen of Sheba, from whom Hailie Selassie, the last Emperor of Ethiopia, maintained he was descended. But the story of that Queen (known as *Bilqis* in Arabic) probably derived from centuries-old Ethiopian–Arab trading connections before

Arabia turned to Islam. In all likelihood she was the ruler of the ancient Sheba, or Saba, now in Yemen, a civilization that went back to the eighth century BC or even earlier, and whose splendid artefacts were on show at the British Museum in 2002. In the Helleno-Roman period, the Nabataeans, an Arab tribe from present-day Jordan, rose to prominence. Their city of Petra, now in south-west Jordan, is a world-famous archaeological site and even appears in Western popular culture, in stories from *Tintin in the Land of Black Gold* to *Indiana Jones and the Last Crusade*. Arabia, therefore, was no backwater.

By Muhammad's time, the two great monotheistic faiths of the Middle East were already well represented in the region by significant Christian and Jewish minorities. Yet most Arabs were still polytheists of some kind or another, with a number of local pagan cults centred on Mecca, where goddess worship had existed for a long time. (The names of three of these – al-Lat, al-Uzza and Manat – have come down to us in what are called the *Satanic Verses* of the Quran.) As the Cambridge and Princeton academic Michael Cook has written, had a sixth-century commentator been forecasting how the Arabian Peninsula would have turned out in the seventh, they might have predicted a conversion to some form of Christianity rather than the dramatic emergence of a new faith and global superpower.

Not all the Arabian Christians were Orthodox, however, and this might have had an impact on the formation of later Islamic doctrine. The Ethiopian Church, for example, has remained what is called Monophysite, which means that it does not fully recognize the simultaneous full humanity and divinity of Jesus Christ as does mainstream Christianity in all persuasions. So Muhammad might have been more familiar with these minorities rather than the majority Catholic or Greek Orthodox forms of the faith. Not only that, but Judaism was very keen to insist that God is one – thereby rejecting the Christian doctrine of the Trinity – and since Islam does the same, it is also quite possible that this too influenced Muhammad as he picked up monotheistic beliefs.

As already mentioned, around AD 600, the centuries-long war between the Roman/Byzantine Empire, and that of Persia, was slowly petering out, with both societies exhausted by so prolonged a conflict. The Byzantines were actively persecuting minority Christian groups, many of which lived in the Middle East. Various client states ringed the edges of Arabia, one loyal to the Byzantines, the other to their Sassanid rivals.

According to Muslim history, the first of the revelations to Muhammad came in AD 610 in the form of a request delivered via Jabril (known as the Archangel Gabriel to Jews and Christians) to recite a message from God. Muhammad continued to have such messages for the remaining twenty-two years of his life. As with the early Christian church, the number of disciples grew by word of mouth, a loyal band of followers began to emerge, and by 615, five years after his early revelations, Muhammad had built up a steady flow of followers. But this alienated some of the more powerful members of the Quraysh tribe, from which he came. Some of his followers were forced to flee as far away as Ethiopia, and from 620 onwards, Muhammad was in negotiations with a nearby town then called Yathrib about taking refuge in it. In 622 they agreed to receive him, and he fled there with his followers, in what we now call the hegira or hijra, and it is from this epochal event that the Islamic calendar begins. Yathrib would soon become Medina (the city of the Prophet), where Muhammad established himself as the secular, military and religious leader of the new Islamic community or umma. The early Muslims were also to raise funds by attacking enemy caravans.

Unfortunately for Muhammad, his kinsmen in Mecca still resented his growing power, and the effect that the new religion inevitably had in reducing the numbers of adherents to the old religion in Mecca, and the profits that leading townspeople made from its worshippers. This resulted in regular military conflict between Medina and Mecca, with a major battle narrowly won at Badr in the Arabian Peninsula in 624 by the nascent Islamic community. However, by the end of 629 the rulers of Mecca had given up the struggle, and Muhammad was able to spend the last two years of his life in charge of the holy city of Mecca as well as of Medina. Eventually all of Arabia, including Mecca itself, came under Muhammad's rule.

Muhammad had no sons, only a daughter, Fatima, married to his (and her) cousin, Ali. No one could succeed him as Prophet. There were other capacities in which a successor could take the leadership of the new Islamic umma, as the Golden Age of the Islamic conquests and expansion later shows, but it was the four caliphs (literally 'successor' in the singular in Arabic) who succeeded Muhammad via the consensus. They became known as the *Rashidun*, or Rightly Guided Caliphs by the reckoning of the 85 per cent Sunni majority of Muslims today.

The first Caliph, Abu Bakr, reigned for only two years, until 634, and was the only one to die peacefully, since internal disputes became evident early on. He in turn was succeeded by Omar, under whom the rapid expansion began, first with the conquest of Egypt (following the Battle of Yarmuk in 636), then Palestine and present-day Iran after the Battle of Qadisayah in 637. He was murdered in 644, and was succeeded by Uthman under whom the Caliphate extended further to the easternmost part of today's Iran and to the borders of Central Asia in the East and northern Africa in the West.

These successes saw a permanent withdrawal of the Byzantines from what was then the Holy Land; after Yarmuk, the Byzantine Emperors were never able to regain the lost territory, and by 751 the Iranian Empire had been vanquished. Uthman, in turn, was murdered in 656, when he was succeeded by Muhammad's son-in-law, Ali. Under Ali there was a civil war, with Ali being assassinated in 661.

The evolution of the Quran

The Quran remains the main source of inspiration and instructions for Muslims today, of whatever variety. Islamic scholars divide it into those passages delivered to Muhammad in Mecca, which are often more poetic or spiritual, and those when he was a ruler in Medina, and which are more down to earth. From it derives God-given law, or sharia, which is still today the official law code of Islamic countries such as Saudi Arabia. Man-made justice, *fiqh*, exists, but does not carry the same weight.

As to the Quran's evolution, since the text was finalized after Muhammad's death in the reigns of the Rightly Guided Caliphs, it is not possible to know for sure what revelation came when.

The Quran is a completely different book from the Jewish and Christian parts of the Bible. Taking Islamic chronology as correct (which 'revisionist' authors such as Michael Cook and the Cambridge academic Patricia Crone would not), the whole corpus was written over the course of just those twenty-two years. The Bible, however, was composed, by both conservative and liberal accounts, over centuries. It has sixty-six books, almost as many authors, and was put together in many languages. It is consecutive, and gives, for example, the lives of Abraham, Moses, David and Jesus sequentially, from their beginning to their end. There are different genres – historical narrative, poetry, prophecy, and teaching – often with particular books specializing in one form or another.

None of this is true of the Quran. One cannot, for example, deduce anything about Muhammad's life from it, since he scarcely appears. The different genres are all interwoven, with themes appearing in different places. (The index in the Penguin Classic Quran is very helpful here for those for whom the text is unfamiliar, although no translation is ever valid in Islamic eyes.) The only acceptable version is the Arabic original, with the diacritical marks finalized some years after Muhammad's death.

Inevitably non-Muslims will find there are parts of the Quran they cannnot accept. However, this should not preclude accepting a large part of Islamic tradition as historically true; furthermore the substantial amount that is persuasive in the works of revisionists, such as Cook and Crone, is no reason to upturn centuries of deeply held Islamic traditions on what happened and when. This is regardless of whether or not we believe Islam to be *spiritually* true, which is an altogether different matter beyond the scope of this book.

The faithful, of all kinds, will of course have their own views. I have in the past been in trouble from Christian scholars who, in rejecting Islam, also reject that, for example, Muhammad really was born in 570. Yet there is nothing to suggest that the Islamic tradition on Muhammad's dates is wrong. Where Crone and Cook have a good case is that very few documents from the dawn of Islam actually survive. This is indeed so, but as to the historicity of *when* the Quran was written, there is no reason to prevent an early date unless evidence appears to the contrary.

The Quran is only canonical in its original language, Arabic, and is thus not written in the language of most Muslims today, who speak a much later and more popular form of Arabic that is often a local variety of the classical original. Classic Arabic is much older, for example, than the language of the King James (or Authorized) Version of the Bible, but because of the insistence in the Muslim world that only the original version is canonical, its style of classic Arabic has become *the* accepted version throughout the Arab world. To the non-Arab Muslim majority – we need to remember that most Muslims live in countries such as India, Indonesia, Malaysia, and Central Asia – the Quran is in a foreign language.

The Quran's structure – the largest suras, or groups of verses, first and the shortest ones last (a problem that a good index can help solve) – means it is not easy to read straight through, although extended study does provide a fairly basic knowledge of Islamic doctrine by the time the end is reached.

However, to many Muslims its directness is an advantage – the doctrines in it are clear and presented in a way that still appeals to increasing millions of people worldwide as Islam, like Christianity, remains firmly in expansion mode. In Islam the great debates have historically been around issues such as whether or not the Quran always pre-existed in eternity with Allah, or whether there was a moment at which it was created.

Next to the Quran itself are the Hadith, or recorded non-Quranic sayings of the Prophet. Here, the two main varieties of Islam possess different Hadith, depending upon whom they regard as authoritative in passing them on. All Hadith always give their source, which, writers such as Michael Cook explain, indicate their original oral history. Finally comes the sunna, or the example of the life of Muhammad – and it is from this word that the 85 per cent majority of today's Muslims, the Sunni, derive their name.

(This percentage of 85 per cent Sunni and 15 per cent Shiite is also the one quoted in most newspapers and scholarly journals. The reasons for this split will be examined later.)

Notwithstanding the various schools of Islamic interpretation, the main thing to remember is that Muhammad was, unlike Jesus and Abraham, creating a state as well as a religious belief system, and that Islam therefore reflects that. Christians often live in countries where they are not in charge, or are actively persecuted, but, as Bernard Lewis points out, that has not been the case with most Muslims until very recent times.

(It is true that the Children of Israel became a state, many centuries after they began, and that books of the Bible such as Deuteronomy demonstrate that. But statehood was not instantaneous, as it was in Islam – and most Jews have not lived in a Jewish state for millennia. The Torah is not the law of Israel, nor the Ten Commandments of any country, however Christian.)

Muhammad did not think he was founding a new religion. For him, Islam (which literally means 'submission') was the final revelation of God, and he, Muhammad, was the final Prophet. Certainly the idea of the oneness and unity of God is as strong in Islam as it is in Judaism, although the Quran does not understand the Christian Trinity. It holds that the Trinity is God the Father, God the Son and Mary, whereas Christians hold that it is the first two, with God the Holy Sprit as the third member.

Patricia Crone has speculated in *The Cambridge History of the Islamic World* that early Islam was deeply influenced by Judaism. Many leading characters in the Hebrew Scriptures appear in the Quran, with Arabic names, such as Adam, Moses, Aaron, David, Solomon and the Queen of Sheba (who was from the Arabian Peninsula) to name just a few. The well-known Arab Caliph, Harun al-Rashid, of 1001 Nights fame, has the same name in Arabic as Moses' brother, Aaron in the Hebrew Scriptures when translated into Arabic, namely Aaron the Wise. Suleiman the Magnificent, the illustrious Ottoman Sultan, is Solomon when translated from the Arabic back into the original Hebrew.

However, the stories are often different in the Quran from the earlier version in the Hebrew Scriptures; for example in the former, Abraham nearly sacrifices Ishmael, from whom Arabs claim descent, rather than Isaac. Muslims would argue that the Jews (and later on the Christians) got the details wrong, and, needless to say, Jews and Christians would argue to the contrary.

At this distance the exact legacy of one faith to another is hard to prove, even though Patricia Crone has considerable validity in what she is writing. Paul Johnson, for example, in his *A History of the Jews* also sees Islam as an offshoot of Judaism, and there remains a very good case for this as a workable hypothesis.

In more recent years another theory of the origins of Islam and of the Quran has gained academic credence, notably through the work of American academic Fred Donner, of the University of Chicago (and his 2010 book *Muhammad and the Believers at the Origins of Islam*). In his fascinating 'believers' theory, Donner suggests that Islam originally (certainly in Muhammad's lifetime) was not as exclusive as it later became. Initially believers of Islam consisted of monotheists, including the group that later became known as those who 'submitted' (from which the word *Islam* derives). However, Donner contends that Jews and Christians, some of whom might even have fought in the early armies of the Caliphate and several of whom we know held high office (most notably the Christian writer later called John of Damascus), were also included in this group.

It was not until well into the Ummayad Caliphate, this theory states, and in particular the rule of Caliph Abd al-Malik (685–705), that Islam became the exclusive religion that we recognize today. Now Jews and Christians are viewed as 'peoples of the Book' but exist outside of the umma or community of believers. Donner's thesis argues that because of the early lack of distinction during the early conquests, non-Muslim peoples, overrun by the armies of the Caliphate, would have been less likely to resist since they would not have seen Islam as a foreign or oppressive religion at that time.

In considering other scholarship about this early Islamic period, Donner states that there is a major 'problem of sources' since none dates from the foundations of Islam itself, but from much later. However, unlike other scholars, Donner suggests a much shorter timeframe (thirty-plus years rather than, for example, a whole century and more) between the foundation of Islam and its earliest sources. It follows, according to Donner's theory, that though the early sayings and stories of Islam might not have been contemporary to Muhammad, they are certainly not as far away from his lifetime, and from those who would remember him, as others have suggested.

Donner's thesis is certainly appealing. Among other things, it describes Muslims, Jews and Christians as far closer together at the dawn of Islam than both the traditional story and scholarship to this date, which posit Islam against Christianity from the outset. If Donner is right, his theory should benefit the civil relations and human rights of Christian minorities in Islamic countries. But, like David Rohl's equally attractive thesis on Egyptian chronology that we saw earlier, Donner's theory is also very hard to prove given the lack of concrete evidence either way. Needless to say, his is not a proposition that will find supporters in strict Islamic circles and maybe not even outside of the Western academic community. But it is an interesting angle to consider nonetheless.

Islam's five pillars and jihad

Islam has five pillars upon which all Muslims agree. The first is the statement made upon conversion, the second is prayer, the third is alms-giving, the fourth is fasting (particularly during the holy month of Ramadan) and the fifth is the pilgrimage to Mecca.

However, from the seventh-century Kharijites – a group who felt that any doctrinal compromise was wrong – to twenty-first-century fanatics, there is a controversial sixth pillar, that such people would add. This is jihad.

Jihad means different things to different Muslims, and has also, some would argue, changed meaning over time. Like Muhammad himself and as with the Crusades, the concept of jihad has become a political football in the debate on what Islam is really like. Those who would defend Islam as a genuine religion of peace take one interpretation, and those who would declare war on the infidel West, and those Muslims not of their own opinion, would interpret this term very differently: with violence.

According to an early Hadith, Muhammad distinguished between the Greater Jihad, namely the internal struggle for a Muslim to lead a more holy life (akin to the Christian concept of sanctification) and the Lesser Jihad, or holy war, taken in the name of God against infidels.

Bernard Lewis and others are surely right to say that the original concept of the word – warfare in God's name – was the prevalent *early* meaning. Not only was Muhammad a conqueror but his successors, the Caliphs, embarked on a massive campaign of global conquest after his death. Furthermore, interpreters such as Ibn Taymiyya in the fourteenth century also took this view. However, over the course of time many Muslims clearly decided that the Greater Jihad – non-violent inner struggle – was the essential real meaning of the term.

This is what Akbar Ahmed argues in his books *Islam Today* and *Discovering Islam*, and American academic John Esposito in *Islam: The Straight Path*. Some commentators such as David Pryce-Jones and Daniel Pipes will not accept this, and neither of course do those radical Muslims for whom the first century of Islam remains an inviolate role model. Nor, as Pipes pointed out in 2002, is there any academic consensus on the matter. It is a shame that in many books there is no *via media*, or area of grey, with religious belief being seen either as perfect or as perfidious. Once more, readers will have to judge for themselves.

Islam: wider issues

With Muhammad, as with Abraham the original Jew, and Jesus Christ the founder of Christianity, the same issue presents itself – no independent narratives of his life exist outside of the texts of the religion that he inspired. In Muhammad's case the difficulty is greater, because, unlike the Hebrew Scriptures or the Christian New Testament, the Quran does not refer directly to the life of the Prophet Muhammad himself. Piecing together his life is thus problematic, since not even Muslim sources tell us a great deal about his life before he began receiving what he believed to be revelations from God. As Jonathan Bloom and Sheila Blair say in their book (and acclaimed TV series of the same name in the USA), *Islam: A Thousand Years of Faith and Power*, 'Little is known about the early life of Muhammad, and most of it has been embellished by later retellings.'

Speculation about Muhammad can even be dangerous. With Christianity, the Church has not persecuted for centuries. In Judaism, the modern Reform version has existed equally peacefully with the more conservative Orthodox varieties. But Islam is still, in many parts of the world, a state-linked faith where heterodox opinions can lead to death, persecution or exile in some countries, such as Saudi Arabia, even today.

As a result, many of the critics of traditional Islam have been outsiders, such as Patricia Crone. Her book, *Hagarism*, jointly written with Michael Cook, takes the same view of the origins of Islam as a myth that many similar commentators do of the existence of characters such as Abraham or Moses. It is however a minority view, as the book admits. The best-known internal critic, Ibn Warraq, the author of commentaries on the text of the Quran, has had to write under a pseudonym for fear of what would happen to him and his family if his true identity became known.

(Michael Cook has written two popular works on the origins of Islam – *Muhammad* and *The Koran: A Very Short Introduction*. The books by writer Karen Armstrong, such as *A History of God*, would be more representative of Western thinking. But to be fair, as Cook points out, heterodox opinion in the Islamic world can lead to death threats. This has occurred recently, when the Egyptian scholar Abu Zayd had to flee for his life for expressing views on the Quran that would be considered normal if applied to the Bible in Divinity faculties in the West. The same became notoriously true in the West when the novelist Salman Rushdie wrote *The Satanic Verses*, a work considered highly blasphemous across the entire Islamic world and which led the Iranian leader, Ayatollah Khomeini, to sentence Rushdie to death.)

Ironically, conservative Muslims often quote from theologically liberal Western New Testament scholars to attack

Christianity, while not allowing that kind of dissent about the Quran. However equally theologically traditional Christian scholars will quote from Abu Zayd and Ibn Warraq on the Quran, while disliking redaction criticism of the Bible.

Even a well-known apologist for moderate but theologically conservative Islam, like Akbar Ahmed, has come under far more attack from hard-liners on his own side, despite his defence of the Muslim faith to worldwide audiences in the West. (Ahmed also points out in *Islam Under Siege* that to refer to Muslim fundamentalists is misleading. In a theological sense, most Muslims are fundamentalist, but equally the majority is also strongly opposed to both violence and fanaticism.)

Unfortunately, discussion on Islam has also become embroiled in the culture wars in the USA, with the neo-conservatives now attacking Muhammad in a very personal way. This is particularly unhelpful, since civilized discussion is highly desirable in an era in which religious terrorism has sadly become a major issue of our time. Mutual understanding is surely preferable to trading insults.

A classic example of this is the success of a recent book, *The Politically Incorrect Guide to Islam (and the Crusades)*, whose title reveals a great deal. Such polemics only increase heat between Muslims and the rest of the world, with the unfortunate consequences that are all around us. As will be argued later, the Crusades were a complete disaster from a Western, let alone an Islamic, point of view, and to defend such past activities only stokes the fires of discord.

Islam, an unknown commentator once remarked, is the only major global religion founded by a businessman. While that is a good description of Muhammad's career as a successful merchant before the new faith began, that is not how Muslims would see it.

Like Abraham, Muhammad never proclaimed himself to be divine. Also like Abraham, he found himself a monotheist in a society in which polytheism was the tribal norm. In both cases each man felt God speaking to him, revealing a direct message that was not just to an individual, but with major consequences down the centuries.

Unlike Abraham, however, the revelations were not just to Muhammad and his descendants, but to all those who would listen, regardless of their ethnic origins. This is similar to Christianity and the message of Jesus. Here too Islam starts to diverge radically from both Christianity and Judaism, as several writers have pointed out. Neither Judaism nor Christianity has political or military origins. The first 400 years of Judaism saw the children of Israel as slaves in Egypt. For its first three centuries, Christianity was an illegal, persecuted faith. Islam however was both a political entity and military force right from the beginning.

The implications of this radically different origin of Islam have had consequences down to our own times. Judaism was finally separated, for all intents and purposes, from its original kingdom in the first century AD, although the process had started long before that. It therefore developed as a religion quite independent of state power and continued so to do until the creation of the Israeli State in 1948. Yet even now, most Jews continue to live outside Israel, and some parts of the faith – notably the ultra-conservative Hasidic Jews – reject the very concept of a Jewish state until the Messiah has returned.

There are still countries where Christianity remains the state religion. But as we shall see, from the seventeenth century onwards the links between Church and State became looser, with toleration given firstly to Christians who did not belong to the official Church, and, later on, to those of other beliefs and none at all. This is a split that has yet to take place in many Muslim countries, and the origins of this issue go right back to the creation of Islam itself.

It is the combination of religion and political power, and the role that the state plays in relation to religion and religious practice, that demarks Islam from Christianity and Judaism. Jews were under alien rule from the eighth century BC onwards and the Christians, as we saw, were persecuted for their first 300 years, and have, in the West, long ceased to make religious adherence compulsory. But it is not the same with Islam, and this key differential today makes it hard for Muslims, principally those in the West, to be under the rule of those who do not accept the Islamic faith.

Western writers usually put it in terms of there being no Church–State distinction in Islam. While true of the Jewish kingdoms and of Christianity in much of its history, such a lack of distinction is a result of history in these two faiths rather than being inbuilt from the very beginning. Islam has, in that sense, always been a religion of state power, with no political/religious divide. This is why the loss of such power to the Europeans in the nineteenth and twentieth centuries has been so traumatic, as the final chapter will show. (The same applies too to Muslims living in the West, outside of the domain of Islamic law.)

5

THE GOLDEN AGE OF ISLAM

Sunni and Shia

In AD 661 Ali, the last of the *Rashidun*, was assassinated – the third to meet a violent end. To his supporters, however, Ali was the first Imam, the lawful successor of the Prophet.

The new ruler was Muawiyya, of the Umayyad clan, one of the families that had originally opposed Muhammad when Islam had first begun. Muawiyya was the Governor of Syria, and moved his capital to Damascus from Mecca, where it remained as long as his family retained the Caliphal title. Although from the same family as the Caliph Uthman, he was not a relation of Muhammad, which would soon become very important.

The new Caliph used many Christians both in his army, and in his administration. But the Umayyads in general showed strong favouritism to their fellow Arabs, and most have not been well regarded by traditional Islamic historians.

When Muawiyya died in 680, war broke out again. Ali's elder son Hassan had never made a serious play for power, but the second son, Hussein, was determined to seize the Caliphate that he believed was rightly his. However, his attempt proved short-lived. Unable to garner more than a small following when his meagre army and a much larger opposition loyal to the Umayyads met at Karbala in that same year, Hussein and his followers were all killed.

Thus 680 is one of the most important dates in Islamic history, since it marks the beginning of a split that has lasted to this day. Hussein – reckoned to be the third Imam by his followers – was the leader of the Ali faction. This in Arabic is the *Shia't Ali*, now known as the Shia, and its adherents as Shiites. Today Shiite Islam is thought of as predominantly Iranian, but historically this is false, since the original group was Arabic, and remains so in majority Shiite Iraq today.

Hussein's death was a source of great sorrow for his disciples, and, ever since, the martyrdom of Hussein has been one of the major festivals in the Shiite world. Today, when men are seen flagellating themselves through the streets, it should be remembered that this is a ceremony endorsed by only 15 per cent of contemporary Muslims, the proportion of the Islamic world today that is Shiite. Martyrdom has been a major part of Shiite thinking throughout history, and the mentality of an oppressed minority still pervades Shiite Islam. To the majority of Shia there were nine further Imams (specially anointed successors of the Prophet), the last of whom disappeared in the early Middle Ages, and whose return is still awaited by Shiites even still. (Three plus nine is twelve, making up Twelver Shiite Islam, in which Iran is the major country.) Other Shiites recognized different successors from the same family, the best-known group today being the Ismailis, who follow the Agha Khan, and who recognize five Imams in the line of descent.

To the Shia, the Imams were perfect in their interpretation of the Quran. After the last Imam disappeared, legal scholars emerged who could interpret the sacred texts correctly. As a result, while there are formally no clergy in Shia Islam, those who do interpret the law have a greater prestige and role in Shiite thinking than their equivalents do with the Sunni majority. There is thus no equivalent in Sunni Islam of an Ayatollah or 'person of veneration' to use the literal term. This means that when we refer to Islamic clergy, we are wrong in many senses to use the word when applied to Sunni Muslims, for whom an Imam is simply the legal scholar at the local mosque. But while it is technically also inaccurate in Shiite Islam, their scholars are far closer to the role of the clergy that we have in the West.

Furthermore, while *ijtihad* remains discouraged or even outlawed among the 85 per cent Sunni majority, this is not the case in Shiite Islam. Thus writers such as Milton Viorst, author of *In the Shadow of the Prophet*, argue that Shiites, who await the return of the twelfth Imam, are more forward-looking and open to change. On the other hand, Viorst thinks the Sunni majority, for whom things are immutable, are more stuck in the past. While it is not possible to generalize, there is enough that is correct in such an interpretation to make a difference in the two forms of Islam today.

The late Ayatollah Khomeini of Iran tried to present himself as simply a Muslim, in order that the radical Islamic version of revolution would spill over into predominantly Sunni Muslim countries. There is a case for saying that further doctrinal differences between Sunni and Shiite Islam, other than the key one just mentioned, are in fact small. But perhaps the key difference is that because Shiite Islam was mainly a minority version for so long – except under the Fatimid Caliphs in Cairo – its mentality was therefore different because Shiites often had to hide their faith. (The idea of keeping Shiite Islam private in fact became legitimate in Shiite doctrine.) In addition the cult of martyrdom, so powerful in countries such as Iraq and Iran today, is unknown in mainstream Sunni Islam. So while the doctrinal differences may indeed not be profound, there is a very good case for saying that the mentality of Shiites and Sunnis is therefore subtly different.

The case of Iran, however, reveals the distinctiveness of Shiite Islam. Some would argue that the Shia denomination of Islam enables the very nationalistic Iranians to be genuinely Islamic and also thoroughly Persian at the same time. Though the current regime would deny this, it is a historically respectable position.

As the American expert on Iran, William Polk, has written in his book *Understanding Iran* (2009), where

> Shiism most fundamentally differs from Sunnism is in the assertion that God chose to continue the mission of Muhammad... [and that one effect was that...] in reaction to the rule of the Ummayad Caliphate that a sort of rebirth of what we can term Iranian cultural and religious nationalism began. It found its voice not in a return to the old regime or even to the old religion, but in the appropriation and conversion of Arab and Muslim events and causes.

Orthodox Shiite Muslims – not all of whom are Iranian – would disagree with Polk's distinction. Orthodox interpretation would prioritize an understanding of events in exclusively spiritual terms – that of the correct interpretation of Islam and of the lawful succession to the Prophet. Polk, however, suggests that there is a correspondence between some of the facets of Shiite Islam and the earlier Zoroastrian faith. The 'weeping of the Magi', for example, over failures to act righteously (the Magi are also known as the Wise Men who visited the infant Jesus) parallels the weeping on Ashura, the day of mourning and self-flagellation each year for the failure of the followers of Ali to defend his son, Hussein, the Prophet's grandson, at the Battle of Karbala in 680.

We have also seen that Shiite Islam believes in the twelve Imams (fewer in the case of the Ismailis), including the last Imam, who vanished centuries ago and who is due, as Christians believe about Jesus, one day to return. This, as Polk notes, means that:

> Iranian Shiism treats the result of the withdrawal . . . in a special way that colors the history and politics of Islam. Between the occultation of the Imam nearly twelve hundred years ago and his reappearance on the last day, there can be no legitimate guide or ruler for humankind. Even the most holy and learned man of religion cannot speak infallibly on the most fundamental issues of life on earth.

As historian Bernard Lewis reminds us, the notion behind Ayatollah Khomeini (1900–89), that there can be a kind of substitute figure – an interim 'Supreme Leader' – is thus a highly controversial one. If there is no one legitimate authority from the Twelfth Imam in 724 down to his reappearance sometime in the future, then whatever powers Khomeini gave himself cannot be truly legitimate according to Shiite theology. Khomeini's title in the Iranian constitution, *Vali-ye faqih*, is

variously translated as 'Supreme Jurist' or 'Supreme Interpreter'. It is upon such an exalted titular rank that Khomeini's
power – and thus that of his successors as Supreme Leaders –
derives.

As we shall see, no equivalent for Khomeini exists in the
majority, Sunni, form of Islam. Moreover, as strict interpretations would argue, there is no precedent in Shiite Islam for the
post Khomeini invented for himself after 1979. Many Iranian
rulers – notably Shah Abbas and those of the Safavid dynasty
– have cloaked themselves in Islamic authority and mystique,
but none of them has ever given himself quite the degree of
combined spiritual/political authority as is implicit in the title
Khomeini has bestowed upon himself.

This uniquely Iranian interpretation of Islam once again
demonstrates a degree of Persian distinctiveness that marks the
practice and theory of that faith in Iran as distinct from its
various forms elsewhere, from the Arab heartland through to
India and to Indonesia. The old Zoroastrian religion may now
be limited to a small number of Parsees mainly found in India,
but Iran remains as religiously distinct as it has always been.

With the defeat of Hussein, the Umayyad Caliphate became
hereditary. This was never officially decreed as Islamic
doctrine, but it remained the case until the Caliphate was abolished in 1924. Since the first four Caliphs had been chosen by
consensus, this was a major break and proof that the Muslims
were becoming more like the hereditary monarchs in neighbouring states and the dynasty of the Sassanian shahs, which
they had removed by 651 in Iran.

The one Umayyad Caliph who has earned the respect of
Arab historians was Abd al-Malik, who reigned from 685 to

705. It was he who made Arabic the formal language of the Caliphate, introduced a proper Islamic currency, and reorganized the tax system, all major contributions to the stability of the new and ever growing regime. He spread the lands of the Caliphate yet further still. In this instance, Islamic forces slowly but surely were able to take what is now north-west Africa, the Maghreb, including the lands lived in by the Berber peoples, a non-Arab group. Eventually between the late seventh and early eighth centuries they reached the Atlantic. The Berbers, who converted over time to Islam, were to become the shock troops of the Islamic conquest and subsequent retention of Spain, just to their north. An empire thus came into being which stretched from what is now Morocco in the West to Pakistan in the East, and as far as Central Asia to the borders of Tang dynasty China, thus making the Umayyad territory one of the largest single domains in history.

Six years after Abd al-Malik's death in 711, the Muslim commander Tariq (after whom Gibraltar – the mountain of Tariq – is named) invaded Spain, notionally to help a Vandal commander defeat his local enemies. Spain had been ruled for just under three centuries by the originally Germanic Vandals after the fall of the Roman Empire in the West, but the regime was swiftly conquered by the invading Muslim armies. By the 730s, nearly all of Spain had been conquered. The Islamic armies then ventured, this time with less success, into southern France. Narbonne and the surrounding region were briefly under Muslim rule, but this was not to prove permanent.

The Islamic incursions continued until 732. That year, a Frankish army under Charles Martel was finally able to stop them at the Battle of Tours, which took place somewhere between Poitiers and Tours. In retrospect, this proved to be one of the most important battles in history, since it prevented further Islamic expansion into Frankish territory, and what might well otherwise have been a Muslim conquest of Western Europe.

Spain became Andalus, the land of the Vandals – now Andalucia. This part of the empire soon gained independence, and would become, under its branch of the Umayyads (founded by Abd'al-Rahman, who escaped the fall of the Umayyad dynasty in 750) and the Almohad and Almoravid Berber dynasties, the most enlightened of all the Arab territories.

(The contemplation of how history might have been different is now called counter-factual history, and usually involves discussion of what would have happened, say, if Hitler had won the Second World War, or if the Confederates had managed to beat the Federal forces in the American Civil War. Such thinking goes back centuries, and one of the first people to propose alternative endings was the eighteenth-century historian Edward Gibbon. In writing of the Battle of Tours he reflected as an Oxford man that the dreaming spires and churches of his own time could well have been the minarets of Oxford instead. Had that been the case, Gibbon wrote, it would have been the Quran that was studied in the halls of the University rather than the Bible.)

By the late 740s, the Umayyads were losing their hold on the Caliphate. Different groups arose, some of them Shiite, and others from the east, from present-day Iran. In 750 there was a coup, which resulted in one of the descendants of Muhammad's uncle, Abu'l Abbas as-Saffah, ascending the

Caliphal throne. The dynasty he founded was called the Abbasids, and was to prove more long lasting, reigning in the new capital, Baghdad, until 1258, and then, notionally, in Cairo until 1517.

The new Caliph, Abu Jafar al-Mansur, immediately executed the general who helped him to gain power – there were to be no rivals. Despite the dominance of the Abbasids there is a famous Umayyad monument that resonates with us still – the Dome of the Rock mosque in Jerusalem, where the 2000 Intifada began with the provocative walk taken there by the Israeli politician Ariel Sharon. The site, revered by both Muslims and Jews, is where Jews believe that Abraham nearly sacrificed Isaac, and Muslims believe that Ishmael was nearly the sacrificial victim instead. As a result the whole area remains a major source of contention between Muslims, who want to keep it, and ultra-religious Jews, who want the space back since it is next door to the original site of King Solomon's temple.

As Arthur Goldschmidt Jr in his *A Concise History of the Middle East* puts it, such grand architecture was a sign that the Muslims were here to stay. Mansur's influence can be seen in the building of the new capital, Baghdad, effectively from scratch – while it was near ancient cities such as Babylon, it had been a small town before the Abbasids turned it into a major imperial metropolis, nearer the heartland of Abbasid power towards the East. Although Arabic was the official language, the ethnic advantage that Arabs had enjoyed now disappeared, with Persians becoming increasingly important both in running the Empire, and culturally.

The best known of Mansur's successors was Harun al-Rashid, or Aaron the Wise, in translation, the legendary

Caliph of the 1001 Nights, and one of the ablest of the Abbasids. Paradoxically, under him, the Caliphs themselves became less powerful as they began to rely increasingly on bureaucratic dynasties, often of Persian origin. Among these were the Barmakids, the *wazirs*, or more familiarly the viziers, a term which came to mean a senior official in Muslim countries. Persian influence increased still further when, after a civil war, Harun's half-Persian son, Mamun, became Caliph, reigning from 813–33. Mamun was one of the major patrons of learning, when he established the *Bayt al-Hikmah*, the House of Wisdom. It is for discoveries in the realm of science, medicine and philosophy that the Abbasid Caliphate is rightly known as the Golden Age of Islam.

From the Arab Renaissance to Fatimids and Turks

Many eminent Arab physicians and philosophers (with the two categories often overlapping) became well known in the West. The Arabs not only preserved much ancient Greek knowledge but, crucially, improved upon it. At this stage in Islamic history, enormous amounts of Western works were translated, and then used and updated by Islamic scholars.

To take a few examples from medicine: Rhazes (more correctly al-Razi, 865–923), Avicenna (Ibn Sina, 980–1037), and the two Andalusians, Avenzoar (Ibn Zuhr, c. 1091–1162) and Averröes (Ibn Rushd, 1126–1204) not only translated Greek works, but came up with innovative medical discoveries. As a result of what they found, these innovations, when in turn introduced to Europe, transformed medicine. Not only that, they led the way until the much later discoveries of the seventeenth century.

Furthermore, as Ahmad Dallal points out in his chapter on science and medicine in *The Oxford History of Islam*, many of the original documents are no longer extant, so the actual discoveries of these physician philosophers were almost certainly greater than we realize. Al-Razi's known magnum opus, the *al-Hawi fi al-Tibb* (The Comprehensive Book on Medicine) runs to no fewer than twenty-three volumes, and this is an incomplete edition. He was an expert on therapeutics, and was able to criticize the ancient authority, Galen, on several clinical issues. Al-Razi in turn was superseded by Ibn Sina, whose masterwork was *al-Qanun fi al-Tibb* (The Canon of Medicine), a definitive text on anatomy, physiology, pathology, and the treatment of disease. Another specialist, al-Nafis from Syria (d. 1288) discovered the minor circulation of the blood, again long before it became established knowledge in the West.

As well as medicine, Islamic mathematics was also both vital and permanent in its effect. As mentioned in the introduction, we refer to Arabic numerals; although these actually originate in India, it was through the Arabs that we received them, thereby transforming Western mathematics as well with a system of numbers far superior to that used by the ancient Romans. In particular, because the Islamic world spread so far, from Spain to Central Asia, it was easier for knowledge to spread widely and be discussed by experts over great geographical distances.

In astronomy, Francis Robinson shows (in *The Cambridge Illustrated History of the Islamic World*), that the Arabs soon realized that the Ptolemaic calculations dominant in the West (and with which Galileo also disagreed, centuries later, to his cost) were seriously flawed. As early as the twelfth century Islamic scientists in Al-Andalus and northern Africa had already established that the earth goes around the sun, and not the other way around as was still believed in Europe. While many of the names of constellations that we use are from Greek or Roman times, the star names, such as Aldebaran, are Arabic.

The Arabs, Robinson points out, were experts in computation and number theory, one of the leading experts being from Central Asia, al-Biruni, who died in 1046. He was able to solve the so-called chessboard problem. A ruler asked him the amount of grain which would equal the number of grains arranged on a chessboard, placed in such a way that there would be one on the first square, two in the second, four in the third, and so on, up to the full sixty-four squares. To the ruler's astonishment, he realized, when al-Biruni explained the answer, that there would not be enough grains left in his entire kingdom! (The answer is 18,446,744,073,709,551,615 grains!)

A major breakthrough in calculation was made by al-Uqlidisi in 950, when he invented the fraction, making precise mathematical solutions much more attainable. As mentioned in the introduction, algebra is an Arabic discipline, the word itself derived from *al-jabr* (restoration). The inventor of this subject was the great ninth-century mathematician, al-Khwarazmi, from whose name the word algorithm is derived.

One of the great mysteries Robinson raises is why the golden age of Islamic discovery came to an end. Like other writers, he concludes that the kind of knowledge they were discovering was, ultimately, incompatible with a Quranic world view around which everything had to revolve. He also reminds us that the Chinese similarly spent many centuries far in advance of the West, and then went backwards. It is therefore inaccurate to call it a uniquely Islamic problem, since culturally and spiritually the Arabs and Chinese were and are completely different. Perhaps, as Robinson suggests, the real mystery is why the Europeans, once they finally established their lead centuries later, were able to go on and maintain it. This is a continuing debate – even in newspapers, with an article appearing in the *Guardian* on 26 May 2006 by the eminent European scholar Timothy Garton Ash that discussed this very issue – but without a consensus being reached. As Garton Ash mentions, the smaller scale of West European states, in comparison to the large Caliphate, and then Ottoman Empire in the Middle East, and Balkans (in the latter case), might be a key cause. But as he admits, even then we cannot be certain.

By the middle of the tenth century the actual as opposed to nominal power of the Abbasids themselves was beginning to fade. In 945 a Turkic family, the Buyids, seized power in Baghdad, and retained it for many years. The Buyids were Shiite, but allowed the Sunni Abbasid dynasty to remain in titular authority, thereby not disrupting the delicate balance of power within the empire.

The Buyids, however, did not control as much territory as the Abbasids did at the height of their rule. Egypt moved in and out of their direct sovereignty, with the rise of the Mamluks, slave soldiers (literally 'owned people') taken initially from what is now the Caucasus in the late ninth century by the Abbasid Caliphs with the idea that such soldiers would be more loyal to their overlords than ordinary troops.

The emergence of the Mamluks in Egypt found a parallel in the onset of a new Arabic power in North Africa. This was the Fatimid dynasty, a Shiite family notionally at least descended from Muhammad's daughter, Fatima. Starting from what is now Tunisia, they worked their way eastwards across northern Africa, and took Egypt in 969. Here they moved the capital from Fustat to the new city of Al-Qahirah, known to us today as Cairo.

While they were strongly Shiite, and active in evangelizing the Shia version of Islam, they did not try forcibly to convert their subjects, who remained – as today – overwhelmingly Sunni, with a substantial Coptic Christian minority. The Fatimids built the Al-Azhar Mosque in 972, which, along with the university, remains one of the most revered centres of Muslim faith in the Middle East, albeit now Sunni not Shiite.

In parallel with the rise of the Fatimids came increasing incursions by the Turks. Originally a fringe people on the outskirts of the Caliphate, as time progressed they began to edge ever nearer to the heartland. While some – notably the Khazars, who converted to Judaism – were of varying religions, the main bulk of the Turkic peoples converted to Islam, an event that would in time alter for ever the nature of Islamic rule. In around 1040 one group, the Seljuk Turks, named after an able Turkish chieftain who converted to Islam in 956, successfully invaded Syria and Mesopotamia (present-day Iraq). In 1045 they captured Baghdad, but once again the Abbasid Caliphs were permitted to stay on as nominal heads of state. The Seljuk rulers called themselves Sultans, and when their Turkic cousins, the Ottomans, came to power in later centuries, that was the title they used for themselves. And after 1517 they also used the title of Caliph.

It was this internal conflict – the Seljuk occupation of the Abbasid Caliphate, and the Fatimid occupation of Egypt – that would form the backdrop to the Crusades. Between then and the arrival of the Crusaders 130 years later, the area we now call Palestine was in contention between the Fatimid Caliphate and the various Seljuk states to the north, with their power bases in Syria and Anatolia. This rivalry between Sunni Seljuks and Shiite Fatimids, which no side fully won until Saladin's conquest of the 1170s, effectively created a power vacuum into which the Crusaders were able to move, especially since neither Muslim side (Seljuk or Fatimid) wanted their Islamic rival to control the territory.

6

MANZIKERT, CRUSADERS, MONGOLS

Manzikert

Waterloo, Gettysburg, the Somme, and the Battle of the Bulge – these great battles are well known around the world. Books galore have been written about them, and counter-factual historians have had a great time speculating what would have happened had they gone the other way – as seen earlier regarding the result of the Battle of Tours in 732.

Yet one of the most important, indeed pivotal, battles ever fought is almost entirely unknown in the West, even though it affected Europe, and changed the Middle East for ever, with consequences right down to the present day. The Intifada and the atrocities of 9/11 are its direct descendants, yet most people today have never heard of it. It is the Battle of Manzikert, fought near Lake Van in Armenia in 1071 in which the Byzantines, under the Emperor Romanus IV Diogenes, were defeated by the Seljuk Turks, led by the Sultan Alp-Arslan. This was followed by Seljuk conquest of most of Anatolia. Spurred by Seljuk raids and incursions into Byzantine-ruled Anatolia, Romanus had assembled a large army to re-establish the security of the Byzantine Empire's eastern frontier there. In the spring of 1071 he led this army into parts of Turkish-held Armenia, entering it along the southern branch of the Upper Euphrates river. Near the town of Manzikert (today's Malazgirt in Turkey), he divided his army, which was composed of mercenaries that included a contingent of Turkmen, sending some ahead to secure the fortress of Akhlât on nearby Lake Van and taking others with him into Manzikert. Learning of the Byzantine foray into his territory, Alp-Arslan hastened to Manzikert, where he confronted the emperor's army. Romanus abandoned Manzikert in an attempt to reunite his forces with the group besieging Akhlât. Trapped in a valley on the Akhlât road, he neglected to send out scouts to assess the enemy's position, and the Turks fell upon him. Romanus fought valiantly and might have won if his position had not been weakened by treachery within his ranks; his Turkmen troops had gone over to the enemy the night before the battle, and one of his generals, Andronicus Ducas, perceiving that the cause was lost, fled with his men. The Byzantine army was destroyed, and Romanus was taken prisoner.

This Byzantine defeat ushered in an age of Sunni Muslim Turkish conquest, that had its finale in the equally Sunni Muslim capture of Constantinople by Ottoman Turks in 1453, and the end of the 1,100-year-old East Roman Empire, begun by Constantine himself back in the fourth century AD. The last event in this historical chain was the expulsion of the last ethnic Greeks from Asia Minor in 1922.

The very heartland of the Christian East was now at risk. The establishment of the Sultanate of *Rum* (so named after 'Rome', the name that the Byzantines still gave themselves), a

Seljuk Turkish principality in central and eastern Anatolia with its capital at Konya, by Suleiman, another Seljuk prince in 1077, was a direct consequence of Manzikert, as was the large-scale settlement in Anatolia of ethnic Turkish nomadic tribes who found the area similar to the steppes from which they had emigrated. Further, as the *Cambridge Medieval History* correctly puts it, the defeat was one from which the Byzantine Empire never recovered. It gave the forces of Islam an advantage that they were to continue successfully to pursue for the next five centuries, and a momentum that did not fully end until nearly 700 years later.

(Following Manzikert, the Armenians were to spend the next 900 years under either Turkish or Russian rule, not gaining their independence until the 1990s. With the Armenians being the victims of the first genocide of the twentieth century, theirs was to be a particularly cruel plight.)

The consequences of the battle for the inhabitants of the Balkans, for example, also became apparent. For instance, the effective successors of the Seljuks, the Ottomans, another Turkish grouping, were to begin their conquest of the Balkan Peninsula as early as the mid-fourteenth century, and rule most of the area right up until the twentieth century and their defeat in 1918. Parts of the Balkans such as Bosnia and Albania remained Muslim after 1918, as we know from the conflict in the former Yugoslavia in the 1990s. This too is a result of the loss of Byzantine power because of the Seljuk victory over the Byzantines in 1071, and recent Balkan history down to the Kosovo conflict shows that we live with the consequences of Manzikert today.

(The Byzantines were also losing their Empire in the West as well – 1071 also saw the loss of their last toehold in Italy to Norman armies. The failure of Christians in the West to support Byzantium against Islam remains a source of anger in Orthodox Christian Europe.)

It was the loss at Manzikert that led the Byzantine Emperor, Alexius Comnenus, to seek outside Western help, in an attempt to regain the territories now lost to the Turkish invaders. Since he asked the Pope, and the Pope passed on the request to land-hungry Western nobles, this was soon to prove a major mistake.

The Crusades

In 638, Caliph Omar had entered Jerusalem, the third holiest city in Islam, following only Mecca and Medina in its sanctity, ever since Muhammad had experienced visions of the city during his time as a prophet.

The Byzantines had been persecutors, not just of those of non-Christian faith, but of many of their fellow Christians as well, since only those who signed up fully to the official version of Orthodoxy were deemed to be properly Christian. As a consequence, the numerous adherents of heterodox forms of Christianity in the region applauded the Islamic invasions, since Omar did not distinguish between different interpretations. As the American author Stephen Glain points out in *Dreaming of Damascus*, Jews and Christians thus warmly welcomed Omar into Jerusalem, glad that Byzantine tyranny was over.

Omar was careful to enter with due humility – another wise move – and he declared the monotheists, the Christians and

Jews, to be *dhimmis*, or protected peoples. On the other hand, Omar expelled all their co-religionists from the Arabian Peninsula itself, including Jews who had lived there for centuries. But the Jews of Jerusalem were to find a peaceful home there for the next six centuries, until the Crusaders came from the West and slaughtered its inhabitants – Jews, local varieties of Christians, and Muslims – all alike.

In Cambridge, a popular tourist destination is the Round Church, the circular part of which is contemporary with the Crusades, and whose official name is the parish of the Holy Sepulchre. (Tour guides who link it to the Knights Templar are wrong, however. The original circular building was founded by a quite separate and non-military group called the Canons of the Holy Sepulchre.) Now a heritage centre, it is keen to apologize to Muslim visitors for the Crusades, and for the acts of barbarism committed by its more gruesome participants. At many a Muslim–Christian dialogue today, the Islamic side is certain to bring up the old chestnut, 'What about the Crusades?'

When looking at events at the end of the eleventh century, we see that in fact the Crusades should not really have happened at all. The Byzantines, worried by their loss at Manzikert, asked the West for help. However, Orthodox and Catholic Christianity, long separated by doctrinal and political issues, had formally separated for good in 1054. The Popes did not want to help an Orthodox power, but they were worried about the increasing difficulty Catholic pilgrims had in reaching Jerusalem.

Consequently, in 1095, Pope Urban launched a Crusade to win back the Holy Land for Christianity. The crowd roared the famous words, 'Deus lo veult' (God wills it!) at Clermont, the French town where the Pope proclaimed his message of crusade, and the Crusades began.

Palestine was not the Pope's to bestow – it had been Byzantine territory until 638, with some minor territorial gains in the years since then. The Byzantine Emperors had certainly not intended a Catholic army to reconquer territory lost over 400 years earlier. But this is what now happened, with Antioch in Syria captured in 1098, and the sacred goal of Jerusalem itself in 1099 AD, 461 years after its loss to the Muslims.

Earlier twentieth-century historiography attributes the Crusades to bloodlust, greed, inherent European imperialism and much else besides. While there was certainly a strong element of this, historians, notably Jonathan Riley-Smith of Cambridge in his numerous books (including *What were the Crusades?*) are now saying that their main motivation was spiritual rather than territorial. For example, absolution for sins could be obtained through taking up the Cross (as going crusading was called), and much spiritual prestige was attached to being a Crusader.

But there was also financial gain for knights who were younger sons. While the eldest brother would inherit the title and the lands, younger brothers would be able to carve out new estates of their own in the conquered territories. So while Riley-Smith correctly reminds us of the spiritual side of taking up the Cross and embarking on a crusade, we should not forget the more material tangible benefits as well.

The problem was that Frankish knights and their cohorts had very different ideas of warfare from those prevalent in the Byzantine Empire and Middle East. When Jerusalem was recaptured in 1099, the invaders slaughtered *everyone* – not just Muslims, but Jews and local Christians as well. (It is important to remember the last two categories of victim – the Crusaders were barbaric all around!)

Furthermore, these were by no means the only Crusades – for example the Popes also launched them, collectively known as the Albigensian Crusade, against the Cathars, a heretical sect mainly based in southern France. There too the Crusaders – led by Simon de Montfort senior – slaughtered everyone indiscriminately, the victims in this case being his fellow Frenchmen.

The actual conquest of what is now Palestine, Lebanon and coastal Syria took until 1099, when the Crusaders, with Godfrey of Bouillon as the most eminent of the Crusader leaders (who included other nobles, such as Raymond of Toulouse), then entered Jerusalem. Godfrey was chosen to be the captured city's first ruler. (He would only agree to be the Protector of the Holy Sepulchre rather than the king, but all subsequent rulers accepted the royal title King of Jerusalem.) The Kingdom of Jerusalem was not the only new state created – other nobles managed to establish the County of Edessa in the north and the Principality of Antioch in the middle. But Jerusalem was always the largest and most important of the new Crusader states.

The capture of Jerusalem had also been held up by squabbles among the Crusaders about who should get which bit of territory. One example is the Principality of Antioch. By the agreement with the Byzantines, it should have been returned to the Emperor, since it had been under Byzantine rule until 1071. But instead, once the Crusaders captured it, they wasted six months quarrelling among themselves as to which nobleman should have it as a fief of his own.

The main quarrel was between the southern French (or Frankish) leader, Raymond, Count of Toulouse, and his rival knight, the Norman, Bohemond, Count of Apulia – southern Italy and Sicily having just fallen to Norman rule, as we saw earlier. In the end, Bohemond ended up as Prince of Antioch, and the main army then proceeded on to the central objective, the capture of Jerusalem. It goes without saying that all this did no credit to the supposedly Christian purposes behind the Crusade.

Eventually, the Franks and others living in the new Kingdom of Jerusalem, and associated states in what became known as Outremer ('beyond the sea'), picked up the more civilized habits of their neighbours, often to the horror of the more rough-hewn knights from Europe. Christian orders of chivalry arose, the most famous being the Templars (after the Temple in Jerusalem), and the still existing Hospitallers (after the hospitals they founded), now called the Order of St John in Protestant countries and the Knights of Malta (after a later residence) in the Catholic world. There was also, briefly, a British Hospitaller Order, that of St Thomas of Acon, linked with the Diocese of Winchester, which did not survive the Middle Ages.

(Serious historians have demolished the gibberish written about the Templars over the years. Reliable writers include the British historian Richard Barber and the American medievalist Sharan Newman. Alas, though, conspiracy theories usually sell better than the truth . . .)

The Crusader states did not last for long. The most outlying, the County of Edessa, fell to the Muslims as early as 1144, and despite the efforts of the Second Crusade, was never recaptured by Christian forces. But as Bernard Lewis reminds us in *The Middle East*, the key battles were between the Sunni forces controlling the rump Abbasid Caliphate and their Shiite rivals, the Fatimid Caliphs in Egypt. The Fatimids had, at their peak, ruled over much of Palestine, and were thus a far more serious threat to the Sunni Caliphate than outside infidels such as the Crusaders.

Here, a new Sunni dynasty, the Abuyyids, came to the rescue. Its most famous member has become legendary – Salah al-Din, known in the West as Saladin, the most famous of Islamic warriors. While some, such as Jonathan Riley-Smith, in commenting on modern interpretations of the Crusades, remind us that Saladin was not always the paragon of both Muslim and Christian legend, he was indisputably a brilliant general and far less disposed to murder and mayhem than his Frankish adversaries. One of the great ironies of Saladin is that he was a Kurd. Muslims have lauded him down the centuries, and Saddam Hussein, a violent suppressor of Kurdish freedom, loved to portray himself as a latter-day Saladin, besting the West and leading the Arabs to renewed power. But Saladin was no Arab, and today, in the twenty-first century, his ethnic relatives are still without a state of their own.

His most important conquest was, in Islamic terms, Fatimid Egypt in 1169, restoring it to Sunni rule after a century of Shiite domination. (He formally proclaimed himself Sultan when the last Fatimid Caliph died in 1171.) Strategically this victory then enabled him to end the Crusader occupation of Jerusalem. After he captured Syria, he launched a jihad against the Kingdom of Jerusalem in 1187, and was able to recapture that Holy City for Islam. The attempts of English King, Richard the Lionheart and the Third Crusade proved fruitless. While a rump Crusader state lingered on until 1291, the Abbuyids were able to rule over both Egypt and Syria until 1260, and although Jerusalem was once more in Christian hands in 1229, this only lasted for ten years. There was a second Christian interregnum between 1240 and 1244, when the city was sacked by the Turks; three years later it fell to the Mamluks. The era of European rule in the Middle East was over until 1917, when the British under General Allenby recaptured Jerusalem.

The Crusades: effects and interpretations

Today, Crusader is frequently a term of abuse. In his fatwas of 1998, 2001 and on several other occasions, Osama bin Laden refers to the forces of the West as the 'Crusaders', having also derided George Bush as a kind of twenty-first-century version of Godfrey of Bouillon. On 18 June 2005 bin Laden's number two, the Egyptian al-Zawahiri, released a video. In his statement he referred to 'kicking out the invading crusader forces and Jews' from the Middle East, and made further crusading references in his video of 4 August 2005 in his attack on Britain and on the West's presence in Islamic lands.

Unfortunately among certain groups in the West, there now seems to be a trend to defend the Crusades because of the Islamic attack on the USA in 2001. Even a respectable magazine such as *Commentary* published an article in July 2005 by Daniel Johnson called 'How to Think About the Crusades', arguing that we should not denigrate the Crusades in the way that has become normal in recent years. The anti-PC lobbies are also now defending the Frankish Crusaders. The title *The Politically Incorrect Guide to Islam (and the Crusades)* says it all, and the author, Robert Spencer, while admitting Crusader atrocities, aims to show that they were there to reclaim lost territory. While that is technically true, there is also the small matter of the 461-year gap between the loss of Jerusalem to the Muslims in 638 and its recapture in 1099.

What such books also omit to mention is that the Crusades not only failed in the long term, but were also a disaster for the war against Islam from the viewpoint of the West. One Crusade that is seldom mentioned in Western Europe or the USA, but is remembered in places like Greece as if it happened yesterday, is the Fourth Crusade. Here the Crusaders never reached the Holy Land at all. In 1204, spurred on by the greedy merchants of Venice and Genoa, they instead captured Constantinople and established a short-lived Latin Empire of the East. This proved catastrophic in the long run, because it removed the one major Christian power that had managed to keep the Islamic armies out of the Balkans and south-east Europe.

While a much-battered Byzantine Empire was back by the 1260s, it was never the same again. We shall see what dreadful results there were for the Orthodox Europeans from the four-teenth century on in the next chapter. When Pope John Paul II visited Greece towards the end of his long Pontificate, one of the conditions was that he apologized to the Greek Orthodox Church for the Crusades – especially for the Fourth – which resulted with the Balkan peoples spending 600 years under Ottoman Turkish rule. However, there are proper historical issues involved, to which we can now turn.

Despite the fact that the First Crusade took place over 900 years ago, the brief Crusading interlude of Middle Eastern history appears to be as hot an issue now as we presume it must have been then. But as authors as diverse as Bernard Lewis and Richard Fletcher have reminded us in their more detailed studies, this is far from being the case. It is, rather, anachronistic in the proper sense of that word to read twenty-first-century opinions back into the Middle Ages.

To begin with, two key points to remember: first, the Crusaders lost and the Muslims won; second, the people who truly lost out were the Orthodox Christians of the Byzantine Empire. They never recovered from the fall of Constantinople in 1204 and the onset, albeit brief, of the Latin Empire. So the Crusades *at the time* were a Muslim victory and a Christian disaster. Furthermore, there are two different perceptions of the Crusades – those believed at the time, and those held by countless Muslims worldwide today – that must be borne in mind in order to understand properly what the Crusades were all about then, and why they still matter.

It is surely right to argue that from the point of view of the protagonists, the Crusades were, in effect, a sideshow to the main battle. This is the irony of those who in that part of the world today – for example, Islamic extremists such as bin Laden – are being entirely Eurocentric in their view of history in attributing significance to the Crusades in the same way in which we do in the West.

The *real* epic struggle in the Middle East was not between Muslims and Christians. The Crusader occupation of

Jerusalem lasted less than a century and the whole Western presence in the Middle East less than 200 years. Bernard Lewis is surely right to say, therefore, that the key fight was the long-term inter-Islamic battle about the kind of Islam that would prevail in the Middle East. The protagonists were the Sunni Turks, Kurds (like Saladin) and Arabs who supported the remains of the Abbasid Caliphate, and the Shiite Fatimids, who supported a very different brand of Islam, and whose claim to the Caliphate split the originally united *Dar al-Islam* (Realm of Islam) in two. The Sunni version prevailed, thanks to Saladin, so that outside of Iran no Muslim country would be ruled by Shiites, until Iraq after the overthrow of Saddam Hussein in the twenty-first century. Saladin's key conquest was that of Fatimid Egypt, and the end of the Shiite Caliphate there, rather than his victory over the far less powerful Crusaders – the need to get rid of a few infidels being comparatively unimportant.

So, as Lewis argues, the actual reason why the Crusades matter so much in our own time is not the perception of Muslims in the Middle Ages, the victors of the war. Rather, it is of those in the nineteenth century, and beyond, when once again Christian Europeans started to invade the *Dar al-Islam*.

This will be explored later, in connection with the fall of the Ottoman Empire – the main beneficiary of the Turkish invasions of the eleventh century – above all in 1918, when it was defeated by the Allies. For it was the slow decline and then collapse of the one last major Muslim superpower in recent years that people like Lewis and I would argue is the real cause of the current accusations of Crusader-style behaviour made by Muslims throughout the Islamic world today.

To put it another way, the root of the problem is twentieth-century Western imperialism, not what a group of knights got up to in the eleventh century. When the West feared the Islamic world, which it did, with good cause for over a thousand years (632–1683), minor irritations like a temporary setback in Syria and Palestine could be forgotten.

It was only when the West finally gained the upper hand after Napoleon's capture of Egypt in 1798 and the Ottoman loss of Greece and Algeria in the 1830s, that the bad memories of the Middle Ages came back to haunt the Muslim world. For to the inhabitants of the Middle East, all Crusaders were *ferengi*, or Franks, whether or not they came from what is now France. What was the country that temporarily occupied Egypt at the end of the nineteenth century and 30 years later conquered Algeria and then ruled it for over 100 years? The answer is France. The Crusades, therefore, are now not forgotten, and certainly not by Al Qaeda and their kind. The deeds of a band of West European soldiers at the end of the eleventh century have come back to accuse us, and now to our permanent disadvantage.

The Sunni triumph did not last long, however, because a much more deadly and efficient foe was already gaining considerable power well to the east of the lands of Islam.

The Mongols

In 1242 the great invading Mongol armies, who had slaughtered hundreds of thousands of conquered peoples since Genghis (or Chinggis) Khan began his massive campaigns of world domination, finally reached the Middle East. That year they beat the remains of the Seljuk Empire and in 1258, under Genghis' descendant Hulagu, they reached Baghdad.

Here we encounter the European legend of Prester John, the mythical Christian king far beyond Europe's borders, to whom many generations of Catholics looked for salvation from the Islamic empires. Prester means Presbyter and the idea was that he was a great Christian ruler far beyond Europe, who would come to the rescue of a Europe under pressure from the Islamic threat. No one ever met this fabled character, but the illusion that such a person existed persisted for centuries.

Prester John was, in reality, probably no more than a legendary version of the Christian rulers of Ethiopia. But in the twelfth century, Western missionaries, such as Friar William of Rubruk, had visited the capital of the Mongol Khans, thousands of miles distant in Karakorum, in Mongolia. There they had encountered the sad remnants of the once widespread Nestorian Christians, one of the many heterodox Christian groups who disagreed with the Council of Nicaea's decision on the person of Christ, and who had therefore fled from the Byzantine Empire. (Named after their original leader, Bishop Nestorius, they reached as far as China and Marco Polo came across many Nestorian Christians in Asia during the course of his much later travels.) At this stage, the Mongol Khans gave freedom of religion to Christians and Hulagu, along with other of Genghis Khan's Mongol commanders, had a Nestorian wife.

But any rosy European twelfth-century view of the Mongols was an illusion. The idea that European knights could combine with the Mongols to defeat Islam, and that the West could maintain its independence from Mongol invasions, was a fantasy. The grandsons of Genghis Khan were no different from their forbear, and had their invasion plans of the Muslim world and Europe succeeded, the carnage would have been terrible. Those parts of Europe that were conquered, mainly present-day Russia, suffered badly.

By 1258 the Mongol Empire, now divided among Genghis' descendants, stretched from the Korean border in the East to the Polish in the West, perhaps the single biggest contiguous land empire that has ever existed. Hulagu launched his attack on Baghdad, and as with other Mongol conquests the slaughter was catastrophic, with perhaps as many as a million put to death (Christians and Jews were spared, probably due to the intervention of his wife) and a glorious civilization, symbolized by the House of Wisdom, destroyed. Furthermore, the Mongols also obliterated the ancient waterways that had irrigated so much of the desert.

What saved the rest of the Muslim world and Europe from inevitable defeat was the death of Hulagu's brother, the Great Khan, Mongke, in 1259. Wishing to be the next Great Khan himself, Hulagu raced back to Karakorum, leaving a much smaller force behind. As a result, when the now depleted Mongol army tried to capture Egypt, they were defeated in 1260 at the Battle of Ayn Jalut (the Spring of Goliath) by the Mamluk army. The Middle East was saved. The Mamluks then invaded Syria, and liberated it from Mongol rule. They then deposed the Abbuyids, and until 1517 a series of Mamluk Sultans ruled Egypt, Palestine and Syria.

However, as Arthur Goldschmidt Jr reminds us, the Mamluks were not Arabs, but Turks, and later Circassians from the Caucasus. For the next 700 years the Arab peoples of the Middle East were to be under non-Arab, albeit Muslim, rule until 1917. The Golden Age of Arabic supremacy was over. It is nostalgia for such an era that resurrected in the twentieth century a powerful sense of Arab nationalism, wholly secular in the case of the Egyptian ruler, Nasser, and strongly religious as regards the Islamic terrorist groups.

In his book *What Went Wrong?* and elsewhere, Bernard Lewis examines how the Islamic powers eventually lost their lead over the West. In military terms, he is surely right to say that until the late seventeenth century, and the Ottoman failure to capture Vienna in 1683, the Muslim world certainly had the edge over the West. However, there is a good case for saying that much of the eventual decline can be attributed to the fall of Baghdad in 1258. By that time too the Spaniards had made major headway against the Moorish-ruled parts of the Iberian Peninsula, and the great Islamic culture, from the Atlantic to the Chinese border, was fragmented, and in decline. Even under the Abbasid Caliphs, the ability to control a single empire from the Hindu Kush in the East to Spain in the West became problematic. The Abbasid solution was to allow local governors to become hereditary, effectively building up semi-independent dynasties of their own, some of which, like the Shiite Buyyid dynasty, became the real rulers under the later Abbasids. So while Islamic culture remained, as the travels of Ibn Battuta attest, the actual *political* unity was breaking up, and the emergence of a Shiite rival Caliphate under the Fatimids, from 969–1071, demonstrates that not even theological unity could always be maintained.

The career of more hard-line Muslim thinkers such as Ibn Taymiyya (1268/9–1328) suggests Islam was changing as well.

Over a century earlier, even the legendary Sufi mystic al-Ghazali (d. 1111), hailed as the Renewer of Islam, had shown he had severe doubts about the new science in his influential book *The Incoherence of the Philosophers*. The situation in Europe had once been similar, with Greek and Roman knowledge being lost for centuries before being rediscovered by the Arabs and then the Renaissance.

Finally, the Golden Age of Islamic civilization was a mix of Arabic and Persian, and for most of that era Iran was in the same empire as the Arabic parts of the Middle East. The Mongols separated Persia from the Arab world, and as the Turkish Ottomans were never able to conquer that country for their own empire, the two civilizations, while both Muslim, have been politically separated ever since. This is not to say that invention ceased, or that there were no more great Islamic thinkers – we shall encounter some of them shortly. But the era in which the Islamic world was medically, intellectually, culturally and technically way ahead of the West was now coming to a close.

Western Europe was fortunate that the Mongols turned back before going on to seize the rest of Europe. One only has to look at the history of Russia, the part of Europe that was conquered by the Mongols, to see the devastating effects that a Mongol invasion could have. Westerners should realize that there was nothing intrinsically better about them, and that if Hulagu had not stopped the Mongol Empire would have stretched from the Pacific to the Atlantic. We in the West are not in any way superior, simply very lucky!

It was hoped in the West that the Mongol rulers of what was then Mesopotamia and Persia (now Iraq and Iran) would convert to Christianity. As with the mythic Prester John, this too was an illusion, although we should not forget that prior to the Islamic conquest of Mesopotamia in the 630s, most of that region was in fact Christian, and that a large Nestorian minority existed in Persia. Nonetheless, the hopes of the Christian West were not fulfilled. The Il-Khans, as they became known, converted instead to Islam and established a brief dynasty. But it was not that simple, and therein lay an opportunity for the Mamluks.

Ibn Taymiyya, the Islamic thinker, was born in around 1268 or 1269, just nine years after the Mongol destruction of the Abbasid Caliphate in Baghdad. Until recently, he was regarded as interesting, but not necessarily important, and certainly not on the same level as Ibn Sina (Avicenna) or Ibn Rushd (Averröes). Now, in the light of his twenty-first-century followers, he has emerged as one of the key thinkers of medieval Islam.

The reason, as the American strategic specialists Daniel Benjamin and Steven Simon show in their book *The Age of Sacred Terror*, is that one can draw a direct line of thought and influence from the thirteenth-century Ibn Taymiyya to the eighteenth-century Arab Islamic scholar al-Wahhab, and then on to the twentieth-century writer and political philosopher Sayyid Qutb and the twenty-first-century Al Qaeda and Islamic terrorism. If we want to understand bin Laden and the attacks on the USA in 2001 and Britain in 2005, we must first understand Ibn Taymiyya.

When the Mongols converted to Islam, as the Il-Khans, they still retained much of their shamanistic Mongolian roots and lifestyle. While they were therefore technically Muslims, many in the Middle East regarded their adherence to Islam as wafer-thin. In terms of thirteenth- and fourteenth-century power politics this mattered, particularly for the Mamluk rulers of Egypt who wished to recapture much of the territory lost to the Mongols and place it back under the rule of Cairo. But technically speaking, there was a major problem – Muslims were not supposed to go to war with one another.

This was the issue which Ibn Taymiyya, who had succeeded his father as a teacher of the rigidly orthodox Hanbali School of Islam, was able to solve for them.

His solution was that an unrighteous Muslim ruler can be lawfully resisted, if he does not live piously according to the strictly interpreted criteria of the Quran. To him, the Il-Khans were not legally Muslim but apostates, whatever their outward profession. Resistance to them was therefore lawful, if not actually a good idea. Not only that, but jihad, in the military sense of the term, could and should be waged against them, as much as one would against overtly infidel rulers in the *Dar al-Harb*, literally 'the realm' or 'the abode of war', the name Islam gives to areas not under Islamic rule. It was therefore fully within Islamic law for the Mamluks to invade the Il-Khans' territory and recapture lost provinces, as Ibn Taymiyya duly pronounced in a fatwa to that effect.

However, as Benjamin and Simon point out:

> By asserting that jihad against apostates is justified – by turning jihad inwards and reforming it into a weapon for use against Muslims as well as infidels – he planted a seed of revolutionary violence in the heart of Islamic thought.

In the twentieth century these arguments would be re-employed by Sayyid Qutb against the nominally Muslim rulers of his own country – Egypt – to say that Nasser could be lawfully overthrown. From this comes the Al Qaeda doctrine that similar Muslim regimes are also unlawful, and can legitimately be opposed, with violence. The link between the Middle Ages and the present is therefore apparent.

Ibn Taymiyya remains controversial within Islam, as one could argue that in redefining jihad, he was exercising individual interpretation, or *ijtihad*. This, as we saw, was the ability of Muslim thinkers to come up with new interpretations of the Quran in order to adapt its eternal teaching to new situations and circumstances. But since such matters had, according to most Sunni interpretations, been closed in the tenth century, his reopening of the gates of *ijtihad* can in itself also be perceived as unlawful. This is because, according to mainstream Sunni thought, going beyond the consensus of the faithful is not permitted, and thus new interpretations of the Quran have been ruled out since the closing of the gates eleven centuries ago.

(Shiite Islam continues to allow *ijtihad*, and, as we shall see, the Ayatollah Khomeini took full advantage of that after the Islamic revolution in Iran in 1979. But with Ibn Taymiyya we are dealing with a Sunni Muslim-dominated world.)

The idea of seeking a new interpretation has not worried his twentieth- and twenty-first-century disciples, however. Thus from Qutb in the 1960s to the 'Arab Afghans' fighting the Russians in the 1980s, his thought has remained pivotal in its influence. The need of the Mamluks back in medieval times to go to war with the Il-Khans – the situation that Ibn Taymiyya was asked to regularize, so that one Muslim state could go to war with another – has led, down the course of time, to a new application of Ibn Taymiyya's teaching: it is always all right for good Muslims to attack bad ones, as theologically astray Muslims are apostates or in error, and therefore can be attacked by Muslims who correctly follow Muhammad's teaching. Sayyid Qutb's interpretation of Ibn Taymiyya inspired Al Qaeda, led in turn to 9/11 and the deaths of Muslim victims as well as Western tourists in places as far afield as Egypt and Indonesia. Thus, mass murder, centuries later . . .

7

THE OTTOMAN EMPIRE: THE STORY OF AN ISLAMIC SUPERPOWER

Imperial expansion in Europe and Asia

In his famous series *The Venture of Islam*, Marshall Hodgson entitles his third volume *The Gunpowder Empires and Modern Times*. Militarily this is a helpful way of looking at the changes brought in by that invention. But it is surely preferable to refer to the Ottoman Empire as the 'Islamic Superpower'. The term might be modern, but it does give an idea of the sheer size and power of the territory over which the Sultans ruled. Hodgson also refers to the Safavid Empire in Iran, and the Portuguese Empire in East Asia within this category. Since the latter is outside our frame of reference, and Safavid Iran was more limited geographically, this description of the Ottomans better summarizes the uniqueness of the enormous Ottoman domain.

It has already been suggested that the superpower nature of the Ottoman state is its main feature, and the part most mourned by Muslims around the world today, both moderate and extreme. The Ottoman Sultans were the last in the great line of the Caliphs, and did not really employ that title until

1517. But they were, for most of the time, far more powerful than any state in the West, and although Turkish not Arab they were certainly Muslim.

The Ottomans were named after their late thirteenth-century ruler, Osman, who, in a battle against Byzantine forces in 1301 at Baphaeum near Nicaea and thus not too far from the Byzantine capital itself, established himself and his people as a new player among the many Turkish groups that now inhabited the Anatolian Peninsula. His descendants were to prove even more powerful, being the Muslims who conquered and extinguished the Byzantine Empire in 1453. This wave of military conquest and territorial expansion was to continue for the first three centuries of Ottoman rule, and their conquests lasted right down until the final defeat of the Empire in 1918.

Osman (ruled 1290–1326) began extending his territory towards Constantinople, and by 1326 the Ottomans had a capital at Bursa, the Prusa of ancient times, in north-western Anatolia. Then in 1354 an earthquake created an opportunity for them to expand into south-east Europe. They took the opportunity to fight in an internal Byzantine power struggle, taking the side of Cantacuzenus, a pretender to the Byzantine throne, against another claimant, John Palaeologus. Thus the Ottomans began their long history of European conquest.

(In this case with permanent results – attempts to expel them altogether from Europe failed in 1913. There is still a small portion of Turkey on the European side of the Bosporus.)

By 1358 they had occupied much of Thrace, and in 1361 Adrianople (now Erdine) was captured. The Turks were in the Balkans for the long haul. Their campaigns in the 1380s saw the capture of the Bulgarian capital Sofia. Then in 1389 came the major battle of Kosovo, against a mainly Serbian force led by the leader of the coalition of Christian forces in the Balkans, Prince Lazar. This encounter is still remembered by Serbs, over 600 years later. The folk memory of the Serb defeat at Kosovo has resonated down to our own time, with many Muslim Kosovar Albanians being murdered by Serb forces as recently as 1999.

Slobodan Milosevic, the Serb strongman, exploited the memories of the battle at its 600th anniversary in 1989 as a Communist leader backed up by the full panoply of the Serb Orthodox Church. Hundreds of thousands lost their lives – mainly Bosnian Muslims – in what have been called the Wars of the Yugoslav Succession in the 1990s, notably the 8,000 completely unarmed and innocent Bosnian Muslim civilian men slaughtered in cold blood at Srebrenica in 1995. All this goes back to the folk memory of the Serb loss at the Field of Blackbirds – Kosovo Polje – in 1389. Seldom has so ancient a defeat had such terrible long-term consequences, hundreds of years later, for the distant descendants of those who took part in it.

Both Prince Lazar and the Ottoman ruler Sultan Murad lost their lives at Kosovo, with Lazar being elevated to sainthood by the grieving Serbs. It should be remembered that many of the troops fighting on the Ottoman side were in fact Christian, from those parts of the Balkans already in Ottoman hands. So the famous battle was not by any means a simple Muslim vs. Christian conflict, as generations of Serb nationalists have tried to portray it since.

Murad's successor as Ottoman Sultan, Bayezid, continued the expansion, and was soon reaching the banks of the Danube. This worried the Europeans, for, as Hodgson points out (in volume two), the Serbs were Orthodox, but the Hungarians, whose borders were now endangered, were mainstream Catholics. Crusade was once again proclaimed, and a new army set out to stop the Ottoman advance. But at the Battle of Nicopolis on the Danube in 1396 Bayezid routed Sigismund of Hungary's Crusader army, although it was far bigger and drawn from a much wider part of Europe than the predominantly Balkan army at Kosovo seven years earlier.

Nicopolis was to prove a disaster, because the West never properly followed it up. No further Western armies did anything to try to prevent the Ottoman (and thus Islamic) conquest of the Balkans, and this condemned Orthodox southeastern Europe to nearly six centuries of foreign rule.

Although, because of enduring Serb folk memory, Kosovo is the better-known battle, Nicopolis is far more important historically, because if the West had won, the loss at Kosovo would have become irrelevant. Nicopolis, therefore, joins the ranks of battles such as Tours/Poitiers in 732 (that the West won) and Manzikert (which the Byzantines lost), as pivotal events in the very lengthy history of European/Islamic conflict. This is because the coalition defeat led to over five centuries of Muslim rule over the Balkans, which only really fully ended with the wars of liberation fought in that region in the run-up to the First World War.

With the advent of the new Ottoman Empire in south-east Europe, an interesting political question emerges. What difference is there between, say, the French conquest of Algeria in 1830, and the British of Nigeria a few decades later, on the one hand, and the Ottoman invasion of the Balkans, or their conquest of their fellow Sunni Muslims in Egypt not long after in the sixteenth century? Surely the answer is that there is none at all? Imperialism, surely, is imperialism by whosoever commits it.

However, after its major victories in the Balkans, the Ottoman Empire was nearly felled at birth, not from Europe, but by a far more potent and Islamic threat from the East. This was Timur-i-Leng, known in the West as Tamerlane.

Timur (1336–1405) was, briefly, one of the most successful conquerors in history, with an empire stretching from Cairo to Delhi. Mainly Turkish, but with some maternal descent from Genghis Khan, his domains were mainly seized in the brief period 1370–1405. Every bit as bloodthirsty as Genghis, he began his campaigns from what is now Uzbekistan (where he is now celebrated as a national hero), and but for his death in 1405 he would probably have conquered the Ottoman Empire as well. In 1399, he mounted a campaign against both the Mamluks and Ottomans whom he claimed had seized some of his territories. By the end of 1401 he had taken Aleppo, Damascus and Baghdad (where he massacred 20,000 of its inhabitants), and in the following year he defeated the Ottoman army of Sultan Bezeyid II near modern Ankara. It was his decision then to attack China that possibly saved the Ottomans from extinction.

Although Timur did not leave a permanent empire, his descendants, the Mughals, were able to invade and occupy most of India. Thankfully for their Hindu subjects, they were nowhere near as violent as Timur, and, as Akbar Ahmed reminds us, they were able to create one of the most religiously tolerant regimes in Islamic history.

Even after Bayezid died, things continued to get worse, since his sons fought a ten-year civil war to take over his realm. Not until Sultan Mehmed I's rule (1402–21) did the Ottoman Empire get back to normal.

Murad II (reigned 1421–51) was thus able to continue the takeover of the Balkans, now that there was both internal peace and no major threat of invasion from the east. He beat the Venetians, who had ruled much of the area off and on since the Latin Empire, and captured the Morea, and the key town of Salonika (now Thessaloniki). He briefly abdicated, resumed the throne, and then beat a Christian army at the key battle of Varna in 1444.

Next to ascend the throne was Mehmed II (1451–81), known to history, and with good cause, as Mehmed the Conqueror. He achieved what the Umayyad and Abbasid Caliphs, and the Mongols, had all failed to do by capturing Constantinople and extinguishing the rump Byzantine Empire. On 29 May 1453 the great city, for so long the last remnant of Rome and capital of Orthodox Christianity, fell to the besieging Turkish forces. The Roman Empire was finally no more and the armies of Islam were triumphant.

Constantinople now became Istanbul, and the ancient church of Hagia Sophia (Holy Wisdom) became a mosque, which it remained for 482 years before being converted into a museum in 1935. Istanbul became the Ottoman capital, and stayed as such until the 1920s.

Then in 1517 the Ottomans turned south, and captured Mamluk-ruled Egypt. The nominal Abbasid Caliphate, based in Cairo, was now ended, and Sultan Selim took the title for himself, even though he was Turkish and no descendant of Muhammad. The Ottomans were not merely victorious but had achieved two vital symbolic victories, all within a comparatively short timespan.

It is said that the fall of Constantinople helped the Renaissance, since so many people fled from the fallen Orthodox East to the still Christian Catholic West. While there is much in this argument, recent books have suggested that the interaction between the Islamic world and the West predates the Renaissance as far back as the twelfth century, and helped to influence it. These include Jerry Brotton's *The Renaissance Bazaar: From the Silk Road to Michelangelo* and Rosamond Mack's *Bazaar to Piazza: Islamic Trade and Italian Art 1300–1600*.

The former also makes an important point – 1517 was not just the year of the Ottoman assumption of the Caliphate, but also the beginning of the Reformation, which, it can be claimed, owed much to the Ottomans. Here fashionable counter-factual history allows an assessment of the degree to which the external threat of Islamic conquest dramatically changed the internal history of Western Europe, and in an unexpected way.

The major consideration here is that had Emperor Charles V, the Holy Roman Emperor, not been so worried about the permanent Ottoman threat from the east, he would have crushed the nascent Protestant movement from its outset. As ruler of Austria he faced the Ottomans in conquered Hungary and as King of Spain, the attempts by Muslim rulers in the Mediterranean to menace his possessions there, which included not just Spain but also Sicily and parts of the Italian mainland.

Therefore Luther and the Protestant Reformation owe much to the Ottoman menace to Europe. The ensuing Protestant–Catholic split ended the Habsburg attempts to unify Germany and delayed unification for three centuries, the Ottoman advances in the sixteenth century thereby altering the history of Western Europe permanently.

An interesting minor snippet – we owe coffee and the croissant, the latter being shaped like the Turkish crescent, to the siege of Vienna. Thus does culture spread in unexpected ways.

Although the Ottomans failed to capture Vienna, they did manage to conquer most of Hungary. In 1520 Suleiman the Magnificent became Sultan; regarded by historians as probably one of the greatest Ottoman rulers, he held the throne until his death in 1566. In 1526 he was able to recommence serious war against the West, and in the same year his forces annihilated the Hungarians at the Battle of Mohacs, after which the young Hungarian king, Louis II, perished while fleeing the battle-field. Hungary, which had always seen itself as the impenetrable shield of the Christian West, became an Ottoman domain, for the next 170 and more years. (The rest of Hungary – now Slovakia – went to the Habsburgs. This dynasty ruled Hungary until 1918, including those parts liberated in the 1690s.) Transylvania, now famous for its infamous inhabitant, Vlad the Impaler (or Dracula), was then mainly Protestant, and part of Hungary. The Protestants often preferred freedom under the Turks to persecution by the Catholic Habsburgs, who had made the same mistake as the Nestorian–persecuting Byzantines back in the seventh century.

Problems in East and West

The Ottomans now ruled from the Iranian border to northern
Africa, and from southern Egypt up to the Austrian frontier.
This was the Golden Age of Ottoman rule. They did not
entirely have it their own way, however. While they continued
to make conquests, taking the key Venetian-ruled island of
Cyprus in 1570, for example, they also, like Charles V, had to
watch their backs. (The wars over Cyprus are part of the
backdrop to Shakespeare's play *Othello*.)

In 1501, Ismail, the leader of a Shiite religious group the
Safavids, became Shah of Persia. Ismail was ethnically Turkish,
as therefore was the Safavid dynasty that he now founded. His
accession to power and the establishment of his family on the
throne reignited the border wars between the rulers of Iran
and those of the Middle East.

One could call this an updated version of the same ancient
struggles between the Romans and Byzantines on the one
hand, and the Parthians and Sassanids on the other. Although
both the Ottomans and Safavids were Muslims, the latter were
zealously Shia, and made the Shiite version of Islam the official
belief of Iran, which it has been ever since. Persia, as it was
then called, had always been culturally distinct, albeit closely
enmeshed with Arabic culture during the time of the Abbasid
Caliphate that we saw earlier. Now that it was also Shiite, as
opposed to mainstream Sunni, this distinctiveness grew
stronger – though we should not forget that many other parts
of the world contained Shiites, notably the region around
present-day Iraq, and what is now Pakistan.

Initially the Ottomans were the winners. In 1534 Suleiman, flush from his victories in Europe, was able to seize Mesopotamia, with the Safavids forced to concede defeat in 1555.

In 1571 Don John of Austria (to use his English nickname), the illegitimate son of Charles V, was able to put together a Christian fleet to prevent further Ottoman expansion in the Mediterranean following the Venetian loss of Cyprus, which had devastated the Venetians and made them extremely apprehensive about their other Mediterranean possessions. As G. K. Chesterton wrote in his famous poem, 'Don John of Austria is going to the war.' A coalition of over 200 ships was assembled based mainly on Spanish, Genoese and Venetian vessels, with some from the Knights Hospitaller. At Lepanto in the Gulf of Patras in Greece, the Christian forces under Don John soundly beat the Ottoman navy, capturing no fewer than 117 Ottoman galleys. This victory removed the danger of a seaborne invasion of the remaining Christian parts of the Mediterranean and enabled the Venetians to hold Crete until the 1660s.

One interesting footnote – one of the Spanish sailors was Cervantes, the subsequent author of *Don Quixote*.

However, as Hodgson reminds us in *The Venture of Islam*, the Ottomans were principally a land-based, not seafaring, power. They did not lose any territory as a result of their maritime loss, and the main result of the battle was more to do with enhancing Venetian morale than stemming the flow of the Turkish advance. Not only that but the West did not follow up their naval victory, and so the cause of liberation from the Ottomans was not in any way advanced.

In fact the main threat, as before, came from the east. In 1587, the most illustrious of the Safavids, Shah Abbas the Great, acceded to the Peacock Throne (the name given to the famous chair upon which the Persian Shahs sat).

He moved the capital to Isfahan. His conquests were considerable, as he reached into Arab territory, especially the area now populated by the Shiite majority in modern Iraq. The survival of so large an Arab Shiite group can be said to owe its existence to the highly successful campaigns of Shah Abbas against the Ottomans, with results that have therefore created ramifications for us in the twenty-first century. He was able to seize present-day Azerbaijan, which has remained a predominantly Shiite state, and which has given Iran a large Azerbaijani minority that exists to this day. While his less able successors, following his death in 1629, were unable to keep Iraq, the majority of Arabs in that region have remained Shiite, not Sunni, down to the present.

His reign was the high point of Safavid Iran, although the dynasty continued to rule, with lessening success, until the 1720s, with the Qajar dynasty taking over in 1779 (and ruling until the 1920s).

While the Ottomans were able to reconquer Iraq, the historical consensus is that the truly great days of the dynasty were over, even though they ruled for another two centuries. Increasingly power went to the real rulers, the Grand Viziers. There is no real modern equivalent to these individuals, but regarding the holder as a kind of prime minister would probably indicate the degree of power they had at their disposal. The office could, for brief spells, be filled by one family, and in certain cases it became hereditary as well, with a particularly notable family, the Koprulu dynasty, exercising the role in seventeenth-century Constantinople. But as time went by it was increasingly occupied by *dervishme* men. *Dervishme* was essentially a highly unpopular practice of kidnapping boys from Christian families, converting them to Islam and using them as a caste of dependable administrators.

Interestingly, loyalty to the Islamic faith rather than membership of a particular race was the key factor in employment at the Ottoman court, some of whose senior members and officials were of European origin. In theory the Ottoman Sultan himself wielded enormous power. But, as Efraim Karsh reminds us in his book on *Islamic Imperialism*, not all the Sultans were up to the task. The devolution of power to the Grand Vizier, and the increasing importance of *dervishme* officials created a bureaucratic elite which, cut off from its roots, was loyal to the Sultan. But like all bureaucracies it stultified, and attempts to reform it in the nineteenth century were perpetually stymied, principally by inertia, and later on by Sultans such as Abdul Hamid, for whom the very notion of change was anathema.

The administration of the great Ottoman Empire has been well described as a policy of 'benign neglect'. This is broadly correct, in that there was not always direct Ottoman rule from Istanbul of all the widespread provinces of the Empire, since in the days before rapid communication, this simply was not possible. Rather a system of indirect rule was practised, similar – as we have seen with previous empires – to that of the British in India and other colonies. In theory, many of the local rulers were higher in status than Ottoman officials, such as the Khedive, or Viceroy, of Egypt. But in practice, many of these posts, like those in Egypt and elsewhere, for example the Bey of Tunis, were hereditary, with the post being kept within one family. Similarly, like the zamindar (landlord) tax collectors in British India, the Ottomans also used local people to collect most of the revenue. This too created a hereditary caste of 'tax-farmers', who would extort money from ordinary people, since they could keep for themselves anything above the amount required by the government.

In 1683, the Ottomans tried to besiege Vienna for a second time; again they failed, and their hold on parts of their Balkan territories was weakening. In 1699 at the Treaty of Carlowitz, they had permanently to cede large amounts of reconquered territory to the West. Hungary came back under Christian rule, and, although the Western liberation of the Balkans took until 1913 to complete – 114 years – the momentum was now with the West, not the Islamic world.

Despite military defeats – the Ottomans had to cede yet more territory to the Austrians in 1718 at the Treaty of Passarowitz, for example – there were some attempts by Ottoman Sultans and their Viziers to reform the Empire from within. But such gallant efforts were defeated, especially by the troops, some of European origin, designed to guard the Sultans, the Janissaries. These were a group of *dervishme* soldiers recruited from boys seized from the Christian parts of the Ottoman Empire, principally the Balkans. They were indoctrinated into loyalty to the Sultan, and were converted to Islam. Rather like the Praetorian Guard of the old Roman Emperors, these elite guards became increasingly corrupt, and therefore antagonistic to any kind of change, however benevolent. Nor did continued military reverses help. The

Ottomans were badly defeated by the Russians at the end of the eighteenth century, and had to sign another humiliating treaty, this time at Kuchuk Kaynarji, in 1774, in which the Tsars were able to regain the Crimea from Turkish rule.

As Bernard Lewis points out in his book *The Middle East*, the Ottoman loss was especially important as this was the first time the Ottomans had lost territory containing mainly Muslims, not Christians, to a prominent Christian power.

Even more menacing, this treaty specifically gave the Russians protection rights over the Orthodox Christians in the Ottoman Empire. Under the Turkish *millet* system, in which everyone was classified by their religion, rather than by their ethnicity, (Jews, therefore, being the exception, since theirs was a dual category), Orthodox Christians came under the Orthodox *millet*. The treaty therefore gave the Russians the right to interfere in the internal affairs of the Ottoman Empire, and with the rise of Slavic/Orthodox nationalism in the nineteenth century, this came to mean Tsarist support for independence movements in the Balkans. The Eastern Question, the great debate among the diplomats and chancelleries on how to manage the decline of the Ottoman Empire, had begun.

Wahhabi Islam

Until recently, historians have given only fleeting attention to one of the most significant movements in the eighteenth century – that of Wahhabi Islam. Since this, often stern, version of Sunni Hanbali Islam is now becoming increasingly global, and is the basis of the extremist ideology of Al Qaeda, people have now realized its importance.

Muhammad ibn Abd al-Wahhab (c. 1703–92) was an Islamic thinker from what is now central Saudi Arabia. He followed the precepts of the medieval jurist, Ibn Taymiyya, at whom we looked earlier.

In Sunni Islam, as we saw, the 'gates of *ijtihad*', or individual/new interpretations of the Quran were supposed to have closed around the tenth century. However, al-Wahhab thought that far too much syncretism, or outside religious practice, had entered Islam, and that the religion had become corrupt.

Here we enter a very contemporary debate, namely that Islam should have a Reformation, similar to the Protestant kind that happened to Christianity in the sixteenth century. An essay by the writer Salman Rushdie in the *New York Times* on 7 April 2005 is a classic example of a call for a Muslim reformation by someone of Islamic origin living in the West. Since all well-meaning people hope for good Muslim–Western relations, including millions of those Muslims living peacefully and happily in the West itself, this is an entirely understandable goal.

However, the experience of al-Wahhab suggests this notion is mistaken. Islam has already had its own reformation, and to expect it to undergo something it has already been through is impossible. Here one can agree with the late Edward Said, and say that such calls are in fact arrogant, since what they are really doing is asking the Islamic world to become like the twenty-first-century secular West.

In fact, it should be perfectly possible for Muslims to continue to be authentic Muslims while living in peaceful harmony with the secular West. This is what leading contemporary Muslim intellectuals, such as Akbar Ahmed, who now lives in the USA, and the former Iranian President Khatami, who calls for a 'dialogue of civilizations', have now been arguing for some years.

Martin Luther and his fellow Reformers were attempting to remove the many accretions inherent in Catholic Christianity, and return it to what they felt was the purity of the original. This is precisely what al-Wahhab was also trying to do, and which is why he would not have regarded himself as an interpreter of Islam, a *mujadid*, even though that is what he was doing. Like the twentieth-century ideologue Sayyid Qutb, he was trying to get back to the original Islam of the *salaf*, the revered ancestors of the first Islamic century, although his teachings took part of that faith – those who follow al-Wahhab – in a direction very far removed from the one that secular thinkers in the West would like.

When one reads modern-day callers for a Muslim Reformation, they are usually thinking of thinkers such as Abdolkarim Soroush, the Iranian reformer, about whom Judith Miller has written in *God Has Ninety-Nine Names*. Reformation will lead to a non-violent, modern-friendly, twenty-first-century-compatible, updated version of Islam.

But while, in an age of terrorism, non-violent versions of any religion are welcome (think, too, for example, of Timothy McVeigh, and also of extremist Hindu mobs killing Muslims in India), this attitude is completely to misunderstand history.

As Daniel Benjamin and Steven Simon show in *The Age of Sacred Terror*, al-Wahhab could not have achieved much on his own. To use my analogy, he needed his equivalent of Luther's Elector of Saxony, a secular prince who would support him and help to implement the message. This al-Wahhab found in the al-Saud clan, the tribal leaders of central Arabia. Thus was forged an alliance between a particular interpretation of Islam – now called Wahhabism – and a powerful dynasty, that has lasted right down until and including our own times. Saudi Arabia remains the one place in the world where Wahhabism is the official interpretation of Islam. Furthermore, as we read in *The Crisis of Islam*, once Saudi Arabia became fabulously wealthy through oil, the Wahhabi religious hierarchy was then able to gain access to lavish state funding. As a consequence, Saudi petrodollars are spreading the Wahhabi version globally, as if profits from the top American petrol companies all went to promote the doctrines of the Ku Klux Klan.

(One hopes that King Abdullah, who became king after that book was written, might be able to change things, but, as with so much in the world today, only time will tell.)

In al-Wahhab's own lifetime the Saudi/Wahhabi alliance was able to conquer only central Arabia. But this was only the beginning.

A new study of Wahhabism, *God's Terrorists: The Wahhabi Cult and the Hidden Roots of Modern Jihad*, by Charles Allen, has brought out very well the doleful effects down to our own time of the kind of extremism which al-Wahhab spawned.

Charles Allen shows that al-Wahhab, like Ibn Taymiyya, rejected the theological notion that there were two forms of jihad – the lesser, or military version, and the greater, the struggle to be holy. For Wahhabism, the only kind that existed was the violent version, and the so-called Hadith, or authenticated saying of Muhammad, to the effect that the greater had now supplanted the lesser was in fact false. Only the way of violence was true.

The Wahhabis, who now intermarried with the Saud clan, embarked on a campaign of violent conquest that lasted until its suppression in 1818. But, Allen goes on to show in much detail in *God's Terrorists*, that was by no means the end of the story, as the Wahhabi version of Islam now spread to the Indian sub-continent. There it became popular among much of the Muslim community, who were not used to being a minority under the British, and no longer rulers of the Hindu majority. This in turn influenced the kind of Islam taught in the north-western part of the Raj, now Pakistan, and also over the border in Afghanistan. Much of the Islamic extremism that still exists in the region – the Taliban being a prime example – is thus strongly influenced by Wahhabi theology.

Consequently, although Pakistan and Afghanistan are outside the remit of this book, this phenomenon does matter, since, in the twenty-first century, Saudi Wahhabism and the Taliban version of Islamic extremism have worked closely together.

The nineteenth century: Western expansion, Ottoman retreat

As Bernard Lewis points out in *Islam and the West*, this time without controversy, the Napoleonic invasion and temporary conquest of Egypt in 1798 marks another major turning point. For the first time since the Crusades a Muslim heartland region had been subjugated, and for a brief period would be under Christian rule.

Worse still, it was the British, through Nelson's victory at the Battle of the Nile, who liberated Egypt from Napoleon, not an Ottoman army. In the West, because of the major archaeological discoveries that resulted, we tend to look benignly at Napoleon's invasion — the Rosetta Stone, the decipherment of the hieroglyphs, and many similar achievements resulting from Napoleon's decision to bring both troops and scholars with him. But to the Ottomans, the brief loss of Egypt was a major humiliation, and the foretaste of a century and more of bad news.

However, the plight of the Ottomans was good news for some of their more independently minded subjects. One of these was Mehmet Ali (or Muhammad Ali in Arabic), an Albanian Muslim, who was part of a failed attempt to regain Egypt in 1799. Once the British had evacuated in 1803 he was able to seize power, and founded a dynasty which lasted until its deposition in 1952. Ali was ruthless in suppressing all dissent, and by the 1820s aimed at conquering as much of the Ottoman Middle East as possible.

The new rulers of Egypt were, as for the past two millennia and more, not Arabs of any description. The phrase often used to describe the new power elite is Turco-Circassian. Inevitably many Turks remained. But there were also large numbers of Muslim Europeans, from the Balkans, like Mehmet Ali himself, and also from the Caucasus, from whence the Circassians came, as had many of the Mamluks before them. Most of the major landowners were from this background, since political power and economic wealth remained strongly enmeshed.

The Europeans were, while all this was happening in Egypt, helping Greece to gain independence from the Turks. Greece, with its Christian population, and illustrious Hellenic past, not to mention the romantic support of the poet Lord Byron, was one thing, though, but Egypt quite another. While southern Greece was recognized as an independent kingdom, the Europeans supported the Ottomans against Mehmet Ali's forces.

As Arthur Goldschmidt demonstrates, a compromise was struck – Ali had to give up his conquests in Palestine and Syria, but was able to rule Egypt as a virtually independent domain, only notionally still a part of the Ottoman Empire.

The other, this time more temporary, Middle Eastern beneficiary of Ottoman decline after 1798 was the Saudi/ Wahhabi alliance. (The Serbs were also in revolt, but the Balkans is outside the main scope of this book.) Initially they were immensely successful, capturing the two holy cities of Mecca and Medina. Here, in accord with the hatred of syncretism in Wahhabi Islam, they indulged in the mass destruction of numerous ancient shrines, including the tomb of Muhammad himself, all very reminiscent of the similar destruction of Catholic shrines in the Reformation and English Civil War.

(Syncretism in this context is the way in which local customs, often influenced by ancient pre-Islamic practices, or by outside religions, had merged with what specialists call 'folk Islam'. To the Wahhabis, this kind of popular Muslim culture contaminated the true, original faith that they were trying to re-establish.)

But by 1818 the Ottomans were able to re-establish control, and the Saudis and their Wahhabi allies were once again restricted to their heartland in the Nejd in the centre of modern Saudi Arabia, only to rise again in the twentieth century, after the fall of the Ottoman Empire.

In 1839 Sultan Abdul Mejid inaugurated what has become known as the Tanzimat era of reforms in which he tried to reorganize the bureaucracy of the Empire and lay the foundations of a modern state, following his predecessor Mahmud II's successful suppression of the Janissaries. Here again, interpretation becomes controversial.

Malcolm Yapp's book *The Making of the Modern Middle East 1792–1923* made it clear that the peoples of the Middle East were not helpless before the Europeans. It shows how the British, hitherto unworried by the Eastern Question, became so once they saw the imbalance *in Europe* that unfettered Russian supremacy in the Balkans, and over the Straits, would create. In other words, British support for Greek independence, and for the Ottomans against Mehmet Ali, was dominated by issues of the European balance of power, as opposed to the interests of the peoples of the Middle East. Furthermore, the Ottoman Empire, despite its decline, was not entirely helpless, and, possibly, given different decisions in 1914, might have survived for much longer than proved to be the case.

However, a few years after Yapp's book came a much more controversial work, *Empires of the Sand: The Struggle for Mastery in the Middle East 1789–1923*, by the authors Efraim and Inari Karsh. What has made this book especially contested and the whole subject vitiated is their view on the origins of the Jewish settlement. This takes us into particularly contentious academic and political territory. It has also distorted reactions to their thesis, namely that Middle Eastern rulers, far from being passive, took an active role alongside Western powers in creating the Middle East we know today. But while Malcolm Yapp was able to say something very similar without provoking a firestorm, this was not the case when the Karsh book appeared.

Whether or not the Ottoman Empire was in inexorable decline in the nineteenth century should have nothing to do with taking sides in the twenty-first-century Israel–Palestine dispute. But, alas, such seems now to be the case. So this book takes the view that Malcolm Yapp is right, that the demise of Ottoman power was *not* inevitable, but in a way that does not thereby imply any particular partisan position on some of the thorniest issues of contemporary politics.

As Yapp, Bernard Lewis, and similar writers show, what really began to make the difference were the Ottoman and Persian territorial losses to the Russians in the period of roughly 1800–1812. Many of these were in the Caucasus, where Muslims and Christians both then as now live cheek by jowl. This has remained an area of major instability and, alas, of religious violence, as seen in the horrific massacre of school children in Beslan in 2004. These Russian gains in turn alerted Britain to growing Russian power, with the results just mentioned.

(British concern over Russian advances to India through Central Asia played an important later role, but as Yapp shows, not in the early stages. The era of *Kim* and the Great Game came later and would last until 1907, when Britain and Russia demarcated zones of influence in Persia.)

One of the major concerns of the European Great Powers was to deny others the advantage, or, as the British would see it, maintain the Balance of Power. While neither France nor Britain wished to see Russia become too dominant, both of them nonetheless were happy to carve up parts of the

Ottoman Empire for themselves if it suited their interests. In 1830 France annexed Algeria (initially the coastal areas, with the conquest of the interior coming later) and in 1839 Britain seized Aden, an important stop for trade on the then long sea journey to India. In the former case, the French began actively to settle in the new colony, a decision which very nearly caused civil war in the 1950s, when Algerians wanted independence, and the French settlers, or *colons*, were determined to stop them.

We saw that in 1774 Russia gained the right to protect the Orthodox Christian subjects of the Ottoman Empire. By the early 1850s this had spread, as France sought similar rights to look out for the Catholic minority, many of whom were Greek-Melkite-rite Arab Christians in the Holy Land. (These were Christians who followed Orthodox rites while being spiritually loyal to the Roman Catholic Church.) What began as a comparatively trivial and minor dispute escalated in 1854 into war, with the British and French fighting to preserve the Ottoman Empire on the one hand and the Russians determined to flex their power on the other. Since the conflict took place in the territory regained by the Russians in 1774, we call it the Crimean War, which lasted from 1853 to 1856. (In Britain this conflict is principally remembered for the achievements of Florence Nightingale and the foolish charge of the Light Brigade immortalized in Tennyson's poem.) Eventually the Russians lost, and the Ottomans were able to breathe again.

Thereafter much of the story of the Ottoman Empire seems to be one of remorseless decline. The Ottomans lost territory continuously, right up until their demise in 1922, into which we will soon go in some detail, since today's Middle East is still suffering from the way in which the Empire broke up. But, as the distinguished British historian John Charmley will remind us when his magnum opus on Europe and the 'Eastern Question' is one day published, it was the European not the core Middle Eastern territories that the Ottomans lost. The core Islamic parts of the Empire (albeit with small Christian minorities, such as the Maronites in Lebanon) remained firmly under Ottoman rule.

The importance of this in a history of the Islamic Middle East cannot be exaggerated. What the Ottomans lost in the second half of the nineteenth century were their Slavic, mainly still Christian, European territories. Serbia, then Bulgaria, Romania, northern Greece, then finally Bosnia (with a large Muslim, but ethnically European, population), and Kosovo (ditto) were lost. Technically Egypt was lost de facto in 1882, when seized by the British, and de jure in 1914. The Italians took Libya just before the First World War. But not only were these territories away from the core, but Egypt had in effect been lost a long time before when Mehmet Ali assumed control at the beginning of the nineteenth century. The heartland territories, including present-day Iraq, Syria, Israel, Jordan, Lebanon and Palestine, and the Red Sea side of Arabia – the Hijaz – remained part of the Empire until 1917, when they were conquered by the British.

In other words, the Tsar Nicholas I might have been right to call the Ottoman Empire 'the Sick Man of Europe', because its European domains were now in permanent decline. But the Muslim part of the Empire outside of Europe was doing fine, because unlike nationalist Europe this part of the Empire was both Muslim, like its overlords, and not nationalistic. While some Christian Arabs were nationalistic, this was not true of the Muslim majority, with repercussions that will soon become very important.

One can argue persuasively that European nationalism threatened Ottoman control of the predominantly Christian Balkans. Nationalism meant self-rule, and there were powerful and ultimately successful nationalist movements among the Serbs, Greeks, Bulgarians and Romanians. Their bids for complete independence doomed the European end of the Empire, especially since Russia actively supported the freedom of their fellow Orthodox Christians. But it is much harder to argue that a few Arab nationalists, many of whom were from the tiny Christian minority, posed any kind of real threat to continued Ottoman rule. Furthermore, the Ottoman Sultan for much of this period, Abdul Hamid, was keen to emphasize Islamic identity, as a focus of unity, and on that issue most of the Middle Eastern subjects of the empire were as at one with their Ottoman overlords.

So between 1877, when the Balkans revolted, with Russian support, and the end of the Second Balkan War thirty-six years later, the Ottoman Empire lost nearly all its European territory to the newly independent Slavic states. The end could have come sooner, but for the fact that the European Powers, including Britain, were still strongly suspicious of Russian territorial designs. For example, in Berlin in 1878 the Russian puppet state of Bulgaria was granted much less territory than under the original borders proposed by the victorious Russians at the Treaty of San Stefano earlier in the same year, when Russia and its Balkan allies inflicted a major reverse on the Ottomans.

In fact one could say that what really doomed the Ottomans eventually was a conjunction of two things. First, their decision to abandon the traditional friendship with Britain and France for alliance with Germany in 1914; second, and perhaps even more important, that in the First World War Britain and France found themselves allied with Russia against Germany, and were therefore no longer in a position to do anything to counteract historic Russian designs on the Ottoman Empire. None of this was inevitable – in the 1890s Britain and France nearly went to war over a few desert oases at Fashoda in what is now Sudan. It was not until the Entente Cordiale of 1904 that the prospect of Franco-British conflict evaporated.

One could argue that it was an attempt at internal imperial reform that began the series of events that would in time lead to the Empire's fall. In 1908 the Committee on Union and Progress (CUP), a movement of young Turkish military officers nicknamed the Young Turks, initiated a revolt that spread rapidly. The response of Sultan Abdul Hamid was to announce the full restoration of the Ottoman Constitution of 1876 – the first such in any Islamic country – that had defined the Sultan's powers, but which he had neutralized. But this attempt to rescue his position failed. He was deposed in 1909, and replaced by his brother Mehmed V, more of a figurehead Sultan, who ruled until the Ottoman debacle in 1918.

Then in 1913, following the massive defeats in the Balkans in 1912, and the loss of most of the European part of the Empire, the CUP took power. But instead of thinking of themselves as Ottomans – all Muslims regardless of race in a great Islamic empire – they were in effect Turkish nationalists, and this began an unfortunate process of alienating the non-Turkish, but still loyally Muslim, parts of the Empire.

The CUP dated back to the late 1880s, with a formal beginning in 1889. It was concentrated initially in the Third Army, based in the still Ottoman-ruled Balkans. (Not all the army supported them however.) It was not until 1913 that they became an effective political party. The CUP were in essence a triumvirate – Cemal Pasha, initially Navy minister, then governor of Syria, Talaat Pasha, who became minister of the interior, and Enver Pasha, perhaps the most important of them all, who now became war minister. As Justin McCarthy puts it in *The Ottoman Peoples and the End of Empire*, this triple sharing of power helped, as no one man could claim to be dictator.

Had the Ottoman Empire not gone to war in 1914, the tendency of the CUP to place a premium on Turkish identity over Ottoman might eventually have led to ruptures that could, in the long run, have proved fatal to imperial unity. But even here, one must remember that most of the Arabs stayed loyal to the Ottomans even after the so-called Arab Revolt in 1916. Moreover it was British and Australian military might that eventually destroyed the Ottomans, despite spectacular Turkish victories at Gallipoli and Kut. One could thus argue that while the Ottomans were indeed the sick men of Europe – they had only a slither of territory left in Europe, comprising their possessions in Thrace, by 1914 – elsewhere in that same year the long-term prospects were good. Although they had lost territory in the First Balkan War of 1912, in which Serbia, Greece, Bulgaria, Romania and Montenegro formed a coalition to win territory from the Ottoman Empire and expel it from Europe, in the Second Balkan War in 1913 (Bulgaria against its former allies over the division of the spoils), the Ottomans were swift to take advantage of the falling-out of its former enemies, and thus regained much of Thrace.

Not only that, but as Alan Palmer points out in *The Decline and Fall of the Ottoman Empire* there were those in senior positions in Istanbul who wanted an alliance with the British, with two CUP delegates sent to London in 1908 as negotiators. Sir Edward Grey, the British Foreign Secretary, turned down their request, with all the consequences that followed from that in 1914. (He was against such alliances in principle, and was wary of whether or not the Ottoman reformers could ever fully overcome the corruption.) Despite this, some Ottoman dignitaries remained sympathetic to the British, including Kamil Pasha, the last pre-CUP Grand Vizier, whom the British helped to flee in 1913.

It is not therefore necessary to agree with the other deeply controversial theories of Efraim and Inari Karsh, in their book *Empires of the Sand*, over the way in which the Ottoman Empire ended. (Many writers, as we have seen, consider they denigrate the Arabs.) They state – and on this I agree – that it was the single decision of the Ottomans to join Germany against the Allies in 1914 that doomed the Empire. (The Karsh theories will be considered in the next chapter.) But as that decision might not have been as inevitable as we now suppose, neither was the end of the Ottoman Empire inevitable, certainly not in the way that it happened, namely that of an Empire defeated by external European forces. Combine this with the fact that Russia was now Britain's ally principally against Germany, and the fate of the Empire was sealed, as the

British prime minister, Herbert Asquith, reminded his audience in the London Guildhall, in late 1914.

But had the Ottomans stayed neutral – as Turkey did for most of the Second World War, before joining the Allies in 1945 – then the Russians would have had no excuse to attack Ottoman territory. Without that, the British and French would have had no cause to partition the Empire, as they did notoriously in 1916, and things could have been radically different.

The decline of the Ottoman Empire: Orientalism and after

What one might describe as the 'What Went Wrong?' school of thought tends to argue that 1683, the second Ottoman failure to capture Habsburg Vienna and expand the Empire, marks one of the key turning points in history. It is true, on the one hand, that proponents of this view – as we saw in the preface – tend to exaggerate the relative decline of the Middle East over time. But 1683 can be considered as good a date in which to see the beginning of the decay of Muslim political and military power in relation to that of the West, underlined by the Treaty of Carlowitz in 1699. (It should be added that this does not contradict what was said earlier about the fall of Baghdad to the Mongols in 1258, and the sad decline of Arabic culture and civilization that flowed from it.)

This view, which Bernard Lewis defends in books such as *The Crisis of Islam*, seems to be the commonsense version of history. By the nineteenth century the once mighty Ottoman Empire only failed to be conquered by the Russians because the Western powers did not let them.

However, to hold such an opinion is, in the eyes of the late Edward Said, to be an 'Orientalist', to look at the Middle East through Eurocentric eyes. Said was an Egyptian-raised Palestinian Christian, Protestant rather than one of the many varieties of Catholic found among the Palestinian population, and of Lebanese ancestry. He was a professor of English Literature, not history, and spent most of his working life in the USA. As a result of Said's best-known work, *Orientalism*, Lewis is now strongly criticized for being one of the worst offenders in the Orientalist canon.

To Said, the West portrayed the Middle East as the 'Orient', but more importantly as the exotic and alien 'other', an altogether different place from the West. Not only that, but to Said, one could not separate the way in which Western scholars looked at the Orient from European colonialism, the two things going together like a hand in a glove. This work has also now spawned a whole new sub-discipline, namely post-colonial studies, and also 'subaltern studies' – the idea that colonial history is best studied from the viewpoint of the colonized rather than from that of the inevitably Western colonial powers.

Much of this makes sense, especially the study of history *after* the start of Western colonization. The Western conquest of most of Africa began in the late nineteenth century. In the Middle East, the Western invasion started de jure in the early twentieth, although on the periphery of the Ottoman Empire Algeria had been lost as early as 1830 and the British had taken de facto control of Egypt in 1882, although they did not seize it formally until 1914.

Unfortunately Said dates 'Orientalism' to much earlier – even going back to the Middle Ages in some of his analysis when Spain, for example, was attempting to free itself from being a colony rather than the other way around.

In his *Islam and the West* Lewis defends himself, correctly I think, by saying that much of what Said says is inaccurate or simply unfair. Not only that, but the facts indicate a major decline relative to the West starting after 1683, and all the more so after 1798, when Napoleon seized Egypt.

Perhaps a better place to understand Said, however, is in another book of his altogether, one in which Lewis is hardly mentioned. This is his later work, *Covering Islam*. Here the major criticism of Lewis is anonymous, in a two-page quotation in the third chapter from one of Lewis' articles. He particularly dislikes what Lewis writes about the lack of intellectual curiosity shown by inhabitants of the Middle East towards European archaeologists who seek to dig up the past of the countries in question.

However, I think that the real issue here is twofold. First of all, people in closed communities, without access to outside knowledge, have enormous difficulties in gaining intellectual concepts of matters denied to them by their totalitarian rulers.

It is true, just to think of one example, that many in the Middle East even today believe the lies of that infamous nineteenth-century Russian secret police anti-Semitic forgery, *The Protocols of the Elders of Zion*. But then so too did millions of people in Tsarist Russia, for whom it was invented, and in Nazi Germany under Hitler. Ignorance of the outside world was also fairly universal in the days before mass education, and communication, and that applies as much to those living in the West as it does to those in the Islamic world.

But perhaps the real difference of view has nothing what-soever to do with past events and whether the Ottoman Empire was, or was not, in a state of decline, but over more recent twentieth-century and contemporary issues much closer to home.

The fact is that, after 11 September 2001, Lewis advised the Bush administration on Middle Eastern affairs, something that in and of itself has nothing to do with historiography, but which has only, alas, exacerbated the situation. Lewis has become part of the American culture wars, with neo-conservatives such as Victor Davis Hanson praising him, and followers of Said the opposite. In other words, Lewis on the one hand and Said on the other are now often used as proxies, by intellectuals who disagree with one another about many things, the notion of 'Orientalism' being merely one of them.

(For non-American readers, the 'culture wars' is a term used in the USA in the ideological conflict between the culturally conservative right and the equally culturally liberal left – it is not just a political issue, as it is in other countries. James Davison Hunter, a sociology Professor at the University of Virginia, made the term famous in his academic study of the same name back in the 1980s, and it has stuck ever since. It now seems to apply to virtually every intellectual area possible, with protagonists on each side looking out carefully for signs of enemy activity.)

2006 saw the publication of *For Lust of Knowing: The Orientalists and Their Enemies*. Helpfully in terms of the debate, its author Robert Irwin is British, and is thus someone not involved in internal American cultural/political debates. Irwin takes apart most of the arguments that Said uses, and does so on historical grounds. To Irwin, much of what Said writes is sheer fantasy, with only a tenuous relationship to the actual past.

For example, he shows that serious study of the Middle East, and of the Arabic language in particular, began in the seventeenth century. This was long before Western imperial encroachment on the area, and was, historically, still at a time when Europe was far more scared of the power of the Ottomans than the other way around. Academic study of the 'Orient' therefore long predates Western imperialism.

Not only that, but Irwin shows that many of the leading 'Orientalists' were German, and thus from a part of Europe that never colonized the Middle East. Irwin's work is important as it completely demolishes the arguments upon which Said bases his work, and has been written by someone who has not been criticized by either side.

Many older readers will know of the famous pastiche history book *1066 and All That*. In this work, Charles I and the Cavaliers are called 'wrong but wromantic' (sic). I would argue that in many respects the same is true of Said's work on Orientalism. Having heard him defend the Palestinian cause in front of an audience that comprised as many Jewish and Israeli students as Palestinian, it is hard not to be moved by his lifelong commitment to a noble cause. As Irwin reminds us, Said was as strongly and correctly opposed to the corrupt coterie around Yasser Arafat as against terrorism as a solution, and believed in genuine freedom for Palestinians, not the substitution of one kind of oppression for another.

But the problem is that because it is easy to sympathize with him on that issue, people automatically buy into his critique of

Western studies of the Middle East as well. Yet the two issues are surely completely different.

Post-colonialism has rightly become a major discipline, along with 'subaltern studies'. Furthermore the fact that devastating critiques, say, of British rule in Kenya or of German oppression in what is now Namibia are all completely on target, does not in and of itself mean that Said was right in *Orientalism*, the book of his that set the ball rolling for such groundbreaking studies. In other words, the successors might be correct, but their originator is not.

We cannot read the very real and thoroughly discreditable imperialism of the twentieth century back into the past, since in the seventeenth century the major imperial power, so far as the Middle East was concerned, was the Ottoman Empire, not Western Europe. Native Americans, South Asian Indians – all these people have every right to complain about Western seventeenth-century imperialism, since they were its victims. But the peoples of the Middle East were still under Islamic rule, and in much of the Balkans it was Europeans under Islamic rule and not the other way around, until into the twentieth century.

It is perfectly permissible, therefore, to share Irwin's conclusion that it is possible both to sympathize with Said on Palestine and at the same time believe that he seriously warped and misread history, with the result that much of the accuracy of *Orientalism* is thus deeply open to question. People can, I would put it, be noble, sincere, and wrong, all at the same time.

All this manipulation of the past for present-day purposes is a shame, as the proxy wars being fought over past events make it much more difficult to look at the actual arguments over what happened and why in their own right. As indicated elsewhere in this book, the issue here has nothing to do with the orient, or indeed with Islam per se, since in earlier times, the Islamic world was far ahead of the more backward West. Rather, it is concerned with size and the division of Europe into much smaller competing states.

China, to use the example given in Joseph Needham's multi-volume history of the science and technology of that country, also lost its lead over the West for a long time, because of the inevitably stultifying effects of an enormous empire that effectively closed itself off to outside interaction and ideas. What is interesting about the Golden Age of Islam is that there was a free market in ideas, one that for all intents and purposes did not exist to anything like the same extent after 1258.

Now both China and Japan, and increasingly also India as well, are catching up very rapidly with the West, and might, as the twenty-first century progresses, overtake the West altogether. It could well be that the two to three centuries of Western intellectual paramountcy might prove to be a temporary blip in the longer history of non-Western supremacy. It is in that context that I see the comparative rise and fall of the Ottomans in relation to the West, in a global perspective, and not through any occidentalist lens.

Ian Buruma, the American-based British author of *Occidentalism*, wrote a review of Lewis' *From Babel to Dragoman* in the *New Yorker*. There Buruma points out that because Lewis praises the Bush administration's policy on Iraq, it does not necessarily mean that he is mistaken about what he described in his massively influential 1990 *Atlantic Monthly* article as 'The Roots of Muslim Rage' – issues which will be examined further in the final chapter. A similar point is made by Michael Hirsh in the *Washington Monthly* in 2004, which demonstrates that it is possible for Lewis to be wrong over twenty-first-century Iraq but right about his major area of expertise, Turkey, and its predecessor, the Ottoman Empire.

Buruma and Hirsh are surely correct. It is, or certainly should be possible to agree with Lewis about the post-1683 decline of the Ottoman Empire in relation to the West, and have all kinds of different opinions about the rights and wrongs of American foreign policy in our own time.

In my book *Winston's Folly*, published in the USA as *Churchill's Folly*, on Churchill's creation of Iraq in 1921, it is made clear that Western attempts to meddle there have proved a disaster. At the time of writing it is too soon to say whether or not democracy will work in Iraq, although, now that we have intervened, however mistakenly, we must hope it will now prove to be a success. So for readers for whom such things are important, I agree fully with Lewis on the seventeenth century, but differ with him on American policy in the twenty-first.

Nor is Lewis right in seeing the Middle East as a place of failure. The UN-sponsored *Arab World Human Development Report* shows that the woes of parts of the Middle East are self-inflicted – political oppression, poor literacy and the suppression of women being the main causes given by the *Arab* authors of the report. On the other hand, some parts of the region, like Dubai, are prospering economically, and Jordan does not have anything like the same kind of religious/gender oppression found in Saudi Arabia. Not only that, but other parts of the Islamic world, such as Malaysia and Indonesia, are well ahead of the Middle East economically, so Islam is clearly not a factor.

But the Middle East is also the place of origin of Judaism and Christianity, the region where the Pharaohs ruled, and a place that was miles ahead of the West in terms of medicine, knowledge and technology for centuries. The 'triumph of the West', in which Irwin argues those such as Lewis believe, could therefore be brief. In other words, the 'Orient', if such a thing can be said to exist, is not the 'other', because we in the West owe our civilization to the Middle East. We are, if you like, its Western descendant, and we cannot therefore by definition be the 'other' to something from which we ourselves descend. The world is a much smaller place that we think, far more interconnected and mutually interdependent.

8

THE FALL OF THE OTTOMANS AND THE BIRTH OF A NEW MIDDLE EAST

Turkey's choice

The fall of the Ottoman Empire is the key to the shape of today's Middle East. Since 11 September 2001 it has also affected the West, since the restoration of the Islamic Caliphate that accompanied the Sultan's title is one of the main aims of Islamic terror groups worldwide.

In 1998 and in many pronouncements since, Osama bin Laden began to refer to the 'suffering of the past eighty years'. Since we are used to statements from Palestinian nationalists, and their anger over the creation of Israel in 1948–50 – not eighty years before 1998 – this might at first seem puzzling. But although bin Laden has now added the Palestinian cause to his list of grievances, it was indeed to the events of 1918 he was referring, namely the defeat of the Ottoman Empire.

In the twenty-first century we live with the consequences – Islamic terrorism, Palestine vs. Israel, the Intifada, the war in Iraq, Saudi petrodollars, and even the wars in Europe's backyard, in Bosnia and Kosovo. All these stem from the

Ottoman Empire's demise. In the same way that historians have attributed the Second World War to the unfinished business of Versailles in 1919, we can do the same with the results of the Ottoman defeat in 1918 in relation to the conflict in the contemporary Middle East.

While I was writing this chapter, Hamas, the radical Islamic group, won the Palestinian elections, to considerable comment in both the Middle East and the West. Although it is too early to predict the consequences of their victory, it has certainly increased the stakes in the Palestinian conflict, since Hamas, unlike the more secular PLO, rejects the very right of Israel to exist. Thus do the decisions of the Allies back in 1918–21 still reverberate strongly.

At the beginning of this book a warning was given against the dangers of reading the present back into the past. The history of both World Wars is a classic example of writing what happened in the light of the known ending. There were many times, beloved of counter-factual historians who love to explore different endings, when both wars could have easily gone the other way. We are very aware of this in relation to the wars against Germany, how 1914 nearly repeated the French defeat of 1870, and how the actual defeat of France in 1940 almost led, had the Battle of Britain gone the other way, to a British disaster as well. In both wars the intervention of the USA made all the difference towards the final Allied victory.

In the Second World War, the immense, and sadly all-too-easily-forgotten, bravery of the Red Army made the crucial difference to the outcome of the war in Europe. But in the First World War, the Russians were, for all intents and purposes, defeated, with the Soviet decision in 1917 to cease fighting. The Russian juggernaut, so crucial to victory in 1944–5, played no such role in Allied victory by 1918.

The historian John Charmley argued in his book review in the *Guardian* of *Winston's Folly* on 27 November 2005 that the Ottoman defeat was by no means inevitable. This is surely correct, for the reasons that we saw in the last chapter. In fact we are so used to the nineteenth-century story of the Sick Man of Europe that we tend to see history from 1798 onwards as leading to the Empire's inexorable disappearance. But such a view, while understandable, is mistaken. Yes, the Ottoman Empire did fall in 1918, to be abolished in 1922 (and the Caliphate in 1924). But nothing that happened was foreordained.

To begin with, what proved fatal to the Empire was the decision of the Young Turk-dominated government to join Germany, and the other Central Powers, in the autumn of 1914, some weeks after the war in the rest of Europe had already begun. This was a major shift in policy, since the Ottomans had traditionally been friendly with both Britain and France. But as these two powers were now allied to the traditional Ottoman enemy, the Russian Empire, the strategic situation had thus changed from the Ottoman perspective. In addition, the Kaiser of Germany had been actively courting the Ottoman government, and the Germans helped to train the Ottoman army in the same way as the British had been giving active assistance to their fleet.

Here Churchill made a foolish move. Turkey had ordered two brand-new battleships – Dreadnoughts – from Britain. But when war broke out Churchill, as First Lord of the Admiralty, impounded them for the Royal Navy, which infuriated the

Turks. Germany, seeing an opportunity, promptly gave two of its battleships that were at the time in Ottoman territorial waters to the Ottoman government. This proved immensely popular, and combined with the close links now being established between German officers and the Ottoman military elite, enhanced German–Ottoman relations. Churchill's major diplomatic blunder had played straight into the hands of those Young Turks, such as Enver Pasha, who wanted the Ottomans to switch allegiance to Germany.

Had the Turks decided to stay neutral, as they chose to do for all but the last few weeks of the Second World War when they joined the Allies at the end in 1945, there would have been no defeat. Without losing a war, the Empire could well have tottered on for several more years, and then, possibly, have imploded from within rather than being conquered from without.

Now however the Ottoman government was firmly allied to Germany and Austria-Hungary, and since these two powers were on the losing side, the Ottomans were to be as well, albeit in the long run rather than the short term, as we shall now see.

Two things could, even after the Ottomans took their fatal decision, have still resulted in the war going the other way. These are the Desert Revolt, in which Arab rebels, with British help, fought against their fellow Muslim overlords, and secondly, the consequences of the Ottoman victories over the Allies at both Gallipoli and Kut, a town to the south of Ctesiphon, on the river Tigris.

With the revolt in the desert, we are misled, especially by the self-propagated legend of Lawrence of Arabia, not to mention the nature of the revolt itself. For, as historians such as

David Fromkin and Efraim and Inari Karsh have demonstrated – along with a recent, non-hagiographical biography of T. E. Lawrence by Michael Asher – the whole story of *The Seven Pillars of Wisdom* is more fantasy than truth. It is not just a case of events happening very differently from the way that Lawrence portrays them, though that is now probably the case. It is also the uncomfortable fact that *most Arabs did not join the revolt and were happy to continue under Ottoman rule*. In terms of what happened later in the Middle East, this is important to remember, as it has twenty-first-century consequences.

War against the Ottomans: Gallipoli and Iraq

When war broke out in late 1914, the British decided to attack the Ottomans on two fronts. The first, and far more famous assault, reflected the daring of its inventor, Winston Churchill, the First Lord of the Admiralty.

If one looks at a map, it is clear that the Ottoman capital, Istanbul, was highly vulnerable to a seaborne attack, through the Dardanelles and into the Bosporus. Capture the capital city, and the whole empire could fall quickly. Churchill, with his usual flair for thinking the unthinkable, realized this and began planning a sea and land invasion to finish off the Ottomans in one bold stroke.

Had he been successful, there is little doubt that the war could have ended much more quickly, millions of lives would have been saved, and events would have taken a radically different turn. The British and French could then have opened up a second front against Germany's more precarious ally, Bulgaria, which would in turn have meant that the Germans would be fighting a war on three fronts: in the Balkans, in the West, and in the East. This might in turn have helped sustain the increasingly rotten edifice of Tsarist Russia, which was to collapse in 1917, in large part as a result of the corrupt and gross mismanagement of the war.

Had it succeeded, as the Cabinet Office War Rooms Museum in London reminds us, Churchill might even have become prime minister sooner rather than later. As it was, the inefficiency, inter-service rivalry and lack of co-ordination, and numerous other factors doomed the British, Australian and New Zealand forces trying to capture the Dardanelles from the very beginning. Almost as soon as they had landed at Gallipoli, the invasion started to go wrong, and after much carnage the Allies had ignominiously to withdraw.

Here it is fair to say that although Gallipoli is remembered with much bitterness in Australia and New Zealand, since the ANZAC forces suffered huge casualties, many British lives were lost as well. It was, in short, a military disaster for the West, and for Churchill's career in particular. He lost his post in the Government, and the Secretary of State for India, Austen Chamberlain, had to resign over Kut. It only confirmed the view that many held of Churchill as a rash, self-promoting adventurer, whose reckless gamble had needlessly cost far too many lives. While there is much truth in this, the real tragedy is that if his stroke of the imagination had succeeded, far more lives would have been saved on all fronts of the war than were lost in the Gallipoli debacle; in addition the main assault on the Ottoman Empire would not have had to wait another two years and one of the worst incidents of the war could have been averted, namely the massacre of the Armenians. This still rankles, with the whole subject remaining a strong taboo in twenty-first-century Turkey, as we shall see.

It was not just Western bungling that led to the disaster. The West seriously underestimated their Ottoman enemy, as they would do at several other battles; they had witnessed Ottoman forces losing to Balkan armies in 1912–13, and made the probably racist assumption to the effect that European armies were innately superior to those of Turkish origin. This proved very far indeed from being the case: Turkish soldiers proved themselves to be some of the very best in the world, and consistently so throughout the conflict.

In addition Western leaders were ignorant, until too late, of the brilliant generalship of the Ottoman commander, a Turkish general from the Greek part of the Empire called Mustapha Kemal (later Kemal Ataturk) who would ironically win a major war over the Greeks in 1922. He learned many lessons from his victory, and would soon put them to excellent use.

Gallipoli was not the only British disaster against the Turks. Less remembered today, but no less important, was the equally major loss to the Ottomans of the siege of Kut. This was a town in Mesopotamia to which the British-commanded troops – a mix of British and Indian – were obliged to withdraw ignominiously after being hammered by strategically superior Turkish troops just outside Baghdad at Ctesiphon.

The British commander, Sir Charles Townsend, had become famous years earlier through his brave leadership in 1895 of the British forces besieged in Chitral, a town on the Indian North-West Frontier. Now, in 1915, he was asked to lead an army all the way from Basra, the port town that the

British had captured easily, to Baghdad, the capital of the Ottoman *vilayet* (province) of the same name.

(It is important to remember that no such state as Iraq existed in 1915 since all the borders of the present-day Middle East are the artificial, post-1918, creation of the European powers.)

This was a tall order; the temperature was often well over 100°F, the British and Indian soldiers were drastically under-equipped and the troops lacked the protection needed both from the excessive heat and from the ravages of upset stomachs. The best way forward was by boat, but apart from inadequate local barges no major transport ships were available. Nor were there really enough troops for the job, such were the arrogant assumptions of Western superiority over Ottoman troops.

But despite these numerous shortcomings – of which Townsend was not unaware – the British/Indian flotilla began its slow journey up the Euphrates in the autumn of 1915.

Initial progress seemed most promising – by November they had captured some key towns along the river, and had reached Ctesiphon, the ancient capital of the Sassanian Empire that had been destroyed by Muhammad in the seventh century. But here everything began seriously to unravel. The actual battle at Ctesiphon, in November 1915, can best be described as a draw. But Townsend realized that he did not now have anywhere near enough troops to proceed on to Baghdad, since the Ottoman positions were exceptionally well fortified. Once again, Turkish troops showed that they easily matched their opponents and were the equal of any European army.

Townsend therefore retreated to the town of Kut with all his wounded, many of whom died en route because there were not proper stretchers to convey them. But the Anglo-Indian army was no sooner embedded at Kut than it was surrounded by Ottoman troops. The siege of Kut, the longest in the history of the British army, had begun. Townsend, with his victory at Chitral, knew all about sieges, and in theory a relief force should have been swiftly upon its way to relieve the garrison. This however proved not to be the case.

For as month after month went by, no relieving force came, and when some finally arrived, several months later, they were utterly unable to dislodge the Turks, break through along the Euphrates, and rescue their besieged comrades. So after five months of attrition, starvation and utter despair, Townsend was forced to surrender to the Turks.

This was a military catastrophe for the British, one of the very worst in the history of the British Empire. Worse still, while Townsend and some of the top officers were taken to luxury imprisonment in Constantinople, the vast bulk of the ordinary soldiers endured forced marches across the desert into captivity, with many dying in the blistering sun en route.

But far worse than any British suffering in Mesopotamia or Australian losses in Gallipoli was the massacre of hundreds of thousands of innocent Armenian civilians by Turkish soldiers and also by Kurdish auxiliary forces. This was, as has now been realized, the first genocide of the twentieth century. Since the Turks escaped any responsibility for this atrocity, Hitler in the 1930s sometimes asked, 'Who remembers the Armenians?' Sadly all too few people do – it is the forgotten Holocaust, even though it was every bit as savage as that of the Jews in the

1940s and the tragically, equally forgotten near-million who died in the Iran–Iraq war of the 1980s, together with those many more whose lives were adversely affected by it.

As recently as 2005, the Turkish author Orhan Pamuk came very close to being prosecuted and imprisoned for telling the truth about the Armenian massacres, so sensitive a topic does this remain in twenty-first-century Turkey. The American bestseller *The Burning Tigris* by Peter Balakian, about the massacres, shows that the Armenians have just as much right to be remembered as genocide victims as their equally tragic Jewish counterparts twenty and more years later.

Carving up the Middle East: the Sykes–Picot Agreement and the Balfour Declaration

As we saw from the earlier bin Laden statement, the Arab sense of betrayal, stemming from the First World War, remains acute to this day. In discussing this part of Middle Eastern history, we are entering a historiographical minefield! Who said what to whom has become part of the debate on the foundation of the state of Israel, since without the decisions made by British and French soldiers and politicians in this period, the very existence of a Jewish state might never have taken place.

Efraim and Inari Karsh, in their highly influential (and thus equally controversial) *Empires of the Sand* show that the sequence of events leading to the Arab Revolt, and the actual fighting itself, was also very different from the popular version. Their argument in a nutshell is that the key Arab players were not betrayed pawns, as David Lean's 1962 film *Lawrence of Arabia* and Arab myth would have us believe, but active participants in a complex series of games in which they won some and lost some. In other words, they argue that the powerful Arab/ Islamic sense of victimization that has permeated the Middle East for decades is from this perspective unjustifiable.

This is what has made their work so debatable, and in reality a step too far. The situation, while easy to explain, was actually more subtle than that, and the Arabs do have good cause to feel at least some grievance at what happened next.

When the British found themselves at war with the Ottoman Empire, they also found themselves with two major problems. In some ways the less important was the geographical/security issue – the protection of the Suez Canal route to Asia. This was the vital artery to the Raj, the Jewel in the British Crown. It had to be defended, and so holding on to Egypt became vital.

(Two British historians, Ronald Robinson and John Gallagher, argued in their book *Africa and the Victorians* that this also led to the decision to colonize vast swathes of Africa in the late nineteenth century. While debatable, it does show the critical importance of the Suez Canal route to India, something that obsessed the British imperial class for many decades, right down to the Suez crisis of 1956. This was nine years after the granting of independence to India, but still at a time when Britain had a large presence in East Asia.)

Procuring the safety of the Suez Canal in 1914 proved easy. Nominal Ottoman suzerainty over Egypt was replaced with a British Protectorate, which made the country into the British-ruled state it had been to all intents and purposes for the previous thirty years. All Ottoman attempts to seize both Egypt and the canal failed – the British position remained safe throughout the war.

There was, however, a much bigger problem that worried the new Secretary of State for War, Lord Kitchener. This was the presence in the British Empire of tens of millions of Muslim subjects. While these were mainly in India (which in those days included present-day Pakistan and Bangladesh), other imperial possessions also had large Muslim populations, from Kenya with an Islamic minority through to the Malay states and their large Muslim majorities. The same applied to the Russian Empire, which had from the late eighteenth century onwards similarly acquired millions of Muslim subjects, from Chechnya to Samarkand. France, too, ruled over large swathes of Muslim Africa, including Algeria and territories such as the present-day Senegal.

When the Ottomans declared war on Britain and Russia, the Sultan, simultaneously, in his capacity as Caliph and Commander of the Faithful, also issued a fatwa, declaring jihad on the Empire's enemies. (This move was done with enthusiastic German support.) Had the numerous Muslim subjects of the British, French and Russian Empires obeyed the call to overthrow their Christian overlords, the effects would have been catastrophic for the three European imperial powers. The suppression of vast rebellions would have taken more manpower than was available, quite apart from draining vitally needed resources from the war in Europe against Germany. In fact such revolts never happened. For Britain this was especially fortunate, since thousands of soldiers were drawn from the Indian Army, who fought not just in Asia, but also on the Western Front.

But we have hindsight, and Kitchener did not. He had the problem of not only preventing rebellion, but also of persuading

Muslim troops under British rule to fight against their spiritual leader, the Caliph, since that same person was also the enemy Sultan.

Here, as David Fromkin, the Karshes and others have shown, came the opportunity for which the leaders of the ambitious Hashemite clan of the Hijaz had been waiting for so long.

The great Abbasid dynasty, as has been shown, was drawn from the tribe of the Prophet Muhammad himself – the Quraysh. However, plenty of members of the Prophet's own immediate clan, the Hashemites, still existed. Much revered in the Muslim world on account of their blood kinship with Islam's founder, members of the Hashemite clan had been chosen over many years as custodians of the two holiest Muslim shrines, in Mecca and Medina. Bona fide descendants of the Prophet were known – as they still are – as sharifs, and the Sharif of Mecca and Medina was the official guardian of the two cities. At the beginning of the twentieth century, the current holder of the post was Sharif Hussein, of the Hashemite clan.

We now know that he dreamed of restoring a large Arab empire, not perhaps as vast as that of his Abbasid ancestors, but certainly including all the Arab parts of the Ottoman Empire. Sharing his ambitions were his sons, the most important being Abdullah and Feisal, the latter spending much of his time in Istanbul as a representative in the Ottoman parliament.

Even before Britain and the Ottoman Empire went to war, Abdullah visited Cairo, to see if the British would help with the Hashemite goal of liberating the Arabs from Ottoman rule. Here the story begins to be controversial, as authors such as

Efraim Karsh and Inari Karsh attribute the machinations of the Hashemites to personal ambition rather than their professed goal of liberating the Arabs from Turkish oppression. At this distance, and without sufficient firm documentation, it is perhaps impossible to tell – and there is no reason why Abdullah and his family could not have had both ambitions, personal and ethnic, at the same time. Few of us always have pure motives in all that we do and there is no reason to suppose that the Hashemites were any exception, so there seems no reason not to give them the benefit of the doubt, something that *Empires of the Sand* chooses not to do.

But whatever the motivation, the British authorities in Egypt realized that a golden opportunity was presenting itself, all the more so when war was declared. Here it is important to remember that the British now spoke in two distinct voices. For those in London and Cairo, winning the war was the essential objective, especially on the all-important Western Front. Anything that could help achieve this was worthwhile, including talking to Arabs prepared to help against the Ottoman enemy.

For the Raj however, moves that helped nationalists of any description were unhelpful. While Gandhi was not as famous as he was soon to become, ideas of independence from imperial overlords were not seen as something to be encouraged, especially as they would make British rule in India more difficult to maintain. While British troops in Cairo were commanded from London, those in the Middle East in general, including thousands of Indian Army troops, were under the Raj.

Kitchener realized the potential of a direct descendant of the Prophet Muhammad leading a rebellion against the Ottomans.

No one could accuse the Sharif of Mecca of being un-Islamic, and any British conspiracy in which he was involved could thus be defended on religious grounds. From the Hashemite point of view, they had nowhere remotely near the resources to overthrow Ottoman rule themselves. However, aided by no less than the British Empire anything might be possible. British wartime necessities and Hashemite dynastic/ethnic ambitions thus combined in an alliance of convenience against the mutual Ottoman enemy.

On one thing the Lawrence legend is correct – the British *were* duplicitous. But the actual picture is far more complex than the simplicities of *The Seven Pillars of Wisdom* or *Lawrence of Arabia*. The India Office wanted the Arab lands to be British ruled. If a suitable Maharajah-style figure could be interposed between the British and the natives, that would be fine so long as the British were the *real* rulers, as in certain of the Princely States in the Raj, such as Hyderabad or Mysore.

However, in 1914, the British also had allies and a war in Europe to win. This meant being nice to the French and the Tsarist Russians. It also meant giving part of the Austro-Hungarian enemy to the Italians, as a bribe to switch sides. This succeeded. Italy entered the war against its own former Allies Austria-Hungary, Germany, Bulgaria and the Ottoman Empire.

Italy was also promised some Ottoman territory, mainly in the Aegean – the island of Rhodes, which should by rights have gone to Greece, is one example. But when it came to carving up the Arab Ottoman territories, the spoils were to go to Britain, France and Russia.

This was the infamous deal named after its two organizers – the professional French colonial official, M. Georges Picot, and the amateur diplomat, the British aristocrat, Sir Mark Sykes. Both were, in their own ways, old Middle East hands, and in early 1916 they duly produced what their masters wanted – a carve-up of the Arab territories of the Ottoman Empire.

This was old-fashioned imperialism of the worst kind. Although the agreement allowed for an Arab-ruled state, such an entity would still have been under the protection of European governments, and would certainly not have been the genuinely independent Arab kingdom dreamed of by Hussein and by the Arab nationalists. In essence, Britain, France and Russia would take over much of the Ottoman Empire and rule most of it themselves – there was no room here for Hussein's wishes, or for anything that he thought that the British High Commissioner in Egypt, Sir Henry McMahon, had promised him.

Sykes–Picot gave Britain the two Ottoman *vilayets* of Basra and Baghdad outright, and France the Lebanese and Syrian coastlines. Palestine, which many people wanted, was to be put under international rule, which would include the still-Imperial Russia. (This was before President Woodrow Wilson of the USA had created his idea of a League of Nations, as America was still neutral at this stage.) In the middle was an Arab zone under British and French protectorate – with the French getting the oil-rich Mosul *vilayet* of what is now Iraq, and some of the Kurdish areas of present-day Turkey. Britain gained what is now Jordan.

(Russia's main gains were to be their long-desired presence in Constantinople and some territorial gains in the Caucasus.)

Needless to say, all this contradicted what Sir Henry McMahon had agreed with the Sharif of Mecca. In essence, in a correspondence between McMahon and Sharif Hussein – regrettably not all of which still exists – McMahon promised a large new territory to the Hashemites with no mention of French and British zones, and which looked to Hussein as if the British were giving him nearly all of what he dreamed. This, of course, completely contradicted the other British policy of carving up the area with their French, and initially also Russian, European allies. It is this feeling that the British were duplicitous – saying one thing to Arabs to enlist their support against the Turks, and another to their French co-belligerents – that has caused the story of the great British betrayal to arise, and not without reason.

At the time, Hussein, believing the British, launched the rebellion against his Ottoman overlords that we now know as the Arab Revolt. In reality it was a sideshow despite the aura of romance associated with it in Lawrence of Arabia's memoirs.

This point, while perhaps new to many, was in fact established back in the 1950s by the London University historian Elie Kedourie, and was eventually published in book form in his work *The Chatham House Version*. Needless to say, it too is controversial, since it substantially reduces the impact made upon the course of the war by the Arab forces under the nominal command of Hussein's son Feisal, and helped by Lawrence and the British. On their own, the Arabs involved were certainly able to annoy the Ottomans, but all the major victories that were eventually to be won were by British, Australian, Indian and other regular troops on the two fronts, Egypt/Palestine, and Mesopotamia.

However, unfortunately for the British and French, the Tsarist regime was overthrown in the first of the revolutions in

Russia in 1917. The second uprising saw Lenin and the Bolsheviks seize power by promising to take Russia out of the war against Germany. They surrendered substantial territory – including today's Ukraine – to the Germans and concluded the war formally in the Treaty of Brest Litovsk in 1918.

(Thankfully 1917 also saw American entry into the war, and this considerably offset much of the damage caused by Russian withdrawal.)

The Bolsheviks refused to sign up to any imperialist agreements, and, to the embarrassment of Britain and France, they made public the Sykes–Picot Agreement of 1916, drawn up when the Russian Empire still existed and was fighting the Turks alongside its British and French allies. Needless to say, the difference between the Sykes–Picot plan and the Hussein–McMahon correspondence became apparent to all.

Many Arabs felt betrayed at the time, and have continued to feel aggrieved ever since. Sykes–Picot has entered the infamy of Western imperialist treachery towards the Arabs, and has not been forgotten. This feeling was not entirely unjustified because, although the British were indeed duplicitous with their Arab ally Hussein, they simultaneously began to regret just how much they had conceded to the French. In fact, the situation was even more complex, as Margaret Macmillan (Lloyd George's descendant) shows in *Peacemakers*, her book on the peace treaties.

First of all, the leading British politician, Lord Curzon, himself no mean expert on India and the Middle East, felt that the Sykes–Picot deal was 'unfortunate' from the beginning. More important, so did Lloyd George, and he was prime minister. In addition, it made no mention of any Jewish entity in the lands that were to be taken after what everyone hoped would be the Ottoman defeat. But this precise point was at the heart of what became by far the most controversial offer of all, that by British Foreign Secretary Arthur Balfour, in a public letter to Lord Rothschild known as the Balfour Declaration of 1917. In essence, this signified full British agreement to a Jewish homeland in Palestine, in what were then still Ottoman territories but already under British and Australian assault.

This completely contradicted Sykes–Picot, under which the core of Palestine was to be in the international zone. If the Balfour Declaration Jewish-homeland plan was to work, however, the British would need to control Palestine directly, and the relevant parts of Sykes–Picot would need to be over-turned. The Declaration also flatly contradicted the promises made to Sharif Hussein, since the latter contained no mention of Jewish immigration to an area that Hussein thought was going to be under his own control. Here we cannot say that McMahon was being deceitful, since his correspondence predates Balfour's decision on a Jewish homeland. But there is no question but that the latter promise was completely incompatible with the earlier pledges made to Hussein. This too is one of the major causes of the Arab sense of betrayal by the West that has vitiated the Middle East ever since, and from the Arab point of view, with due cause.

By 1917, therefore, in terms of Sykes–Picot, Lloyd George, Curzon and other leading British politicians, already with the ink barely dry, much regretted their decision to allot so much to the French. Furthermore, with the Russians out of the war, and in ideologically hostile hands, all concessions to the old

Tsarist regime were now worthless. Far from wanting to carve up the Middle East in accordance with the Sykes–Picot Agreement, Britain wanted now to grab as much of the area for itself as possible, including Palestine, where the Jews were to go, and Mosul, which Lloyd George suspected, correctly, of having large oil reserves.

(It should be noted here that both Winston Churchill, soon to play a key role in the Middle East, and Curzon, Foreign Secretary after 1919, did not rate the oil reserves highly – and no major oil finds were made until the late 1920s. But Lloyd George was right, as we now know: Iraq, in the twenty-first century, is second only to Saudi Arabia in oil reserves.)

So Britain, therefore, especially after 1917, wanted to do all possible to tear up Sykes–Picot and start afresh. If the British were duplicitous towards the Arabs – and there is a good case for saying so – Sykes–Picot had nothing to do with it, and the Lawrence legend that it was *that* agreement that betrayed the Arabs is wrong. This is because Sykes–Picot, from 1917 and the Balfour Declaration onwards, was no longer British policy.

In other words, as shall become obvious, the West *did* betray the Arabs, but it was events *after* Sykes–Picot that caused that to take place, not that notorious agreement itself. Britain now wanted to seize as much Ottoman territory as possible, and for the French to have far less than was originally allocated in 1916 by Sykes and Picot. There was also now the new dimension of the promise to the Jews for a homeland, something that Lloyd George believed in strongly for religious reasons, as shown in the Duchess of Hamilton's book *God, Guns and Israel*. The Arabs were going to be betrayed, but for reasons very different from those in the Lawrence legend and Arab mythology, since

Sykes–Picot was a dead letter almost as soon as it had been written.

But in order to implement any plan for the Middle East, the Allies first had to beat their Ottoman foes. When Sir Mark Sykes and Georges Picot were meeting and drawing lines in the sand, the situation, from the Allied point of view, was going very badly. Not only that, but in some respects the Ottomans were actually winning.

The Arab revolt and its aftermath

By 1917 the British had finally learned the lessons of the debacles in Gallipoli and Kut. This time, with far better logistics, a two-pronged invasion was launched against the Ottoman Empire, the main thrust being from Egypt, under Lord Allenby, with a second in Mesopotamia. Both proved successful. Baghdad and Jerusalem were captured in 1917, and by 1918 the Ottoman Empire, like its German and Austro-Hungarian allies, was forced to surrender.

There was one difference, however – whereas the German and Austrian empires disappeared, the Sultan initially remained, along with a vestigial Ottoman administration. Not only that, but events were certainly not as T. E. Lawrence and the myth of Arab betrayal have portrayed. This is entering contentious territory, since present-day twenty-first-century disputes are read back-wards, and history is used in contemporary political battles. Since one of the most controversial of these is the struggle between the Arab world and Israel, the history of this period is a minefield.

A treaty with the Ottoman Empire – the Treaty of Sèvres – was finally signed in 1920. Not only did the Empire lose all its Arab lands, but it was obliged to give territory to a new Armenian state – a Kurd state still being an unresolved issue – and, perhaps most controversial of all, cede large swathes of territory to Greece, including land around Smyrna, present-day Izmir. This proved profoundly controversial within the rump Ottoman lands. But unlike in Germany, the Turks rebelled and war broke out between the official government and the rebel army under Mustapha Kemal.

Meanwhile, the British and French had not agreed among themselves what to do with the Arab territories. As we saw, Britain wanted to get out of as much of Sykes–Picot as possible, and to gain far more land than that agreement had allocated them. Fortunately for Lloyd George, Clemenceau, the French prime minister, was far more interested in crushing Germany than in creating a Levantine empire for France. It therefore proved easy for Britain to gain Mosul from the French zone, and to have Palestine under a British League of Nations mandate rather than under international rule. The sticking point was Syria, and it is here that the legend of the great Arab betrayal, beloved of people from T. E. Lawrence to Osama bin Laden, really begins.

It had been British and Australian forces that had liberated Arab territory from the Ottomans – not the campaign waged by Arab troops under Feisal and Lawrence that has become known as the Arab Revolt. In fact, historians, such as Efraim and Inari Karsh, Elie Kedourie and David Fromkin, have now proved that the Arab Revolt made virtually no military difference at all. Its real benefit was in public relations, since in terms of the war, Feisal's troops were little more than an irritant. Not only that, but the key thing is that *most of the Arabs stayed loyal to the Ottomans.*

The importance of this cannot be over-emphasized. Not merely did the Arab Revolt change little, but most Arabs failed to support it. They were Muslims, and Ottoman rule had suited them fine. In fact, many of the early Arab nationalists were Christians, from Syria – including Michel Aflaq, the later founder of the Ba'ath Party, the Arab nationalist party through which Saddam Hussein ruled Iraq, and another branch of which rules Syria to this day.

That is not to say that there were no Muslim Arab nationalists. They certainly existed – but in Egypt, over which the British had established a protectorate in 1914, having, as we saw, effectively ruled it since 1882. But these – the *Wafd* (delegation) – were not anti-Ottoman, but wanted independence from Britain, their colonial overlord.

Nor is this to overlook episodes such as the Arab capture of the Red Sea port of Aqaba in 1917, an incident considerably played up by Lawrence in *The Seven Pillars of Wisdom*, and in David Lean's film. It is not that the Arabs played no role, but rather that the actual effect that they had is much smaller than many before and since would like to attribute to them.

So the people who wanted Arab independence from the Ottomans were, in essence, the Hashemite dynasty: King Hussein, who proclaimed the independence of the Hijaz, and his most important sons, Feisal, of the Arab Revolt, and Abdullah.

Britain, as John Charmley has pointed out, traditionally ruled its empire through collaborators. The Maharajahs in India, the Sultans in Malaya, various Kings in Africa – all were part of the British policy of *indirect* rule. It was one of the reasons why the British were able to rule such a vast empire with so few troops and officials, and at comparatively so little cost.

In 1914 the Hashemites in effect offered themselves as Britain's collaborators in the Arab world. They wanted to rule much of the Middle East, and Britain, as well as needing help in winning the war, needed an intermediary local ruler in classic British imperial style. Hashemite ambition and British necessity thus happily came together in 1918, when the post-war settlement was being worked out.

Part of the legend of betrayal is evident in the scene set in Damascus in *Lawrence of Arabia*. Feisal had thought that he could be King of Syria, but the wicked British deprived him of power and broke all their promises to the Arab people. Such an argument certainly makes for powerful emotions, but it seriously compresses events, since Feisal was in Damascus for several months in increasing chaos until expelled by the French, a sense that you do not get from either watching the film or from Lawrence's autobiography.

The legend, therefore, is in fact misleading.

Left to themselves the British would have been happy for Feisal to stay in Damascus as King. However, while Clemenceau could cheerfully concede Palestine and Mosul to Britain, domestic opinion at home prevented him from similarly conceding Syria. So long as British troops controlled Damascus, Feisal was at liberty to stay, accept the Syrian throne, and do whatever he liked. When, however, in 1920, French forces took over, he was instantly expelled, and found himself stateless, with only Lawrence to plead his case. France generally believed in direct rule, and there was no room for puppet rulers in Syria or Lebanon. When the League of

Nations formally gave France the mandate, Feisal's dreams ended.

This was European realpolitik in action; it was not that the British were against Feisal, but more that they had to concede Syria to their French wartime ally, even though British and Australian troops had liberated the territory in 1917. Pleasing Clemenceau was strategically preferable to allowing Feisal to continue on the putative Syrian throne.

Britain, however, still needed an intermediary ruler for its exclusively Arab mandate territories – Mesopotamia (now including Mosul) and Transjordan, the part of Palestine that was not open to Jewish settlement under the 1917 Balfour Declaration. By 1920 the need for a local collaborator had become especially pressing, particularly in the three Mesopotamian provinces, where a major anti-British rebellion had broken out, with not inconsiderable British casualties.

Also by this time, Winston Churchill had returned to office, thanks to the patronage of David Lloyd George. As Secretary of State for War in 1920, Churchill realized that the British Empire was massively over-stretched, and simply did not have the ability to maintain, let alone pay for, a large army in the Middle East. Then in 1921 he became Colonial Secretary and, despite serious reservations by his officials, made T. E. Lawrence one of his key advisers.

Churchill believed in the British Empire. But he was also realistic, and understood that direct rule was no longer feasible. Britain had a debt of honour to the Hashemites, and Feisal, in particular, had a firm ally in both Lawrence, and in Gertrude Bell, an archaeologist who had become one of the mainstays of British policy in the region. They felt that they had let Feisal down in Syria, and wanted to make it up to him. A local collaborator would save money, and in the Hashemites, such people were available. Britain could have its collaborator, and the debt to Feisal could be paid.

As I showed in *Winston's Folly*, Churchill's main aim in 1921 was to save as much money as possible, while also saving British face. His knowledge of the area was woefully small; he had no idea about the difference between a Sunni and a Shia, for example, and while he sympathized with the Kurds, he never delivered when it came to creating an independent Kurdistan. So when Churchill, Lawrence, Bell and various other assorted British officials met in Cairo in early 1921, Churchill opted for the cheapest solution – a new state, to be called Iraq, under Feisal as puppet ruler, and British protection.

Iraq, it is vital to remember, had never existed before. It is an entirely artificial creation, like so many colonial entities all over the world. It was simply the three Ottoman *vilayets* under British mandate put together as one country – predominantly Shia Basra, Sunni Baghdad, and largely Kurdish Mosul, with, for example, the single largest ethnic group in Baghdad not being even Muslim, but Jewish. A referendum was duly rigged that enabled Feisal, who had never lived in the country before, to be invited to become King. Real power however still lay with the British, even after the mandate ended in the 1930s, right up to the violent overthrow of the Hashemite dynasty in 1958.

Feisal was a Sunni, and while the Sunni Arabs remained – as they are today – very much a minority, they dominated the country right up until the elections of 2005, since both the Hashemite regime and those that followed, such as that of

Saddam, were all Sunni as well. Genuine democracy was never able to take root.

Also in 1921, Britain suddenly became concerned with Abdullah, Feisal's brother. He launched an attempted invasion of Syria against the French. His army was in the Transjordan, when the British stopped him, and bought him off by offering him the Transjordanian throne, again under British protection. Here the story for the Hashemites proved happier, since his descendant, the half-British King Abdullah II, is still on the Jordanian throne. But here again the country created was artificial, with local Bedouin in the same state as town-dwelling Palestinians.

Egypt also gained its nominal independence in 1922. But here the British insisted on reserving all the key powers, such as control of the Suez Canal, a veto on foreign policy, a continued say over the national debt, and the right to maintain an army on Egyptian soil. Since the kings – Mehmet Ali's descendants – remained corrupt and incompetent, the situation for ordinary Egyptians stayed as bad as ever.

However, the really controversial British decision, fully endorsed by the pro-Jewish Churchill, was the creation of a mandate in Palestine to which Jews could come. This was then as today not accepted by the local Arab population. Their resistance against both British rule and Jewish immigration lasted up until the creation of Israel in 1948. Here the important thing to remember is that Israel was the result of British policy, and that the cause of all that is happening in the region today dates back not to 1948 but to decisions made by Churchill and other Western leaders between 1917 and 1921.

The losers were the Kurds, Armenians, Greeks and ironically, the Hashemite King Feisal. While Efraim and Inari Karsh
are right to say that the al-Saud dynasty were winners, so too
were the Turks, and the Zionist activists who were busily
creating a new Jewish state.

The Kurds, Armenians and Greeks all lost because of the
military victories of Mustapha Kemal. Greece wanted too
much former Ottoman territory, and after a series of major
military defeats, both Greek troops and civilians were expelled
from Asia Minor in 1922, in what we today would call ethnic
cleansing. (One of the losing Greek generals was Prince
Andrew of Greece, father of Britain's Prince Philip.)

The expulsion of the Greeks, with much violence in
Smyrna, ended thousands of years of Greek presence in
Anatolia, going back to the time of Xenophon, the Graeco-
Persian wars, Alexander the Great, and the Byzantine Empire.
Similarly, all Turks were expelled from Greece, where many
families had also lived for hundreds of years. (Mustapha Kemal
himself had been born in Thessaloniki, for example.)

Lloyd George, a great hellenophile, had wanted to help the
Greeks. But the Conservatives in his coalition government
regarded this as a war too far, and overthrew him in 1922.
(This was not the only reason so far as many Conservatives
were concerned – their prime reason was domestic politics
rather than overseas strategy. But the risk of dragging a war-
weary Britain into yet another conflict certainly gave leading
Conservatives the excuse that they had long wanted.)

The French had refused to support Britain against the Turks,
and the result was another British withdrawal, this time
without conflict, and victory for Mustapha Kemal, who now

renamed himself Kemal Ataturk, or Father of the Turks. Lloyd George, the victorious prime minister of the First World War, left power, never to hold it again.

The successful Turkish campaign also put an end to hopes of a greater and independent Armenia, and to any kind of Kurdistan. The original hope was for a greater Armenia to arise, under some kind of American protection or mandate. But this fell through, along with any US involvement in the League of Nations. That part of Armenia conquered by Russia was absorbed into the new USSR, and the rest was seized by Mustapha Kemal's victorious campaign. Similarly Kemal and his forces overran the northern part of Kurdistan, and this led the British to conclude that the southern Kurdish areas that they protected should be unified with the rest of the new Iraq, rather than become an independent state. The reduced Armenian state finally achieved independence in 1991, but the Kurds, many of whom live in present-day Iran and Syria as well as Iraq and Turkey, never achieved a country of their own.

New rulers, new dynasties: Turkey, Iran, Arabia

Kemal Ataturk became president of the new Turkish Republic in 1922, after unifying the country under his rule. He abolished the Ottoman Empire straight away, although initially permitting one of the former ruling family to continue as Caliph of Islam. But in 1924 the Turkish Parliament abolished this post too, thereby ending an office that had existed, off and on, since the death of Muhammad in 632, nearly 1,300 years earlier. Ataturk then began a major modernization programme, reducing the role of Islam, abolishing the Islamic fez, liberating women, introducing the Western alphabet, and much else besides. Turkey was not a pluralistic democracy under his rule, but nor was it a monarchical dictatorship or theocratic state.

The former decision – to opt for a republic over a monarchy – was the opposite of the one taken by Ataturk's contemporary, Reza, in Persia, which now became Iran.

As we saw, Persia survived Western conquest by being in between the Russian Empire and British Raj in India. After the Bolshevik Revolution, Britain retained an army in Persia, both to stop Soviet incursion and also to protect its oil investments, especially after the huge oil fields of Baku, on the Caspian Sea, became part of the USSR.

The Qajar dynasty was now tottering fatally, and Reza overthrew it in 1925. But instead of establishing a republic, as Ataturk had done in Turkey, he proclaimed himself Shah instead, establishing a new dynasty. This proved fatal to Iranian liberty, and was an instrumental cause of the Shiite theocratic takeover of Iran in 1979.

The decision to opt for a theocratic-based regime was taken by the other major winner of the post-1918 settlement in the Middle East, the al-Saud dynasty. Originally just rulers of the central Arabian state of Nejd, Abdul Aziz al-Saud, known in the West as Ibn Saud, decided to embark on a series of dynastic conquests, with the aim of ruling over as much of the Arabian Peninsula as possible.

The Ibn Rashid state of Shammar in north-western Arabia proved easy to conquer, as that dynasty had foolishly backed the Ottomans. Another, smaller state called Afar on the borders of Yemen, was also captured – the region which would produce most of the 9/11 hijackers in 2001.

Yemen itself however proved impossible to conquer, and both Aden and many other Gulf states (such as Oman, Dubai, Bahrain and Qatar) were under direct British protection. The borders of Kuwait were uncertain, and here Ibn Saud was able to gain much more terrain, under British adjudication, than originally thought possible. He also wanted to take present-day Jordan, and to expand his frontiers at the expense of Iraq, but in both of these the British frustrated him, as they wanted to keep all the territory in their new mandate.

The key area he needed to seize was the large coastal kingdom ruled by the Hashemites – the Hijaz. This was the sacred land of Mecca and Medina, and since, in the days before oil, revenue from the Haj was the most lucrative source of state income, Ibn Saud determined to have it.

Here the ambitions of Hussein played into his hands, with effects that are with us today.

In Islamic terms, the Hashemites – like their modern descendants in Jordan – were moderates, following the main-stream schools of Muslim thought. By contrast the al-Saud followed the very hard-line Hanbali School of interpretation, thanks to the eighteenth-century reformer, al-Wahhab. The deal made then – the Wahhabis would support the al-Saud, in return for the al-Saud clan's support of Wahhabi Islam – had continued down to the twentieth century (and remains fully in force today). The Wahhabis had a religious shock troop army, the Ilkwhan, and these were the dedicated, elite forces the al-Saud used on their conquests.

With the abolition of the Caliphate, King Hussein had coveted the title, as a descendant of Muhammad, as did the King of Egypt. Neither obtained the title, which was in any case not theirs to demand. Hussein was also angry with the British over Feisal's failure to gain Syria, and the restrictions placed upon his sons in Iraq and Transjordan by Britain. As a result, he lost the right to British protection, and, in 1924, this proved fatal.

Using his fanatical Ilkwhan holy warriors, Ibn Saud invaded the Hijaz, and conquered it by the end of the year. Mecca and Medina, the two holiest cities in Islam, were now in the theological hands of the hardest-line Muslim group in the Islamic world. Those shrines deemed syncretistic, or somehow un-Islamic, were destroyed, Ibn Saud proclaimed himself ruler of the Hijaz, and in 1932 his conquests were consolidated into a new state, named after his own dynasty, Saudi Arabia. Only the Wahhabi form of Islam was permitted, the version of the Muslim faith not only practised there today, but, thanks to Saudi petrodollars, now spread around the entire Islamic world.

So Turkey became a republic, Iran continued as a monarchy under a new dynasty, and most of the Arabian Peninsula fell under the rule of a clan closely allied to the Wahhabi sect of Islam.

Fareed Zakaria points out the vital importance of all these events in his *Newsweek* articles written in the aftermath of 9/11 ('The War on Terror Goes Global' 13 September 2001 and 'The Politics of Rage: Why Do They Hate Us?' 15 October 2001).

First of all, Turkey lost the war but won the peace. This is crucial. For as Zakaria shows conclusively, the Turks were able to feel good about themselves, despite defeat in 1918 and the loss of their entire Arabic empire. Ataturk was a victorious hero, so modernization, and Europeanization were associated with success, especially as the Turks had beaten a European power – Greece – and humiliated the great British Empire in the process. As I write this, Turkey is a pluralistic parliamentary democracy, a linchpin of the NATO alliance and may soon also be a member of the European Union, French, Greek and Austrian public opinion permitting. Not only that, but the human rights Turks enjoy, while harsh towards the suppressed Kurdish minority, are far ahead of anywhere else in the Islamic world. Furthermore, the Turks' democratic rights were not forced upon them externally, but introduced by themselves in the aftermath of victory over the Greeks in 1922.

Turkey, one could also point out, was the one losing power of the First World War successfully to be able to negotiate its post-war treaty. The Treaty of Sèvres was torn up and the Treaty of Lausanne, in 1923, recognized Ataturk's conquests and the withdrawal from Turkish soil of all European armies. This is in contrast to Germany, where German defeat and humiliation in 1918 and the ravages of the Great Crash of 1929 led to Nazi Germany and the Second World War. Turkey, by contrast, stayed neutral for most of the latter conflict, was essentially sympathetic to the West, and joined the Allies just as fighting ended.

This is not the case, however, with the Arab world. While, as has been argued, the myth of betrayal is historically oversimplified, it is, nonetheless, still widely believed in the Middle East today, along with the *Protocols of the Elders of Zion* and the post-9/11 myth that all Jews were told not to turn up for work on 11 September 2001. Yet a myth is no less potent for being false or illusory, as the continuing rage of the Islamic world against the West gives credence. We too in the West have many myths, some so potent that we fail to see them as myths at all.

What is especially important is that Muslim Turkey abolished the Caliphate, not the West. Nor did Ataturk try to revive the old Ottoman Empire. He did not, contrary to Churchill's fears at the time, even attempt to occupy the Mosul province of Iraq, despite its not inconsiderable Turcoman ethnic minority (which is still there). Turkey gained the tiny Alexandretta province of Syria (now called Iskanderun) in 1938 from the French, and has made no territorial demands ever since. Turkey has been ruthless to the Kurds, and also helped Turkish Cypriot separatists in 1974. But the Turkish victories in 1922 enabled the Turks to start their new state on a wholly positive note, and the psychological benefit this has brought is therefore enormous.

In the Arab world it is very different. There, liberation from their fellow Muslim Ottoman Turks was replaced with Western rule, direct in the case of Syria, indirect in the case of the British-mandated areas (except for Palestine). As we saw in the chapter on the Crusades, the Muslim world forgot about the brief loss of territory to the Crusaders, especially since the Muslims won. Now French and British rule, along with the legitimatization of Zionist wishes for Palestine, engendered an Arab/Muslim sense of humiliation and betrayal that still burns in our own time. Not until Nasser's triumph over Britain and France at Suez in 1956 and the murder of the British-puppet Hashemite dynasty in 1958 could the Arabs feel that they had overthrown the colonial yoke. Then there was Israel, not just after 1948 but after 1967 as well.

The Pakistani academic Akbar Ahmed has pointed out in his many books on Islam that there is a major culture of *shame* in the Islamic world. While sorrow for events now long past should, one can argue, now be overcome, such a sense of shame is potent and most of it, in the early twenty-first century, can still be attributed to the circumstances of the fall of the Ottoman Empire.

As Efraim and Inari Karsh remind us, the one *Arab* victor of 1918–24 was the al-Saud family. While the West did not realize it at the time, this was a costly victory. In the light of 9/11, and the Saudi petrodollar-financed spread of Wahhabi Islam to the rest of the hitherto moderate Muslim world, it would have been far better to back Hussein of the Hijaz, whatever his sulk towards the British.

This is, historically, a perfectly legitimate position, and also the fairest. But the unavoidable conclusion is that we still live in our present century with the consequences, often for ill, of the fall of the great Ottoman Empire.

9

THE CREATION OF ISRAEL AND AFTER ...

A Jewish dream realized

In his classic work *England and the Middle East*, the historian Elie Kedourie refers to the often violent metaphysical disputes that have arisen about interpreting the origins of the present Middle East. This is an understatement: few areas of history are perhaps as controversial and fiercely polemical as the story of our region since the creation of Israel in 1948. Furthermore, as already seen, much of this involves reading history backwards, of using the past to fuel current debates about the rights and wrongs of Israel's presence in Palestinian areas, or indeed of the very legitimacy of the Jewish State itself. To take a particular stance – for example, attributing agency to Arabs between 1914 and 1923 rather than seeing them as wholly passive – is to be regarded as actively supporting Israeli military action against Palestinians in 2005, because pro-Israeli historians, such as Efraim Karsh, author of *Islamic Imperialism*, make such an attribution, and to agree with him on 1918–23 is interpreted therefore as agreeing with him on events in 2005, even though these issues are quite separate and are decades apart. Taking a historical position on events of eighty or more years ago is doing no such thing, but because of the controversial nature of the debate that is how it is often seen today.

While this particular chapter was being written, the Jewish settlers in Gaza had been expelled by the Israeli army, and Hamas, the hard-line Islamic party, had confounded much international opinion by winning the often-postponed Palestinian elections. This is an area in constant flux in which presumptions are frequently shown to be false. In addition, there are numerous areas of grey in a dispute in which the protagonists see things entirely in black or white.

Having therefore given the context for what follows, let us begin the story of Israeli independence and its aftermath.

Britain, having created the area of Jewish settlement in the first place by the Balfour Declaration of 1917, spent much of the 1930s backtracking on its promises to the Jewish peoples of Europe about allowing them to settle in the land of the Palestinian mandate. Further Jewish immigration to Palestine was restricted, which had devastating effects because of the Nazi persecution of the Jews. A Commission under Lord Peel, a descendant of the famous nineteenth-century statesman Sir Robert Peel, decided that Palestine should be split. However, it was also decided, in 1939, to restrict Jewish immigration because of its unpopularity with the Arab population. While this may have been understandable from a logistical and policing viewpoint, the timing was disastrous. Hitler was already persecuting the Jews in Germany and the tentacles of the Third Reich were expanding, to the detriment of Jews all over Europe. Just when they needed to escape, a number of countries, the USA and Switzerland included, were placing barriers in the way of Jewish immigration, as were the British in Palestine.

We know that over six million Jews were slaughtered in the Holocaust along with millions in other categories, such as Gipsy, homosexual, and Slav, all deemed lesser beings, or *untermenschen* by the Nazis. (Perhaps as many as twenty million Soviet citizens died as a direct result of the war, for example, with a very large proportion being civilians, not Red Army soldiers.) As Elie Kedourie writes in *Arabic Political Memoirs and Other Studies*, the 'advent of Hitler in 1933 introduced an entirely new and unforeseen element in the Palestinian problem'.

Suddenly, as a consequence of the Holocaust, a Jewish homeland made much sense to a guilty Europe. Nearly all countries had collaborators who took part, in some way or another, with helping the Germans round up and murder Jews. The controversial writer Daniel Goldhagen, author of *Hitler's Willing Executioners*, would not agree with such a view, since he insisted on taking the traditional route of ascribing special blame to the German people. Such a view could be considered both old-fashioned and historically inaccurate. The historian David Caesarini is surely right to point out that anti-Semitism was by no means only a German phenomenon. Europe was rife with it, and so a minority of peoples, including for example some of the British inhabitants of the Channel Islands, willingly collaborated with the Nazis in their pursuit of Jewish genocide. To single out the Germans is to ignore the crimes of countless others.

Jewish immigration to Palestine increased exponentially, as Jews felt that only with their own state would they be safe from future Hitlers. From the Jewish viewpoint, this was more than understandable. The problem, as we know, was that the long-standing Arab inhabitants of the region had different feelings about an enormous number of foreigners coming to their part of the world, and as exculpation for European sins of genocide of which the Arabs were innocent.

In other words, both sides, Jewish and Palestinian alike, had strong moral grounds for the cases that they now put to the wider world, which were entirely incompatible. After the annihilation of six million Jews, the Jewish national wish for safety was entirely comprehensible as was the Palestinian desire not to lose their ancestral land as a result of mass immigration from outside. It is important to remember that after the Second World War both sides therefore had equally strong moral claims for their particular viewpoints, and the fact that neither could coexist with the other one was now the real dilemma.

In 1947 the newly created United Nations agreed with the British decision, which had been made a decade earlier, that partition was the only solution to the Palestinian problem. By 1948 the Jewish population had risen to over 650,000 from well under 200,000 some twenty years earlier. By now this was the result of an enormous emigration of surviving Jews from Europe; the homecoming of Muslim-world Diaspora Jews had not yet happened, and would result from the expulsions from Arab countries *after* the creation of the new Israeli state. Most of the inhabitants of Palestine as a whole remained Arab – not just Muslim, but with a large Christian Palestinian group as well.

Had a Palestinian state been created in 1947 as the UN envisaged, decades of war could have been avoided. But the

Arab states, especially Jordan, were determined to avoid recognizing Israel's very existence, and acceptance of the UN two-state solution entailed accepting Israel as a separate and predominantly Jewish state, distinct from the rest of Palestine. The Palestinians were, as they have been since, a pawn in a much bigger Arab game, and their one chance for an internationally recognized state of their own went by the board. Furthermore, no Arab state wanted any other Arab state to grab too much of the territory that would be available were Israel to be strangled at birth. The different rulers therefore mistrusted each other, adding to the divisions.

By this time the British were in a no-win position, with Jewish terrorist groups, including two future Israeli prime ministers among them, Menachem Begin and Yitzaq Shamir, alongside Arab groups that did not want a Jewish state to exist. So Britain, still wanting a powerful military presence in the Middle East, withdrew from Palestine in 1948 and recognized Israel's independence, while maintaining an army in Egypt to protect the Suez Canal, and ensuring close military ties with the two Hashemite kingdoms of Iraq and Jordan.

On 14 May 1948 David Ben-Gurion became the prime minister of the newly independent Israeli state; on 19 May the country found itself at war, attacked by five of its Arab neighbours.

Here it is important to recall the fall of the Ottoman Empire. As Sir Richard Allen wrote in *Imperialism and Nationalism in the Fertile Crescent*, without it there would have been no Jewish homeland and no Israeli State. The problems of today's Middle East are often attributed to the events of 1948. But on this, Osama bin Laden is right to agree with Sir Richard – they actually go back, as already argued, to 1917 and the origins of the post-First World War settlement in 1918–23.

The initial fighting itself lasted one month, with the Jewish State able to gain more territory than had been allocated to it by the UN. Despite all the nearby Arab states joining in the attack, the war was, from the Arab viewpoint, a complete disaster. Not only did Israel continue to exist, but the Arab states lost territory, and then gained 750,000 Palestinian refugees as well. The UN tried to mediate, but then the UN Swedish negotiator, Count Folke Bernadotte, was assassinated in September 1948 by a Jewish group. He was replaced by an American diplomat, Ralph Bunche. By July 1949 fighting had finally ceased.

As with all claims and counter-claims right up until the present, each side has accused the other of committing massacres against innocent civilians. Those sympathetic to the Palestinians do not hesitate to remind us of the slaughter of Palestinians at Dayr Yasin, a village in which over 200 civilians were killed by Israeli terrorists. Similarly, Israelis do not let us forget a similar mass murder at Mount Scopus, where nearly 100 Jewish medical workers were butchered.

Arthur Goldschmidt in his *A Concise History of the Middle East* is surely right to say that both sides committed atrocities and that statistics from this period are notoriously difficult to prove, since each side exaggerates the numbers involved of both the dead and of those who fled. Jordan gained most of the 22 per cent of the Palestinian state that was left in Arab hands – today called the West Bank, as it lies west of the river Jordan – and the Egyptians took the Gaza Strip, which is contiguous to their territory. Jerusalem was split between the Israelis and

Jordanians. The United Nations set up a UN Relief and Works Agency to house the Palestinians who had fled in 1948. These settlements were supposed to be temporary. But only Jordan gave Palestinians citizenship – other Arab countries kept them as permanent stateless refugees, since the hope was that, with the elimination of Israel, they would be able to go back and reclaim their lost homes.

As we know, this did not happen, with a million Palestinians condemned to effective refugee status. This proved disruptive to all recipient countries, but perhaps above all to Lebanon, independent from France since 1945, and, as Albert Hourani points out in *A History of the Arab Peoples*, without the restrictions that Britain had placed over Iraq at the latter country's nominal independence in the 1930s, and with a constitution that presumed a now non-existent Christian majority. The seeds of the later Lebanese civil war were planted with the coming of the Palestinian Diaspora.

The Palestinian flight transformed the demographics of the region. While well over 100,000 Palestinians remained within Israeli territory, large areas now became available for Jewish settlement. Furthermore, hundreds of thousands of Jews from all over the Middle East were now expelled from countries such as Iraq, but also from Arab parts of northern Africa where they had lived since Biblical times. Baghdad, for example, a city with a substantial Jewish minority, now became overwhelmingly Arab in population.

Since the original 2006 edition of this book, the debate on the origins of Israel have further been inflamed by a debate within that country itself about whether ordinary Palestinians were primarily evicted by Israelis, or at the behest of neighbouring Arab powers

In one sense this argument is literally academic, the topic of many polemical discussions at university seminars both in Israel and in numerous other similar institutions around the world. But in another sense it is a profoundly partisan issue, since the identity of the Palestinian cause – namely the desire for an independent country or, in the case of many Palestinians, their wish either to return to their pre-1948 'home' or their desire to expel the Israelis altogether in some instances – is strongly linked to a sense of Arab victimhood and Zionist aggression. If there is a historical basis that proves that the representation of victimhood at the hands of Zionists is factually inaccurate, then much of the Palestinian argument becomes seriously undermined, which in turn brings with it strong political repercussions in the current dispute.

The debate arose with a group of Israeli 'New Historians', notably Benny Morris of Ben Gurion University in Beersheba. In books such as *Righteous Victims: A History of the Zionist–Arab Conflict 1881–2001* (2001), and in his more recent work *1948: A History of the First Arab–Israeli War* (2008), Morris shocked the wider as well as academic world by arguing that the Palestinian case is essentially correct. His argument is that Palestinian inhabitants of pre-1948 British mandate Palestine had been driven out of their homes by Zionist groups, many of whom were bent on creating a Jewish majority state with borders wider than those sanctioned by the United Nations. This was therefore an eminent Israeli scholar supporting the Palestinians' point of view in the debate over who was entitled to live where. Morris is also careful to say, though, that what he calls the 'expulsionists' – those wanting the opposing group to leave the region altogether – were mainly on the Arab side, not the Jewish.

Morris also makes a vital point that other historians of the region often omit, namely that the Arab desire to expel all but a tiny percentage of Jews from Arab soil was not born out of secular nationalism – Palestine for the Palestinians. Rather this desire represents a religious, specifically Islamic, way of seeing the world: that non-Muslims had invaded sacred Muslim soil. In other words, this is not a clash between Israelis and Arabs, which is the secular understanding of the conflict, but a wish by devout Muslims to see what had been Islamic territory since the seventh century return to Muslim rule again, repeating the victories of the Islamic armies of Saladin in expelling Christians centuries before during the time of the Crusades. In a twenty-first-century context, these two different ways of approaching the conflict bring to light one of the complications that the Middle East faces today. It is, as we shall see, why the exclusively Muslim group Hamas (unlike the PLO, which contains Palestinian Christians at all levels) refuses to recognize the existence of Israel and thus rejects a 'two-state' solution that would allow a Palestinian state to coexist with Israel.

However controversial Morris' other views might be considered to be – such as the existence of massacres committed by Israelis against Palestinians, albeit on a much smaller scale than the hideous carnage of the Armenian genocide of the First World War – his distinction here provides a perspective not only helpful in understanding the history of the region, but also in elucidating present-day attempts to find solutions to the Israel–Palestine dilemma.

Subsequent research by the equally controversial historian Ephraim Karsh – whose earlier work we have seen in previous chapters – has shown that such a view is statistically incorrect.

In his polemical (and therefore much disputed) work *Palestine Betrayed* (2010), Karsh shows clearly that it was Arab neighbouring governments and the Arab Higher Committee (AHC) (which included leading Palestinians) that urged the Palestinian people to leave their homes. This, Karsh argues, was so that Arab armies bent on destroying the new state could attack more easily and be in a better military position to invade and eliminate the newly created Israel. In leaving in droves as they did, Karsh continues, the fleeing Palestinians acted in obedience because, like the Arab neighbouring countries and AHC leadership, they all presumed that Israel would be defeated, the Zionists driven into the sea and that everyone leaving their towns and villages would soon return to homes free of Jewish neighbours. As we now know, the Arab attempt failed in the *Nakba*, the great catastrophe, of 1948. Palestinians who thought they had left their homes for just a few weeks found themselves to be refugees.

Karsh's work shows conclusively that there *could* have been a Palestinian state in 1948, and that it could have adhered to much wider borders than those set out by the United Nations. What destroyed the creation of what we now refer to as the 'two-state solution' was firstly the unanimous Arab view that the Israeli state had no right to exist. This meant that, together with the Arab nations and Zionists advocating a 'one-state' solution, the Palestinians believed that the UN offer to sanction a fully independent Palestinian country alongside the UN-created Jewish/Zionist Israel was unacceptable since such an undertaking would have to involve Arab recognition of Israel. As Morris also argues, for *religious* Muslims, this would have entailed recognition of a Jewish state on historically

Islamic land – something quite possible for more secular or for Christian Palestinians, but unlikely for those who saw the issue in spiritual as well as nationalistic terms.

In addition, some of the Arab countries did not want an independent Palestine because they wanted that new state's lands for themselves. As we know, when the invasion of the new Israeli state in 1948–9 failed, rather than allowing a Palestinian state in the remaining territory, King Abdullah of Jordan annexed the West Bank to Jordan instead. (Egypt correspondingly annexed the Gaza Strip.) Had King Abdullah decided differently, some speculate that there could still have been an independent Palestinian state in 1948, albeit on a smaller territory given Arab losses to the new Israeli state. In other words – and this is the most controversial of Karsh's contentions – the reason there is no Palestinian state today is because of the decisions of Arab leaders back in the 1940s.

It is easy to see how academic history can become polemical and partisan. If Morris is right, the Palestinian moral case is somewhat reinforced since it allows that, while not expulsionist, many Israelis also committed wrongful acts. But if the opposing Karsh thesis is correct, then it is fellow Arabs that the Palestinians have to blame rather than their Israeli enemies. Either way, ordinary Palestinians have still been victimized. If blame is to be allocated in the dispute between Palestinians and Israelis, then an honest assessment might be that both sides have committed atrocities, as Benny Morris and the 'New Historians' argue, although details are still contested decades after the original events. For whatever reason – Israeli aggression or Arab rejectionism – hundreds of thousands of Palestinians have found themselves as refugees, with no hope of return. Jordan alone gave Palestinians citizenship rights – no other Arab country did this.

How one interprets the past makes a profound difference to how one sees the present. As we shall see when looking at events in twenty-first-century Israel/Palestine, some Palestinians seek to escape their past while others remain firmly embedded in it. In public, on the West Bank (and probably in private in Gaza), many Palestinians hope for liberation from the tyranny – whether Zionist or Arab – of the past and the legacy of victimhood that the past engenders. To the more secular or religiously moderate Palestinian demographic, the possibility of a twenty-first-century two-state solution (despite the possibility that this may have once been squandered in 1948) remains a viable option.

As we shall see, the Islamic-based group Hamas are loyal to the 1948 stance and refuse to acknowledge the existence of Israel, a view that renders a two-state solution impossible. This stance is derived from religious belief, and is thus distinct from the policy-making processes of secular societies who separate matters of religion from matters of the state. The tenet that religious belief has policy implications is by no means limited to Islam in the twenty-first century – consider for example the role of Christianity in Latin America and Africa, or Hinduism in India today. Those Palestinians who support Hamas create a continuum between the present day and the ideology of 1940s rejectionism, making the past very much alive in the present, even if the alleged Palestinian motivation (faith) differs from that of the (secular) nationalists of 1948.

Jewish settlers had called Israel a 'land without a people'. This had not been true, because of the number of Palestinian inhabitants, Muslim and Christian. But they had fled, creating a new empty space. Now, with the two enormous influxes of new Jewish inhabitants – from Europe, and from the Middle East and North Africa – the land was filled again, with a whole new category of inhabitant.

Now that Israel and the USA are so closely linked, we tend to think that this has always been the case. But as Goldschmidt and other writers remind us, initially it was the Communist USSR that was supportive of Israel, since they saw their backing to the new state as a means of reducing British influence in the Middle East, where the British still cherished illusions of influence and Great Power status in the Arab world. In the USA, the State Department, the US military and many missionaries all tended to sympathize with the Arabs or fear losing good relations with the Arab countries. But 1948 being an election year, Truman did not want to lose the Jewish vote, and neither did politicians wishing to be re-elected to Congress. Since popular support for Israel was overwhelming, not least among American Christians who saw 1948 as linked to a new understanding of Biblical prophecy, the politicians therefore supported Israel as well.

(Many commentators, in writing about the USA, have spoken of the power of the so-called Jewish Lobby. While the lobbying power of Israel is indeed great and much more concerted than that of the Arab world, the issues can be misunderstood. For when a Republican administration is in office, the Christian Right is far more powerful than any Jewish organization could ever hope to be, since it is a major base *within* the Republican Party itself. The Christian Right believes in a nineteenth-century interpretation of the Bible, called 'dispensationalism'; this gives enormous credence to the re-establishment of the Jewish people in their land of origin, and the independence of Israel in 1948 confirmed such American Christians in their views. It is therefore this group far more than any Israeli lobby that drives the policy of the USA, especially if, as was the case with George W. Bush, America has a president who believes such a modern theological interpretation himself.)

Communist support for Israel was to change, especially after 1958 when the Americans invaded Lebanon to prevent extremists from taking power and when Egypt turned to the Soviet Bloc for support. But we should not forget that strategic relationships were not always as they are today.

The sense of loss and humiliation was total, and not just confined to the five defeated Arab countries; 1948 is known as *the* disaster, and, as Elie Kedourie reminds us, fate has been unkind to the Arab world ever since. Increasingly, a feeling arose that Israel was the creation of Western imperialism. Two groups shared this view – Arab nationalists, and Islamic radicals, for whom the presence in the former *Dar al-Islam* (Realm of Islam) of a Jewish, non-Muslim state was a permanent insult.

But while Kedourie counsels against over-estimating the influence of Christian Syrians in the formation of Arab nationalism, it is probably fair to say that this sense of being Arabs together against a common foe was inclusive and open to Christian Arabs as well as the Muslim majority. From 1948 until the disaster of the Six Day War in 1967, Arab nationalism remained the predominant sentiment in the Arabic-speaking Middle East, often mixed, as time went by, with socialism.

Both Elie Kedourie and Bernard Lewis have shown that the states that exist in today's Middle East are new and artificial. Furthermore, both nationalism and socialism are imports from the West. Arab nationalism was thus a clarion call across state boundaries to wider loyalties and a sense of Arabic solidarity, however precarious such an identity might be historically. (Under the Ottoman *millet* system, it was your religion that demarked you, not your ethnicity.) Socialism was new to the Arab world as well. One could argue, perhaps, that the way in which it was interpreted in the Arab world might have been different in the region's predominantly agrarian societies, since what Marx had in mind in the nineteenth century applied more to urban societies in Europe than to their rural equivalents in the Middle East.

So while the Arab world felt bitterly against the West, and against what they regarded as imperialistic interference by Western powers in their internal affairs, it is ironic but true that the main ideology of the ruling classes was in this period entirely Western in origin, as both nationalism and socialism are European ideologies.

Arab revolutions and Arab–Israeli wars

Egypt has been, especially since Mehmet Ali (Governor of Egypt for two periods between 1805–49), the powerhouse of the Arab world. In 1952 it would be again. One of the tragedies of post-war Egyptian history is that the chance for real democracy, which began in 1950, was in effect sabotaged by the discredit heaped upon the ruling elite by the military debacle against Israel and by the understandable lack of trust in

King Farouk, a compulsive intriguer. A group of officers, including two future presidents, Gamal Nasser (Gamal Abd al-Nasir) and Anwar Sadat, began to plot to get rid of the corrupt royal regime, which, despite its nationalist protestations, was seen as being unable to get rid of the hated British occupiers. In a coup in 1950 King Farouk was overthrown – the broadcast being made by a young Sadat – and a new revolutionary regime took power. Initially Egypt was under the nominal leader, General Neguib, but he was soon in turn overthrown in 1954 by the real leader, Colonel Nasser, who was to rule Egypt for the rest of his life, until 1970.

Nasser was the first authentically Egyptian ruler since the Pharaohs, as the Ptolemies were ethnically Greek. He began cautiously, not wanting to alienate the major Western powers, but sooner or later his radical ambitions for the Egyptian people led to an inevitable collision with the West.

Two major issues had to be tackled. The first was the British military occupation, which had been there since 1882 and, linked with it, Anglo-French ownership of the Suez Canal. The second was the urgent need for energy and for irrigable agricultural land, both of which could best be met by building a huge dam at Aswan. But this was well beyond the economic capacity of the still poor Egyptian state. The Americans decided not to finance the new dam, and Nasser soon realized that the other key grievance – the Suez Canal – provided the answer. Ironically Nasser had succeeded by negotiation in persuading the British in 1954 to remove their forces, so the British army had finally withdrawn after a seventy-four-year occupation in early 1956.

But in mid-1956 Nasser announced the nationalization of the Suez Canal, and the appropriation to Egypt of all its revenues. The British, still obsessed with Empire, regarded this as cutting the umbilical cord through the Mediterranean to the rest of the Empire in Asia – the defence of the Suez Canal had been pivotal to British defence policy for decades. Despite the strongest protests from the USA – both President Eisenhower and Secretary of State Dulles were appalled at the idea of imperialist adventures in the Middle East – the British and French secretly colluded with the Israelis to attack Egypt. Israel would invade and then an Anglo-French army would intervene, pretending to separate the combatants but in reality using this as a cover to regain the canal.

War duly broke out, but that autumn Britain and France were completely humiliated by American outrage and global insistence that they withdraw their forces. (All this was happening while the Hungarians were making a desperate but futile attempt to break free of Soviet domination.) France and Britain therefore had to retreat; their dominance in the Middle East was coming to an end, and from now on the Middle East would be part of the wider, superpower, Cold War rivalry between the USA and USSR, and no longer a pawn in power struggles of European countries.

Nasser was perceived throughout the Arab world as the man who had humiliated the hated imperialist powers. He became an instant hero to millions of Arabs who, after all the disappointments of recent decades, needed one. But he was a nationalist and, while notionally a Muslim, essentially a secularist and socialist. Although most adored him a minority, mainly of zealous Islamists, did not – as we shall see in the last chapter. He was also a dictator who would not hesitate to have his enemies executed. So while Egypt was now finally ruled by Egyptians, after two and half millennia of rule by Iranians, Greeks, Romans, Byzantines, Caliphs, Ottomans, and British, its very brief democratic interlude had been extinguished.

If the so-called Arab Street – a name given to the average Arab point-of-view and the equivalent of Joe Bloggs in Britain – adored Nasser, the more conservative monarchies in the Arab world did not. A proxy war was fought for many years in the Yemen between the supporters of the former monarch, backed by Saudi Arabia, and the nationalists, who were helped by Egypt.

The Suez crisis did not help the monarchical cause. For decades the two wings of the Hashemites, in Iraq and Jordan respectively, still longed for the Syrian territories over which Feisal had ruled briefly between 1918 and 1920. But each Hashemite ruler wanted it for his own country, so even here the Hashemite cause was divided. Abdullah was able to gain much of the West Bank and a foothold in Jerusalem, but he was assassinated. His son was mentally unstable and the throne went to the teenage Hussein. King Hussein, fortunately for his small country, proved to be one of the ablest Middle Eastern monarchs of recent times, and survived against all the odds on his throne, dying peacefully in 1999 after a reign of over forty years. He ended up with less territory than he had at the start, but at least he kept in power, unlike so many of the dictators around him.

For the ostensibly more powerful Iraqi Hashemites, 1956 was a disaster. King Feisal II ruled in all but name, with a permanent power struggle in the background between his ambitious uncle Abd al-Ilah, and Nuri al-Said, the arch-manipulator and shadow ruler for much of the monarchical period. Nuri wanted Syria as well and Jordan too, but he was never able to fulfil this dream, not least because of zealous Egyptian opposition (and traditional Saudi distrust of the Hashemites). The Sunni minority, as Kedourie reminds us in his devastating critique in *The Chatham House Version* and other writings, continued to rule over both the Kurds and the Shiite majority.

King Hussein of Jordan was shrewd enough to realize that British support no longer counted for survival in the Middle East. In early 1956, before the Suez debacle, he dismissed Sir John Glubb – known widely as Glubb Pasha – from his long-standing command of the key Jordanian force, the Arab Legion. Glubb represented the old, post-Lawrence of Arabia romantic link between European and Arab, but by contrast to the young Jordanian nationalists, he also represented Western domination and control. His dismissal was therefore highly symbolic from both points of view. Yet Nuri and the ruling elite in Iraq did not understand this new world, and in 1955 they signed a treaty with countries like Britain, Turkey, Iran and Pakistan called the Baghdad Pact, a kind of Middle Eastern NATO (Jordan refused to join).

Three years later in 1958 there was a bloodthirsty revolution, in which an Iraqi soldier, Qasim, seized power, with all the royal family, and Nuri was brutally murdered. (A certain young political activist called Saddam Hussein played a minor role.) Nuri had tried a brief union with Jordan, but this dissolved in July, when the successful plotters proclaimed Iraq a Republic. Britain's domination over part of the Middle East, all but destroyed by the Suez crisis of 1956, was finally and permanently finished. Not only that, but in 1958 Syria did unite with another Arab country, but it was not Iraq. The new state, albeit short-lived, was the United Arab Republic (UAR), and the country with which Syria came together was Nasser's Egypt.

Also in 1958 came the first American-armed intervention in the region. Following the coup in Iraq, there were fears that Lebanon and Jordan would be in danger. American troops landed in Lebanon, already near civil war, to protect that country from invasion, and this time British troops were also welcome in Jordan, since they went there with American approval.

Iraq could also have joined the UAR. However, Qasim realized that neither Egypt nor Syria had oil but that Iraq did in abundance, and therefore he concentrated on his own country. In and out of power during this time were members of both the Iraqi Communist Party, something that alarmed the West, and another, more nationalist, and equally secular grouping, the Ba'ath (literally 'Renaissance') Party, who helped a new regime to overthrow Qasim and seize power in another coup in 1963. But this regime too did not last long, being overthrown within a year.

The Ba'athists, founded in the 1920s by the Syrian-Christian-Arab nationalist Michel Aflaq, were in the context of the Middle East secular and nationalistic. A Chaldean Catholic Christian such as Tariq Aziz, later Saddam Hussein's deputy, could be as active a member as a practising Muslim. While they paid notional allegiance to ideologies such as socialism, what they really wanted was the Arab world for the Arabs and the entire removal of Western hegemony over the region. They were, in that sense, a classic nationalist party, since any Arab was able to join. This sets them apart from Islamic parties, which automatically exclude Christians, Druze, Fire Worshippers and members of other non-Muslim religions.

To leap ahead slightly, in 1968 the Ba'ath Party, of which Saddam Hussein was now a prominent member, took power. This time they were to remain in charge until Saddam's regime was removed by the American invasion of 2003. While Saddam did not become president immediately, he began plotting behind the scenes and was able to establish the terror network that kept him in supreme power for so long. As with all Iraqi regimes it was to be a Sunni-led government, in Saddam's case even more restrictive than usual since he relied increasingly on his own clan from Tikrit to maintain his rule. Soon the Kurds were being massacred in the north, as were all opponents to the psychopathic regime that Saddam operated.

(There is an irony here. Tikrit was also the birthplace of Saladin, who, as we saw, was a Kurd, not an Arab. Since Saddam was active throughout the 1980s in genocidal attacks on the Kurdish people, while at the same time proclaiming himself to be a modern Saladin, there is a considerable incongruity in his actions.)

In 1964 the Arab countries decided that something should be done for the benefit of the Palestinians, on whose side they nominally all were. A meeting in Cairo led to another in Jordan, and the Palestinian Liberation Organization (PLO) was born. However, the really effective opposition to Israel was not so much the PLO but an armed group led by a Palestinian called Yasser Arafat. This was *al-Fatah*, which literally means 'conquest' in Arabic. It is, though, the reversed first letters of 'The Movement for the Liberation of Palestine' in Arabic: *Harakat al-Tahrir al-Filistani*. (Filistani comes from the same root as the biblical 'Philistine', but Arabs are not descended from that ancient race – the similarity is geographical, not ethnic or linguistic.) So effective was Fatah that the PLO leaders invited them to merge, and Arafat was soon leader of both, which he would be for the rest of his life.

By 1967 it was clear that the Israelis were able to hold their own against regular guerrilla attacks from Arab countries. The USSR, which now had numerous advisers in Egypt, became worried about what they felt was a large Israeli presence on the Syrian border. The Egyptians persuaded the UN to withdraw their forces that had been there since 1956, and then began a blockade of Sharm al-Sheikh, which completely cut off Israel's ability to export through the Gulf of Aqaba to the Red Sea. Talks began on a unified command of Arab countries against Israel. Then on 2 June the Israeli prime minister, Levi Eshkol, appointed the great Israeli military hero, Moshe Dyan, who as far back as the War of Independence in 1948 had shown himself to be unusually brave, to be minister of defence.

What happened next, in June 1967 is, as with so much of Middle Eastern history, a source of dispute. One side claims that the Egyptians launched an attack on Israel and that the Israelis therefore defended themselves. By contrast, the Arabs claim that Israel, realizing that there was a considerable Arab military build-up, launched a massively successful air strike on 5 June, completely destroying the Egyptian air force in the process. Whichever version is correct does not alter the indisputable outcome of the very rapid conflict. The Israelis routed the Arab armies so swiftly that the conflict became known as the Six Day War, in no small way thanks to the effortless air superiority they now enjoyed.

Israel seized the entire Sinai Peninsula in just four days, despite having an estimated 800 tanks to the 2,700 possessed by the Arab armies, and a probable population ratio of around twenty-five to one. Jordan too was swiftly routed – on 30 May King Hussein having foolishly put his forces under effective Egyptian command – with the Israelis able to take both East Jerusalem and the entire West Bank. The Syrians did no better, losing their strategic positions on the Golan Heights. It has been reckoned that if it wasn't for the ceasefire agreed to by Israel and Syria through the UN on 10 June, even Damascus would have fallen to Israeli attack.

The world lives decades later with the consequences of that lightning Israeli victory in 1967, since the pre-1967 borders of Israel are those upon which the entire Arab world continues to insist. By contrast, no Israeli government is ever going to want to jeopardize the military security of their country as they see it by reverting to them. Some Israeli conquests, such as Gaza, were abandoned as recently as 2005, whereas others remain fully in place and are regarded as non-negotiable, for example those settlements on the West Bank it is deemed necessary to preserve for Israeli national security.

From the Arab point of view, the war in which they had been humiliated again was a disaster – physically, psychologically and in terms of morale. As Arthur Goldschmidt reminds us, the Soviet Bloc had aided the Arabs for years, and their armies were supposedly much better prepared than nineteen years earlier. Nasser had been in power in Egypt for fifteen years, and the Arab world had thought itself rejuvenated. But in 1967 the Arab nations lost far more land than in 1948, and over 200,000 Arabs fled, creating an even bigger refugee problem than before. In addition, nearly one million Palestinians on the West Bank, denied a state of their own back in 1948, were now ruled not by fellow Arabs but by Israel. Decades of Palestinian–Israeli strife was about to get far worse.

In Resolution 242 the UN asked Israel to return to the pre-1967 boundaries. Israel refused, annexing the formerly Jordanian part of Jerusalem. On the Arab side, none of the countries agreed even to negotiate with the Jewish state whose existence they continued to deny. A stalemate then ensued. As Bernard Lewis reminds us, the PLO now became the real spokesman for the Palestinian peoples, a role it has enjoyed ever since. Initially the PLO settled in Jordan. But in September 1970 it was ruthlessly suppressed after activities by a militant wing, the Popular Front for the Liberation of Palestine, caused a major rift with the Royal Jordanian Army. The Jordanians expelled the PLO to Lebanon, where it remained until seven years into the Lebanese civil war in 1982, when Israel invaded that country and expelled the PLO forces.

Finally, in 1993 the PLO decided to negotiate with the Israelis, something that it has been doing off and on ever since. (Now that in 2006 Hamas controls the Palestinian Authority Area, this might all change, since the PLO no longer speaks for the majority of the Palestinian inhabitants.)

In 1970 Nasser died, still a hero to many but seriously tarnished by the 1967 defeat. Anwar Sadat, his vice-president and fellow 1952 conspirator, succeeded him. Sadat immediately made links with the West, allowing foreign investment and in 1972 expelling his Soviet advisers. But as regards Israel, he was determined to gain revenge for the defeat of 1967.

Peace proved elusive, despite the best efforts of the USA. Jordan was willing to have a new, united Jordan/Palestine and then recognize Israel, but as this would have involved Israeli withdrawal from the West Bank, the idea did not prosper. Terrorism continued, with the murder of Israeli hostages at the 1972 Olympic Games in Munich provoking outrage, as did the Israeli revenge attacks on Arab soil.

In October 1973 Egypt and Syria felt ready for war. They chose to attack on 6 October, the date of the major Jewish festival of Yom Kippur (the Day of Atonement), which gave its name to the conflict. This time the Israelis nearly lost before going on to win, in no small way thanks to emergency weapons supplies sent by the United States. The myth of invincibility, and the idea that Israel could always win unaided, which was the case in 1967 and to a lesser extent in 1948 as well, was now punctured permanently. Israel's counter-attack saw Israeli divisions getting near to Cairo and Damascus, but since the Soviets were supplying the Arab powers the UN decided to ask for a ceasefire lest the situation escalate – this was becoming a rather hot Cold War conflict. After eighteen days the war ended. The UN passed Resolution 388, which, like its famous predecessor, 242, was ignored.

In a sense though, Egypt had won. Sadat had been shrewd enough to gain support from Saudi Arabia, thereby ending decades of mutual antagonism. Saudi Arabia and the other oil-producing Arab countries now used the urgent and permanent Western need for petrol against the West. In so doing, they managed to split the USA – which had plentiful oil supplies of its own – from Western Europe, which in this still pre-North Sea oil era, did not. An oil embargo was introduced against any country deemed to be excessively pro-Israeli – the Netherlands was singled out as the worst culprit – and a decision was made to increase the price drastically.

(Oil went from around US$3 a barrel to as high as US$20, before going back down to around US$11 – still, therefore, nearly four times what it had been early in 1973.)

Sheikh Yamani, the Saudi oil minister, suddenly became a major figure on the world stage. The oil price hike demonstrated Arab power over the West for the first time – finally they had a weapon that they could use to great effect. The change in petroleum values hit European economies very hard, and in Britain the situation was worsened by a decision of the mineworkers to go on strike.

It was this sense of crisis that mobilized Henry Kissinger, the United States Secretary of State, to engage in his famous 'shuttle diplomacy' in an attempt to de-escalate the crisis. He was able to prevent Israel from wreaking even more damage on the Egyptians, correctly realizing, as Arthur Goldschmidt has written, that this would render Egypt more rather than less likely to want eventually to agree on a more lasting peace.

Until July 2006 Lebanon had largely avoided becoming embroiled in the more recent upheavals of the Israeli–Arab conflict around it. But in 1975 this area, in which Christians and Muslims had lived together in peace and whose capital, Beirut, was described as the Paris of the Levant, slid into civil war. According to the constitution, Christians were in the majority, and so held the Presidency. But Muslims had in reality constituted the majority for a long while, and the presence of mainly Muslim Palestinians in the country tipped the scales even more in their favour. Every group had its own private army, or militia. An attack on a Palestinian bus, by

Christian Maronites, sparked a fifteen-year conflict, worsened when Israel intervened against the PLO in 1982.

One of the very few oases of calm was the American University in Beirut, where the students came from all the warring factions. I spent time there in the 1980s with friends and relatives who taught and lived there, and it was an eerie feeling. The campus was peaceful, while beyond it all kinds of death and mayhem could be seen from my balcony window. Even a short journey could be treacherous. Especially noticeable was not just that much of Beirut had been reduced to rubble, but that so much of the damage had been done by small arms fire, by militias of teenage gangs, some of whom, by the end, had known no other way of life. In 1975–6, Goldschmidt writes, some 70,000 people were killed, half a million left homeless and whole parts of the city destroyed.

In 1977 two new leaders came to power: Menachem Begin, the former anti-British activist, became prime minister of Israel, thereby ending decades of left-wing rule, while in the USA Jimmy Carter, the idealist, became president, determined to bring peace worldwide.

As the saying goes, it takes a Nixon to go to China. The same now applied in Israel – Begin was notorious as the insti-gator of the Dayr Yasin massacre, in which large numbers of Palestinian civilians had been killed. He was therefore uniquely qualified to create peace with Egypt, and since President Sadat was thinking along similar lines, this process now began. On 19 November 1977, President Sadat flew to Israel. Unfortunately he was alone among the Arabs in wanting peace; denounced as a traitor by other Arab nations, this embrace of reconciliation would eventually cost him his life in 1981 at the hands of Egyptian Islamic extremists.

Not all Sadat's requests were met – he asked for a Palestinian state, for example, an entity we still await. But thanks to Carter, the US government became fully involved in the process, and at Camp David, the presidential retreat in northern Maryland, Carter was able to bring Begin and Sadat together for talks on what they might be able to agree. After much hard bargaining, in September 1978 two framework documents were produced. One was for peace between Israel and Egypt, and one for peace in the Middle East in general.

It was hoped that the latter would lead to other countries becoming involved, but this proved illusory. The PLO rejected it outright, as did Jordan, Syria (now under the hard-line leadership of Hafez Assad) and the now economically powerful Saudi Arabia, paymaster of so much of the Middle East.

Nevertheless, progress was made on the Israeli–Egyptian front. Israel agreed to pull out of Sinai, giving the peninsula back to Egypt, though, crucially, not Gaza, from which Israel did not retreat until 2005. Egypt spurned the enticements of other Arab states, made in a gathering in Baghdad in 1978, to pull out of the discussions altogether. So in March 1979 Carter flew to Cairo to rescue the now seriously delayed talks. He proved entirely successful. Sadat and Begin came to Washington and on 26 March they signed a peace treaty at the White House ending twelve years of on-off warfare. This treaty has lasted; for over quarter of a century Israel and Egypt have maintained the peace. Some years later, Jordan also recognized Israel's right to exist.

The Palestinian problem was not solved, however, and is with us still. The PLO remained firmly rejectionist, as did

Israel's other neighbours. Not only that, but by 1979 a dramatic change of events in Iran, Muslim but hitherto the West's key regional linchpin, changed the face of the Middle East for ever.

10

REVOLUTION AND RESISTANCE

The Shah and the Iranian Revolution

Iranians have been predominantly Muslim since the seventh century. But over the course of time, they turned increasingly to the Shiite form of Islam, officially so for the past few hundred years. They were also never part of the Ottoman Empire, albeit their ruling dynasties were Turkic in origin. In 1925 Reza Khan rejected the republican option that Kemal Ataturk had taken in Turkey, and so was succeeded on his death by his son, Mohammad Reza Shah Pahlavi.

The new Shah's hold over his throne was initially shaky – the Second World War followed by the threat of the Soviet occupation of northern Iran saw to that. Then, in 1951, came two years of crisis, caused by the Iranian prime minister, Mohammad Mossadeq, who nationalized the Anglo-Iranian Oil Company (now BP). This caused a major rift with the British, since the company's British government links went back to before the First World War. Churchill, as First Lord of the Admiralty, had taken a major government shareholding in it because he realized that the future fuel of the Royal Navy would be oil, and that the Government ought to be able at all times to have access to such fuel. Iran was therefore of crucial geopolitical importance to the British over several decades, even though it was never formally conquered by Britain or any other Western country.

Because of the earlier threat to Iranian territory by the Soviets, the Americans were worried that Iran could go in a Communist direction. In what was, in the long term, to be a foolish move, the CIA under Kermit Roosevelt (a distant relative of Franklin Roosevelt) organized a coup that restored the Shah to power and removed Mossadeq. Iran, as we saw, joined the British-inspired Baghdad Pact two years later in 1955 and became a crucial American ally, keeping an eye, along with Turkey, on the Soviet Union to the north. It received millions in military aid from the USA, and the US–Iranian relationship became very close.

Unfortunately, the Shah used his restoration to rule as a dictator, introducing a dreaded secret police force, the SAVAK, to enforce his will. He inaugurated in 1963 what he called the 'White Revolution', a series of moves designed to modernize the country and increase Iran's power and prestige. Much of this comprised what we would consider good ideas – the enfranchisement and empowerment of women, modern technology and literacy being among the key goals. But all this was introduced, not through democracy as in neighbouring Turkey, but by an absolute monarch who did not really share his power with the ordinary people.

Consequently the reactionary forces in the country – in particular, the bazaar merchants, and the Shiite clergy – were able to use dislike of the Shah's autocracy to oppose his modernization reforms. He also made the major error of forgetting the country's strong Islamic roots. He looked back to Iran's golden age, under rulers such as Cyrus the Great and Xerxes, all of whom predated Islam, and were therefore looked on askance by devout Muslims (in the same way that they also reject Pharaonic civilization in Egypt). One of the Shah's key reforms was land redistribution, again a laudable goal as millions of ordinary Iranians were able to own land for the first time. But some of the major expropriated landowners were Shiite religious foundations, who had used their extensive land-holdings to support religious learning and the mosques.

One of the Shah's key critics was a Shiite Grand Ayatollah, Ruhollah Khomeini. Based in Qom, the Shia theological centre, Khomeini did everything possible to oppose both the Shah's changes and his despotic rule.

Khomeini was initially exiled in 1964 to Iraq, with its very large Shiite population, and then, after Saddam Hussein expelled him in 1978 from the Shia holy city of Najaf, to Paris. From both places he used recent technology – the cassette tape especially – to spread his message: the overthrow of the Pahlavi dynasty, to be replaced by a proper Islamic state based upon Quranic principles, with religious leaders not a hereditary despot in charge.

Oil, some now argue, can be a curse, not a blessing. The revenues often go straight to the capital city to be used by the ruling elite, rather than being spread generously among all the populace. Iran under the Shah is a classic example of this. While the state earned billions, ordinary Iranians saw precious little benefit, with the money going to the Shah's Pahlavi Foundation, which became richer and even more powerful, and to the increasingly Westernized and deracinated upper-middle-classes, many of whom were educated in the West. Other related issues also rankled; for example, Americans working in the oil and similar industries were often exempted from Iranian law, which ordinary Iranians found humiliating.

So while the Shah was modernizing, and making the lot of *some* Iranians much better – especially well-educated women, for example – others were feeling worse off than before. This was especially true of the new urban poor, the millions who came to the big cities – Tehran, for example, rose from one million people in 1945 to five million thirty years later. Corruption also became rampant, again with the middle-classes gaining and the poor feeling resentful. The classic example of hubris by the elite came in 1971, when the Shah decided, without any strong historical evidence, that the Iranian monarchy was 2,500 years old. The celebrations – yet another reminder of Iran's pre-Islamic past, with many of the soldiers dressed up in Achmaenid-period costume – cost around $200 million, at a time when many ordinary Iranians were living in dire poverty.

Above all, average Iranians felt that their country was a pawn of the United States, and therefore not controlled by its own people.

The fall of the Shah in 1979 was, like so many events in history – the collapse of the Iron Curtain in 1989 being a good example – not predicted by the experts. All the expensive intelligence in the world often fails to forecast major world changes before they happen, and the coming to power of the world's first Islamist regime in Iran in 1979 is among such failures. Analysts in the CIA and elsewhere worried about

Iran's Communist Tudeh Party, while ignoring the portents of the real revolution about to happen.

(Western media experts similarly confessed in 2005 that they all failed to spot the huge groundswell of support for the hard-line Mayor of Tehran, Mahmoud Ahmadinejad, who won the Iranian presidential elections in June of that year. This was, they reflected ruefully after the event, in no small way because his voters, the poor, do not move in the same elite, English-speaking social circles as journalists from the West.)

In his book *The Modern Middle East: A History*, James L. Gelvin makes the important point that historians, sociologists and political scientists are not agreed on one overarching cause for the 1979 Iranian Revolution. But does this matter? As Gelvin reminds us, the closer we are to events, the more difficult it is to see them in perspective.

Consider histories of the Cold War written as late as 1988: all are written from the viewpoint that the Cold War was a permanent phenomenon, and that Soviet/American rivalry would continue indefinitely. It was fear of the Soviets to the north, Gelvin shows, that was the prime reason that the USA supported a regime as despotic as the Shah's. Yet in 1989 the Iron Curtain fell peacefully and in 1991 the USSR, seemingly so invincible, collapsed from within.

It is the same point, Gelvin argues, with Iran. Writing in 2005, he felt that Iran – to use a French Revolutionary analogy – was going through its 'Thermidor moment', namely, that part of the revolution's history when moderates take over after early excesses. But at the same time as the book was published Mahmoud Ahmadinejad became president of Iran. At the time of writing, the issue of the production of nuclear material by

Iran has become one of the most pressing of the day, its resolution not helped by remarks by the new president on other
items, such as his wish to see the state of Israel destroyed. As
always, the Middle East remains as unpredictable as ever.

One of the paradoxes of revolutions is that the regime
which takes power is often far worse, and considerably more
repressive, than its predecessor – for example, one only has to
compare Stalin with Tsar Nicholas II, and Robespierre with
King Louis XVI.

The dictum was soon to prove itself in Iran. By early 1979 it
became apparent even to the Shah that his despotic rule was no
longer working. He finally installed a more genuinely reform-
oriented prime minister, Shapur Bakhtiar, but it was too late.
The strikes and riots that had begun in 1978 now escalated
beyond the Shah's control. On 16 January 1979 the Shah fled,
never to return. The following month, Ayatollah Khomeini
returned in triumph from Paris. The army refused to protect
the old regime any longer, and Bakhtiar's government
collapsed. Moderation and a secular solution for the problems
of Iran thereupon ended too, although this was not immediately realized until October of that year.

On 1 April 1979 Iran was proclaimed an Islamic Republic
following a referendum the previous month. One wonders if
most people knew what they were electing, but if any had qualms
it was now too late. Initially, as can happen, a moderate prime
minister took office – an engineer called Mehdi Barzagan, who
had worked in the past with Mossadeq. The calm was short-lived.
Strict Islamic dress codes were introduced, alcohol banned and
links with the West reduced. Then in October came the coup
that enabled the hard-line Shiite theocrats to take control.

The Shah was dying, and was obliged, now that he was a powerless international pariah, to go from pillar to post in search of effective medical treatment. Many in Iran were worried that since he had been reinstalled by the CIA after he had fled in 1953, history would repeat itself. Others in Iran noted with concern the Israeli–Egyptian peace process, which, like their fellow Muslims in the Arab world, they viewed as a betrayal. Then in October, at the urging of Henry Kissinger, the Shah was admitted to the USA for medical treatment, despite Carter's strong misgivings.

Carter's doubts proved well-founded, and this decision probably cost him his presidency. The Iranian government had blocked an earlier attempt by revolutionary students to seize the American Embassy in Tehran – now all restraint was removed. In November 1979 militant students captured the Embassy (except the consulate, whose officials were able to escape disguised with fake Canadian passports), and took the entire diplomatic staff hostage. The siege lasted 444 days, and the hostage diplomats were not released until the day Reagan took office in 1981.

(I was told at the time that the Soviets threatened dire action if any of their diplomats were similarly kidnapped – whether or not this is true I have never discovered.)

But not only were the diplomats held hostage – so too, in effect, was the USA, and its hapless president, Jimmy Carter. Khomeini proclaimed the USA as the Great Satan, and Barzagan was replaced as prime minister by a Khomeini loyalist. The Shah's death in 1980 made no difference and American attempts to rescue their diplomats ended in military humiliation.

Then on 21 September 1980 Saddam Hussein launched a war against Iran. This was to last eight years, with nearly a million eventual casualties, many of them either civilians, or soldiers of child age. It was a savage struggle, with numerous suicide missions only worsening the carnage. The West took Saddam's side on the basis that one's enemy's enemy is one's friend. Not surprisingly, after 1991, and especially after 2003, the West's decision to arm Iraq came back very strongly to haunt it, and with good cause. The war ended in stalemate with no side the true victor, millions bereaved and the two despotic regimes as firmly in power as ever.

In 1980 President Carter publicly underlined the importance of the Persian Gulf and its oil to US strategic interests. Ironically, it was the Iraqi invasion of Kuwait in late 1990 that saw it implemented, rather than any action by the Iranians.

Meanwhile, the threat of outside invasion greatly reinforced the power of Ayatollah Khomeini, whose rule as Supreme Leader, or interpreter of the Quran, the *Faqih*, enabled him to have jurisdiction that, as Bernard Lewis has pointed out, was unknown in Sunni Islam and, until then, in Shiite Islam as well. In 1980 the theocrats were able to take control of the *Majlis*, or Parliament, and the rule of the Western-educated Bani-Sadr as president lasted only until 1981, when Ayatollah Ali Khameini became president. (He succeeded Khomeini as Supreme Leader in 1989 and is still very much in power.)

Both sides in the war wanted greatly to increase their firepower and advantage over the enemy. Both sides therefore tried to gain nuclear weapons. Iraq's attempts failed when the Israelis bombed the Osiris nuclear power plant, and Saddam was unable, as we now know, to effectively resurrect his programme after being defeated in the Gulf War in 1991, although he always tried to make it seem as if he had. With Iran the attempt is still with us, since President Ahmadinejad has made it clear that Iran is still on track to become a nuclear power in the twenty-first century.

Revolution and religion: theories, lessons and implications

How much did the Revolution change? Here again it is surely too early to tell. Much depends on how one sees the issues examined in the final chapter – the return of religion as a major player in world affairs. Are religious revolutionaries of the Iranian kind innately different from what went before? Or are writers like Gelvin correct in saying that while the style of revolution is different, in reality Shiite zealots are no different from their secular counterparts elsewhere in the world? On this there is no consensus – academic or any other kind. The issue upon which experts disagree is known as secularization theory, and it affects substantially the perception of both the Middle East, and issues such as Islamic terrorism.

According to the theory, people should be becoming increasingly less religious as the world progresses with science, innovation and similar processes rendering people more secular. This is essentially a Western concept, tracing its origins to sociologists of religion such as the Harvard academic Harvey Cox. In Western Europe it uses as proof the massive decline in any kind of religious adherence in the twentieth century. In the USA, academics such as Cox argued for much the same phenomenon being seen in North America as well, until the

Reagan era of the 1980s. Then other thinkers, such as Peter Berger, noticed the start of the massive return to religious values that led to Moral Majority, and the decision of millions of Evangelicals to support the Religious Right.

However, all these are Western examples, and what Peter Berger, George Weigel and former Democratic Senator Daniel Patrick Moynihan all noted is that the West is very different from the rest of the world when it comes to the continuing importance of religion.

When the Iranian Revolution happened and militant Islam received a shot in the arm, the results were completely counter to what the secularization theorists were saying. Suddenly, millions of people were becoming *more* religious, rather than less! Iran, for example, had been Muslim since the seventh century, but now, in the late twentieth, the ordinary citizens of one of the most technologically advanced Muslim states were making Islam the core of their national identity.

(It should be said that, like Malaysia, or a Gulf State such as Dubai, a nation is fully able to be both Muslim and highly technologically advanced at the same time. Furthermore, the 120 million Muslims in India are playing a full part in that country's recent technological renaissance, including the nation's current president, Dr A. P. J. Abdul Kalam who, as well as being a Muslim, is also the inventor of India's nuclear weapons programme and Azim Premji, the Chairman of Wipro, the multinational Indian IT company and the richest man in the country.)

Gilles Kepel described the Iranian example above in his book *The Revenge of God*, which looks at the resurgence of religion in Judaism, Christianity and Islam. (It is vital to remember that plenty of other religions have their hard-line followers, not just Islam.) Likewise, as mentioned previously, the American sociologist Peter Berger has written in *The Desecularization of the World: Resurgent Religion and World Politics* that secularization theory is being proved wrong by the day. In many parts of the world, Islam and Christianity are growing more rapidly than ever before, in both cases mainly at the expense of the ancestral tribal religions. This is occurring – as Philip Jenkins indicates in his book *The Next Christendom* – in places like parts of Indonesia and central Nigeria. All this has been very puzzling for the experts, many of whom have found the phenomenon disturbing, since the reality on the ground often contradicts the deeply held personal, secular and some-times anti-religious views of academic specialists.

Gelvin (and, for example, the African writer Lamin Sanneh, in *Piety and Power*) are right to say that what dramatically increased secularism in Western Europe was the Protestant Reformation of the sixteenth century, and the nearly 200 years of warfare that followed as a result of it.

First, there were two completely separate kinds of Christianity – Catholicism and Protestantism – within Western Europe, with belief differences that exceed those of the Sunni and Shia (except for Wahhabi Sunnis, most Sunni would recognize a Shiite as a fellow Muslim). Second, they went into active spiritual competition with each other, and third, there were long periods of active warfare on religious grounds. Eventually by the eighteenth century, the era of religious war was over – some would argue by 1648 in the seventeenth – and in time the ability to choose one kind of Christianity over another led to many deciding not to choose any religion at all.

This, Gelvin points out, made the West different from other parts of the world, whose history, religious and otherwise, is not at all similar.

However, even Gelvin and other writers such as the American academic Benedict Anderson who wrote *Imagined Communities* do not seem fully to recognize that religious belief is different from holding a political ideology – being, say, a socialist or nationalist. When the Middle East was dominated, as in Nasser's time, by Arab nationalism, and by state socialism, secular theorists in the West could understand this, since nationalism and socialism are Western secular concepts. But since 1979 the world has witnessed the outbreak of a wholly new religious phenomenon, which is completely outside the comprehension of most cultural commentators.

In fact, as Peter Berger points out, only Western Europe is almost entirely secular in outlook. (Even countries that were once devoutly Catholic, such as Spain, are becoming increasingly as secular as their European neighbours to the north.) What is surprising about the USA is not that it is religious, since most of the world is profoundly religious, but that it is unlike Western Europe, which is not. Therefore Iran looked at from a global perspective is far from unusual.

Unfortunately, in the USA religion, especially Christianity, is highly partisan and politicized in a way not prevalent elsewhere, such as in Latin America, whose growing number of Protestants hold a wide variety of political beliefs, with many Brazilian Evangelicals, for example, being on the left not the right. Much religious analysis is therefore strongly linked to the American culture wars, which, as we saw earlier, is something unique to the USA. Since the Al Qaeda attack of 9/11, the way in which people consider Islam has also become part of the struggle, so that issues such as political correctness and the like are not seen on their own merit but through the prism of the proponent's stance within America's internal domestic cultural debate.

This polarization is highly regrettable, since it means that much of the world is therefore seen through a prism of internal American cultural conflict. Middle East policy too, for example, has in recent years become part of this secular/religious culture war in the USA, and in a way that is very puzzling to those of us watching the debate from inside. It is sadly easy, to take another example, to find a commentary piece in newspapers which says that those who have religious beliefs are somehow primitive. Political correctness then makes this an awkward statement if applied, for example, to Muslims, since it is wrong to call those of other ethnic backgrounds savage or backward in any way. But then, as we saw in looking at the Crusades, there are others in the USA who defend the Crusades, and who do not hesitate to attribute to all Muslims the views of a small number of extremists.

Much of this debate was caused by the events of 1979 in Iran. In so far as the USA is concerned, it was exacerbated by the capture of American diplomatic staff as hostages, something that had a traumatic effect on the USA, and which has profoundly influenced how many have seen Islam ever since, especially after 2001.

We should always look at other people in the light of how they see themselves, not as we think they are or should be. For many Iranians, it *is* about religion, and the same is true of millions of other Muslims around the world. If we are to understand the Middle East properly, we need to accept that billions of our fellow humans out there have a world view dissimilar from our own.

The 1980s and the First and Second Gulf Wars

In the 1980s, President Assad of Syria was busy killing his own people. The Ba'ath Party there was principally secular, and led by people, like Assad, from the Alawite minority sect of Shiite Islam – most Syrians being Sunni. Assad was worried by the threat posed, both spiritually and politically, by the Muslim Brotherhood. They represented mainstream Sunni Islam, which threatened him as an Alawite. They also posed a specifically Islamic threat to someone as innately secular and nationalist in outlook as Assad.

He attacked the town of Hama in 1982, killing between 10,000 and 20,000 people. In 1988 Saddam Hussein similarly butchered tens of thousands of innocent Kurdish civilians, gassing many of them to death, with results that became infamous worldwide.

No massacre of Jews by Palestinians or of Arabs by Israelis has even approached such carnage. From the 1980s onwards, there was a major increase of Palestinian attacks on Jews, often directed as much against civilian targets as military, especially after the first major Palestinian uprising, the 1987 Intifada.

Yet none of the atrocities committed by Middle Eastern leaders upon their own people has ever received the global publicity or moral outrage that has come from attacks related to the Palestinian–Israeli struggle. Ten people in a pizza parlour achieve far more publicity and create far more anger than the death of 10,000 equally innocent civilians. Why is this?

We saw that, Jordan apart, the Arab states did not give citizenship to Palestinian exiles, however deeply they felt about Israel's actions. As Arafat reportedly said to a friend as far back as the 1950s, the Palestinians would have to achieve liberation themselves, since no one would do it for them. While that might be unfair, it also has a strong element of truth.

However, it is also true that for the Arab world the Palestinian issue is in many senses a defining one. First, Arab states have consistently opposed Israel, and Palestine is the key to the ongoing hostility even if, as with Egypt after 1979, that animosity has been non-violent. Second, more controversially, it has been the perfect way to channel rage against an external enemy, rather than on one within. Most regimes in the Middle East are autocracies of some kind or another, with varying degrees of freedom permitted or denied the inhabitants. The Egyptian elections of 2005, for example, were regarded as not fully democratic by outside observers.

Diverting hatred away from local despotic rulers to Israel is a classic example of what psychologists call projection theory, the best-known example being the Nazi use of the Jews as scapegoats for all that had gone wrong in Germany. Some almost Nazi-like propaganda against Israel has been freely permitted in the Middle East for many years – it is only very recently that Egyptian schools have ceased to teach the nineteenth-century anti-Semitic forgery, *The Protocols of the Elders of Zion*. Hate Israel and it is easy to forget that you are being repressed by a ruler of your own nationality and religion. Furthermore, as Gelvin points out, the conflict with Israel has seen the permanent militarization of many Arab societies – up to 30 per cent of the world's arms sales are in Arab countries.

Egypt has continued in a state of emergency for decades, even though it has been at formal peace with Israel since 1979, and, as Gelvin writes, many Arab societies use the excuse of the struggle for internal repression. It would be ironic if the Palestinians were to gain political freedom while those countries that spoke out on their behalf remained repressed.

In 1982 the Palestinian struggle became internationalized. To get rid of PLO emplacements in Lebanon which were being used as bases to attack Israel, the Israeli Defence Force (IDF) invaded Lebanon, taking much of the south. While this incursion achieved its immediate objectives, it also worsened the already terrible Lebanese civil war. Bashir Gemayal, the Maronite Christian warlord and President of Lebanon, was assassinated, by whom is still disputed by some. In revenge the Lebanese Christian Maronite Phalangist militia slaughtered hundreds of innocent Palestinian refugees in the camps of Sabra and Shatila.

(Those knowing Spanish history will know that Franco's fascist/nationalist forces in the 1930s used the adjective Phalangist as well – the Maronites were strongly influenced by such developments.)

I visited these camps a few years later: the atmosphere was still tense. The IDF had been very close by, but did nothing to prevent the massacres, and an Israeli inquiry not long afterwards strongly censured their own forces, including the commander, General Ariel Sharon, who later became prime minister of Israel until serious ill health felled him in late 2005.

In 1983 the American peacekeeping forces in Beirut were also massacred, when a suicide bomb hit their barracks. Jacob Fellure in *The Everything Middle East Book* recommends his readers watch the Robert Redford and Brad Pitt film, *Spy Game*, to get a picture of what Beirut was like at the time. From my own memories of being in Lebanon during the civil war, the film gives a superb impression of the sheer chaos in the city.

In 1985 the Israelis withdrew, since they now had local Christian Lebanese forces to carry out much of the security work in the border region. By 1990 the civil war was over, but Lebanon swiftly became a Syrian dependency, until the assassination of Lebanese politician Rafik Harari in 2005 led to what some hopefully called the 'Cedar Revolution', in which people power compelled the withdrawal of Syrian troops.

But 1990 is better remembered as the year in which Saddam Hussein invaded Kuwait, under what seems to have been the false impression, gained in a misunderstood conversation with an American diplomat, that the West would not interfere. From his point of view, this turned out to be a highly costly mistake.

(Countries facing similar threats in the 1990s but which did not have oil, such as Croatia, Bosnia and Rwanda, felt understandably aggrieved that the West did not form a coalition to help them as well, but such, alas, are the realities of international politics.)

Saddam's misreading of the situation meant international involvement to liberate Kuwait from the Iraqi attack – and also, perhaps even more important, prevent a further invasion of Saudi Arabia, holder of the world's greatest oil reserves. President George Bush Sr was a firm believer in international coalitions and diplomacy, and was soon able to assemble a powerful group that contained Arab nations as well as Western, Egyptian and

Syrian troops in addition to British and American forces. The coalition was known as Operation Desert Shield and, after the invasion of Kuwait in January 1991 as Operation Desert Storm.

Bush's diplomacy meant that it would be more difficult to see the war as one of Western imperial aggression. For example Syria – who in common with Iraq had a Ba'athist regime – was hardly an ally of the West, had close links with the weakened, soon-to-be-dissolved USSR and remained implacably opposed to Israel and the peace process. In spite of this, President Assad sent troops to fight alongside those from the UK and America. The USSR did not intervene – by the end of 1991 it would no longer exist – and this meant that Iraq like Syria had no powerful Soviet ally to whom it could turn. The losers were the PLO who supported Saddam, and Jordan, which did too, though in the latter case to avert internal strife as the government knew how deeply unpopular support for the US would be, given that so much of the Jordanian population was and is of Palestinian origin. (Yemen also supported Iraq.) The Arab Street also strongly and vociferously supported Saddam. For many ordinary Arabs he became the great champion of the Arab cause against what many regarded as Western imperialism, in spite of widespread Arab government support for the coalition.

The nature of the coalition also meant that there were severe limitations on what the Desert Storm forces could accomplish, and here began a debate that, in the USA at least, has been going on ever since. For once Western troops and their Arab allies, principally Saudi Arabia, had liberated Kuwait in 1991, the war stopped.

Before fighting started, tales of large coalition casualties at the hand of Saddam's elite Republican Guard units proved to be untrue – more British soldiers were killed by accidental American friendly fire than by Iraqis, and while coalition casualties were very low, the Iraqi army was swiftly defeated.

Some therefore, especially neoconservatives in the US administration such as Paul Wolfowitz, advocated going all the way to Baghdad and removing the Ba'athist regime. But removing Saddam was not an option for the Arab members of the coalition, who feared that a post-Saddam regime would be unacceptable, however much they disliked the Iraqi dictator. In particular, it is unlikely that Sunni Saudi Arabia, with its Wahhabi brand of Islam that does not even recognize Shiism, would have wanted a democratic and predominantly Shiite regime to the north. Kurdish separatism together with possible demands for an independent Kurdistan was also unacceptable to the local regimes. In addition leading US soldiers, such as the Chairman of the Joint Chiefs of Staff, General Colin Powell, were keen to have a limited war with clear objectives and minimum casualties – the Powell Doctrine. So Saddam Hussein remained in power.

However, the West encouraged local groups to rebel. The rebellion duly broke out, with catastrophic and near-genocidal consequences for those who were brave enough to revolt against the dictator. In the Kurdish areas north of the coalition-imposed no-fly zone, much of the region was able, after a while, to become semi-independent, albeit in unusual circumstances. But the rebellion in the Shiite areas led to major disaster. Hundreds of thousands of Shiite Marsh Arabs, who had lived for centuries in the southern marshes of Iraq, were killed or displaced and their ancient habitat destroyed in what became a simultaneous human and ecological catastrophe. The rebellion was duly suppressed, and although it had been encouraged by the West, no Western state went to the aid of the hapless rebels, who were butchered unaided. Better the devil you know, reckoned the Arab governments, than a disruptive new regime that might unsettle yours.

For as Goldschmidt reminds us, most Middle Eastern regimes have no popular legitimacy with their own people. They are therefore particularly vulnerable, and Arab unity is difficult to maintain. A post-Saddam regime with legitimacy or an Iraq split into its three component parts could have been highly destabilizing, and thousands of Shiite Arabs and Kurds therefore paid the price.

Should the allied forces have gone all the way to Baghdad? Such a decision remains highly controversial to this day; Lady Thatcher notoriously stated that if she had still been in power they would have conquered Saddam! The decision was regretted by American neoconservatives, who subsequently wrote an infamous memo when back in opposition saying that the conquest of Iraq was Western unfinished business. Since many of its authors, such as Richard Perle and Paul Wolfowitz, took influential positions when George W. Bush took office in 2001, and since Iraq was then invaded under his leadership in 2003, this view has become yet more controversial still.

On the one hand, hundreds of thousands of Iraqis would be alive today if coalition forces had continued to Baghdad. Not only would there have been no massacre of the Shiites and Kurds in 1991, but the huge numbers that died as a result of the economic sanctions against Iraq then imposed by the UN – and manipulated by Saddam against his own people – would also be alive as well. Democracy might then have come earlier.

But on the other hand, the Arab dictatorships would never have agreed to topple Saddam since they would have feared for their own regimes, and it would have been virtually, if not totally impossible for Western forces to have proceeded under such circumstances. Although the decision caused countless deaths and enormous human suffering to innocent people, it was, alas, the only one realistically possible.

The disappearance of the USSR, which left the USA as the only remaining superpower, or hyper-power (to borrow a French phrase), soon made another major impact on the Middle East. This was the Israeli–PLO agreement of 1993, sometimes called the Oslo Accords, since the peace process was begun in secret negotiations by the Norwegian government, and only ratified by the USA when the clandestine discussions became overt. Yitzhak Rabin, the Israeli prime minister, Shimon Peres, the foreign minister, and Yasser Arafat of the PLO were all awarded the Nobel Prize the following year, sadly prematurely, since the peace for which everyone longed did not break out.

Writing more than twelve years later, the great hopes of 1993 remain tragically unfulfilled. There is still no real peace in Palestine, and, if anything, the situation has worsened, with suicide bombing becoming the weapon of choice of the Islamic terrorists.

(Specifically Islamic terrorism will be examined in the next chapter – I consider it different from the essentially secular, nationalist terrorism of the PLO. Christian Palestinians can want a Palestinian state. However Hamas, and similar Islamic organizations seek a *Muslim* state, which is therefore religious as well as nationalist – a seemingly small, but nonetheless vital distinction.)

Of the Nobel Laureates, only Peres is still with us. Arafat died in Paris in 2004 after becoming gravely ill. Rabin, by contrast, was assassinated in 1995 at a peace rally, and not by a Palestinian terrorist but by Yigal Amir, a fellow Jew. Amir was part of an extremist group that regarded any deal with the Palestinians as treachery, and therefore punishable by death. Rabin's murder was a tragedy in many ways. He had been a highly successful general, and had impeccable pro-peace credentials. Without his presence the peace process suffered accordingly. The rise of Jewish terrorism was demonstrated, for example, by the massacre of innocent Muslim worshippers in Hebron by an Israeli extremist. Jews have killed Arabs, Arabs have similarly killed Jews, and the fight has been, to some extent, internationalized – some of the Islamic suicide bombers were British Muslims, for example.

(Interestingly, they were from upper-middle-class homes and privately educated – thus as far as possible from the usual picture of an impoverished Palestinian with nothing to lose in death.)

Ever since 1995 countless attempts have been made, often with the help of the USA, to broker a peace deal in Palestine. Up to and including the time of writing, none has been successful, although, with new Palestinian leadership following the death of Arafat, things might possibly change for the better. In 2000, President Clinton felt he came close, with talks arranged between the then-Israeli prime minister, Ehud Barak – also a former general – and Arafat. But even though Barak conceded much, it was still unacceptable for Arafat, and the stalemate continued. In 2005 the right-wing Likud prime minister, Ariel Sharon, yet another former soldier, was able to make Israeli settlers withdraw from Gaza. But large settlements remain, as of 2006, on the West Bank.

It is very difficult to write about a conflict in which we are still mired, with no end in sight. Of course, one could have said the same about the Cold War, even as late as January 1989. When that conflict ended, the demise was very swift, and equally total.

So details about the many ups and downs in the negotiations over the past decade, accounts of deaths on both sides, and lists of meetings and bombing raids, would in a sense just be retelling the same story without the perspective that a known conclusion, on the lines of 1989 in Europe, can give us. Nothing of real substance has changed.

One possible good sign from the Israeli side is a realization that if they are to remain a democracy they have to do something drastic, otherwise they will either have to be a dictatorship or withdraw to territory that is overwhelmingly Jewish. Gaza and the West Bank apart, there is – as Ehud Olmert told a group of us in London – also the question of the growing Arab population *within* Israel, including those within the old pre-1967 borders. Olmert, who wishes to preserve Israel as a genuine democracy, is very aware of this and it is the rationale both of the withdrawal from Gaza and for the construction of the wall between Israel and the Palestinian Authority area. Since the person saying this was later a co-founder of the new Kadima political party and now prime minister, it might augur well. But it would be a brave person who could predict the future of so long-standing a conflict.

The building of the wall has been likened to the construction of the equally notorious Berlin Wall in the 1960s. But the

Berlin Wall did not work and nor, I suspect, will this new one. It might make terrorism slightly more difficult, but those determined enough to commit atrocities against civilians will, alas, find a way around it, in the same way that those zealous enough at escaping Communism always managed to get out somehow.

The other dramatic event of the Middle East was the fall of Saddam Hussein in 2003. This is a story very much in progress at the time of writing before the long-term consequences of the late 2005 referendum on the constitution is known. In 2006 we have a majority Shiite government with a Shia Arab prime minister, al-Maliki, elected for a full term of office, but with the internal conflict still very much in full flow.

Here again, people have often taken sides not on the basis of the issues themselves, but on how they view the power of the USA. In Britain, some on the socialist left did support Anglo-American intervention, notably the Labour MP Ann Clwyd and Nick Cohen, the radical journalist and columnist. Some on the political right, such as the prominent Conservative MP Kenneth Clarke, opposed the war. What is interesting about the pro-war left was that they included people who had been involved in supporting the human rights of the Kurds, hundreds of thousands of whom had died at the hands of Saddam's secret police. In this case, the deaths were indisputable, with countless bodies being discovered to prove that the massacres, unlike the legendary 'weapons of mass destruction' were genuine.

In my book on Churchill's creation of Iraq, and in the London *Sunday Times* on 26 December 2004 I have written about the very artificial nature of Churchill's creation of 1921.

While the future of Iraq is as deeply unclear as that of the Israeli–Palestinian dispute, it is evident that old allegiances – to tribal or religious groups – are more powerful for many Iraqis than patriotism for a unitary Iraqi state. The Sunnis who ruled, often despotically, for the first eighty-two years of the country's existence now find themselves excluded, an inevitable result of sectarian rather than ideological voting. It is clear that the hard-line elements in Iran are doing their best to support similar factions in Iraq and perhaps also to destabilize their newly democratic neighbour. Whatever the future of Iraq will be, the idealism of the right-wing neoconservatives in the USA who so keenly supported the invasion prior to 2003 now seems rather misplaced, as a repentant Francis Fukuyama admitted on changing from his original hawkish position on invading Iraq. In early 2006, military analysts to whom I have spoken think that the current alliance between secular Ba'athist Sunni Arab nationalists and hard-line Islamic (and also Sunni) extremists might eventually break up, since their visions of a future Iraq – one still secular, the other profoundly religious – will eventually conflict. But we shall see . . .

Whatever the future of the Middle East, the Cradle of Civilization will be at the centre of global attention for a very long time to come.

11

A CLASH OF CIVILIZATIONS? 9/11 AND THE FUTURE OF THE MIDDLE EAST

When I began thinking about this book, Yasser Arafat was still alive, and Saddam Hussein was president of Iraq. No Islamic terrorist attacks had taken place in Britain, and the Middle East and its concerns were still very far from the thoughts of most people in the West. There was hope that moderates would continue to rule Iran, and sorrow that Lebanon would still be suffering under Syrian tutelage.

As it is being finished, Ariel Sharon, the former Israeli prime minister, is now off the political scene following a massive stroke. He founded a new political party, Kadima, which, under the leadership of Ehud Olmert, is now the largest party in the Knesset following an election in which their old party, Likud, trailed in fourth place. Olmert is now prime minister in a coalition that includes the Labour Party.

One of the difficulties about taking history into the present is that events can change so rapidly and unpredictably. The atrocities of 9/11 took place in the middle of my writing a textbook on terrorism, so much had to be altered, and quickly.

Likewise, the death of Arafat has, some people now feel, improved the prospects of a peace settlement between Israel and the Palestinians, even though old tensions between the Fatah base of the PLO and the overtly Islamist Hamas are continuing. But the election of Hamas as the biggest single party in the Palestinian elections of 2006 could change the situation yet again, with PLO and Hamas gangs shooting at each other in Gaza and the instant-comment pundits on television predicting a Palestinian civil war.

Similarly, in 2005, Lebanon became freer with the Syrian stranglehold diminished, although hopes for a reformist president in Iran were dashed in the elections that year. (Just to show the dangers of making predictions, the otherwise excellent *US News and World Report* special edition on Islam entitled 'Secrets of Islam' (no date) predicted confidently that former President Rafsanjani would win, only for him unexpectedly to lose almost immediately the edition was published.) And while the carnage in London of 7 July 2005 did not change British policy, it nonetheless drew the attention of British people to terrorism and issues in the Middle East in a way that might not have been the case hitherto.

Therefore, this chapter will be concerned with themes and broad ideas, in order to avoid the dangers of dating too quickly. While the individuals involved will probably change, the underlying issues are certain to be with us for some while into the future. As American specialist Ellis Billups Jr has remarked, the current conflict between Islamic terror and the West is likely to be around for many years. Similarly former CIA Director James Woolsey has referred to it as the Fourth World

War and also expects it to last a very long time – presumably inferring that the Cold War figures as the third world war.

The key theme of this chapter will therefore be the rise of specifically Islamic terror, and the conflict *within* Islam to which many in Britain woke up on 7 July 2005. I was in the USA on 9/11, when America received a massive alarm call that should have woken the entire West. Therefore the events of 7 July nearly four years later should have come as no surprise, especially in the light of the Madrid train bombings not so long before.

Thankfully, and as all moderates of goodwill predicted, British Muslim leaders denounced the bombings that four of their fellow Muslims had carried out that day in London. For one of the key events of recent years is the impact that the Middle East and its internal conflicts is now having on the wider world, from Bali to Madrid and from London to New York.

Had this book been written not just a few years ago but some decades back, Nasser would have been the obvious choice for one of the most important Arabs of the post-war period, and certainly the most eminent Egyptian. However, there is now a good case for saying that that accolade should go to someone who, at that time, was almost entirely unknown.

In the light of the increase in religious terror since the 1990s, it is clear that by far one of the most influential and important Egyptian thinkers would now be the former school-teacher, Sayyid Qutb. Qutb was executed on Nasser's orders in 1966. The writer Peter Bergen has rightly described him as 'the leading ideologue of the jihadist movement'. His thinking, and in particular his book *Signposts Along the Road* (sometimes translated as *Milestones*) has been crucial in the inspiration of the Islamic terror the world has witnessed since 1998, and in particular including and since September 2001.

At the heart of Qutb's teaching was his confirmation that it was legitimate to attack apostate Muslims as well as complete outsiders. Therefore someone like Nasser, who was theoretically a Muslim, was evil, because his real ideology was not so much Islam as Arab socialism and nationalism. Qutb gained this idea from Ibn Taymiyya, who, as we saw, regarded it as lawful to attack the Mongol Khans in Iran, even though they were, nominally at least, converts to Islam.

(The academic Michael Scott Doran has suggested that bin Laden sees the current world threatened by the West in the same way that the Mongols threatened and then destroyed the great Abbasid empire in 1258 – a possible interpretation of bin Laden's 1998 fatwa.)

As John Esposito, the American academic, has explained, in *The Islamic Threat: Myth or Reality?*:

> For Qutb, Islamic movements existed in a world of repressive anti-Islamic governments and societies. Society was divided up into two camps, the party of God and the party of Satan, those committed to the rule of God and those opposed. There was no middle ground ... The Islamic movement (*haraka*) was a righteous minority adrift in a sea of ignorance, and unbelief (*jahiliyya*). He dismissed Muslim governments and societies as un-Islamic (*jahili*), being in effect atheist or pagan.

As we saw much earlier, early Islam referred to pre-Islamic society as *jahiliyya* or a state of ignorance. To Qutb, Egypt in the 1950s and 1960s was no different – the same now applied to the modern Middle East. As Esposito continues:

> For Qutb, the cause was the displacement of Islam's God-centered universe by a human-centered world . . . [To Qutb] the West is the historical and persuasive enemy of Islam and Muslim societies, both as a political and as a religiocultural threat. Its clear and present danger comes not only from its political, military and economic power, but also from its hold on Muslim elites who govern and guide by alien standards, which threaten the identity and soul of their societies.

Nationalism and socialism are Western inventions. While Arabs like Nasser believed in them, such world views could not claim to be Islamic. Thus the new Islamic threat is against both local tyrants and innocent Westerners alike.

Palestinian terrorism, as we saw, was specifically directed against Israeli targets, including those overseas, such as the Israeli athletes killed at the Munich Olympics in 1972. Both the PLO, as a straightforward nationalist group, and Hamas, as a Muslim nationalist body, do not target anyone other than Israel.

However, what we have now is *transnational* terrorism, aimed both at regimes deemed un-Islamic, even if they are Muslim, and those countries deemed to be allied to such governments, and likely to corrupt ordinary Muslims by undermining their Islamic faith and practice. This latter threat has been called 'westoxification', a term popularized in Iran in the circles around Ayatollah Khomeini. The West is a double source of corruption – both at elite level, persuading rulers to reject Islamic government in favour of democracy or dictatorship, and at a street level, by seducing ordinary Muslims from leading pious lives.

This remains a controversial issue, in both the West and in the Islamic world. On the one hand there are writers such as the former CIA analyst, and now media commentator, Michael Scheuer, the author of books such as *Through Our Enemies' Eyes* and *Imperial Hubris: Why the West is Losing the War on Terror*. Scheuer says that it is what the West *does*, in terms of foreign policy and the like, that matters. On the other hand, those such as the conservative British critic and philosopher, Roger Scruton, who wrote *The West vs. the Rest*, claim it is because of who we *are* that extremists in the Islamic world dislike us.

A middle way between these views is possible – like that held by Thomas Friedman of the *New York Times*. He has popularized the idea of a Jordanian journalist, Rami Khouri, who distinguishes between the Arab Street and the Arab Basement. (Since the Islamic world, thanks to television and radio, is now globally attuned to events in the Middle East, it might be better to refer to the Islamic Street and Islamic Basement.)

Khouri and Friedman argue that Islamic terrorists live in the Basement, but recruit from the Street. I would go on to say that the Basement hates the West and its Middle Eastern allies for who they are, and the Street dislikes them for what they do. Both theories are therefore correct and mutually compatible. The terrorists want a return to a pure Islamic state, a Caliphate, and the Street might, for example, like Coca-Cola and rock music but loathe the way they perceive the West as supporting Israel over Palestine, or the American invasion of Iraq in 2003.

This means that, while the West may not wish to change its nature and thereby lessen the hatred felt for it by the Basement, it can, by judicious policy, prevent recruitment from the Street into the Basement. Much therefore depends on whether or not the West realizes that there is a conflict *within* the Arab world for the soul of Islam, and that when it does, it proceeds to act accordingly.

(The desire of the West to hold on to its own values – such as freedom of speech – was seen dramatically in the riots by angry Muslims worldwide in early 2006 against unpleasant caricatures of the Prophet Muhammad published in a Danish newspaper in late 2005.)

For after 9/11, the instinctive reaction of many in the West was to blame themselves. This was particularly true, for example, in many publications in Britain and the USA, and at the teach-ins held on American campuses to try to explain to perplexed students not just what had happened but why. But this, one can argue, was a completely Western-centred way of looking at the world, always making the West responsible for everything that goes right or wrong and refusing to attribute independent agency to anyone living outside the West's borders.

This is far from arguing that the West bears no responsibility, since Scheuer does have a point. But to say that the West bears sole responsibility is surely not true, and is also insulting to the people living in the Middle East. Unthinking knee-jerk support either for Israel (as in some circles in the USA), or for Palestine (as on much of the political left in Europe) does not help either side in the Israeli–Palestinian struggle, just one example of where Western attitudes have made an impact in the region.

Likewise, while support for war against Iraq has surely helped recruit some to the terrorist cause, for other like-minded individuals a hatred for everything for which the West stands long predates 2003. Therefore the picture is chequered or of uneven shades of grey rather than straight black or white, even though protagonists on the various sides would not see it that way.

In fact it is better to say that the main struggle is often an internal one, with the West often the scapegoat. This one can argue was the case in 2006, when the Syrian and Iranian governments used the Danish cartoon affair to stir up anti-Western hatred, conveniently, especially in the Syrian case, diverting local anger from an oppressive internal regime. To persuade the people to hate a foreign enemy is a good way of preventing them from realizing how freedom is crushed at home.

Again, while some people from the Muslim world were talking peace, others were plotting violence. For example in the 1990s when Palestinians were engaged in peace negotiations with the West, including with Israel under US auspices, Al Qaeda was plotting the attacks on the USS *Cole* and on American embassies in Africa.

All in all, while some people have a conceptual preference for black and white, I think the Friedman/Khouri paradigm of the Street and the Basement works better than any other interpretation. For the Basement, it is a religious struggle – or cosmic, as Mark Juergensmeyer helpfully puts it – and an internal conflict for the soul of Islam. Much of the Street, however, is affected considerably by how the West behaves, or how ordinary people perceive what is happening in Palestine when they watch Al Jazeera. To attribute blanket motives to everyone is to make matters much too simple, and if we are to understand the situation properly we need to be able to see it from several angles at once.

Analyses of the rise of Islam often begin with the tumultuous revolution in Iran in 1979, and the overthrow of the Shah not by pro-Western modernizers, but by religious zealots determined to create a regime radically different from what had gone before. There is much to support such a view, since 1979 was the first time that Islamic radicals had managed actually to take control of a country, and in Iran's case one of the most prosperous, oil-producing and populous nations in the region.

But two cautions need to be made.

First, Iran is a Shia country, and therefore in Islamic terms atypical of most of the Middle East, which has remained Sunni. Only in Iraq and Lebanon, which have large Shia populations, has Shiite Islam and its perspectives made a difference.

Second, and related to this, Sunni Islamic radicalism has been around for a long time, going back to the Muslim Brotherhood and similar organizations. So although Ayatollah Khomeini remains a figure of real consequence, and events in Iran have greatly encouraged Islamic militants around the world by demonstrating that Islamic regimes can come into being and radical Shia organizations, such as Hizbollah, are involved in the active struggle against Israel, it is Sunni Islam from which Al Qaeda and its many imitator groups come, and Sunni militants who have launched holy war against the West.

One of the key – and most controversial – theories of recent years in international relations has been that of a Harvard academic, Samuel Huntington. First put forward in the influential American journal *Foreign Affairs* in 1993, and then published in book form in 1996 under the title *The Clash of*

Civilizations, this was a theory that came back into the news, inaccurately I believe, in 2006 over the issue of Islamic rage against the Danish cartoons.

In essence, Huntington's message was that since the end of the Cold War the old bipolar world – the free West (the USA and its allies) vs. the Communist East (the USSR and its satellites) – had come to an end. Optimistic commentators, like Francis Fukuyama in his idealistic *The End of History*, had suggested that this excluded future conflict. Far from it – there was a new kind around the corner.

· The bipolar Cold War would be replaced by what Huntington called a 'clash of civilizations'. This was based not so much on secular ideology but culture, at whose heart was religion. He divided most of the world into the following groups (surprisingly leaving out Israel, the only Jewish state): the West (as a merger of Christian Catholic and Christian Protestant), the Orthodox, the Muslim, the Hindu, the Buddhist, the Confucian and the Shinto.

Most controversial of all, he stated that the civilization of Islam had 'bloody borders', and that many of the world's forthcoming conflicts would include Islam as a protagonist. So when 9/11 happened, many Americans, in newspaper comment and on television, felt that Huntington had been vindicated. So too did Huntington. But there are good reasons to suggest that such a theory is fatally flawed.

To begin with, it embodies Edward Said's hypothesis that the West looks at the Middle East and nearby regions en masse through a distorting lens. While by no means always agreeing with Said – his criticisms of academics such as Bernard Lewis are often unfair – on this issue, he has a strong case. In reality the Middle East is far from homogenous culturally, economically, and even spiritually. There are secular republics and an Islamic state, moderate countries and totalitarian regimes. A number of countries, such as Egypt, Jordan, Syria and Iraq, have old Christian communities. In some, women are well-educated; in others conditions are similar to the Middle Ages. Some are Sunni, others Shia or with large Shiite minorities. Iran is Persian speaking, reserving Arabic for religious use. In Iraq, from 2003 onwards, many Shiite Iraqis were murdered by Sunni extremists – Muslims killing Muslims.

Outside Islam's historic heartland, Muslim communities from West Africa to Indonesia vary even more widely – to say that Saudi Arabia and Indonesia, for example, are the same would be to stretch a point too far. In Pakistan as in Iraq, Shiite Muslims have been the victims of attacks by Sunni terrorists, pitching Muslim against Muslim once again.

In another of my books, *Why the Nations Rage*, I have quoted from the now former president of Iran, Khatami, a moderate who, when in power, was keen to develop what he describes as the 'dialogue of civilizations', a theme enthusiastically supported by the United Nations. Similar calls have been made by other Muslim peacemakers, notably the Pakistani scholar, Akbar Ahmed. In short, one could use the phrase of another Harvard academic, David Little, who refers both to the 'confusion of civilizations' and the fact that the Huntington thesis is over-simplistic.

Not only that, but the decision of many moderate Muslims to march against the extremists in early 2006 also proves that Islam is far from monolithic, and that many in the Islamic world deeply resent the claim of the hard-liners to be the sole spokespeople for the Muslim religion.

But while the clash of civilizations theory may be flawed, and fails to recognize the rich diversity of life in the Middle East, it does, like all Orientalist theories, inform much Western perception of the region, although in this particular case distorting outside views of the area to the detriment of those living there.

Perhaps a more impressive theory is that of a Muslim academic living in Germany, Bassam Tibi. This theory, which, alas, has had far less attention, is the 'clash of universalisms' in his book *The Challenge of Fundamentalism: Political Islam and the New World Disorder.*

Tibi's argument is that Islam and Christianity are innately different from other religions, in that they claim universal validity. Both of them are active missionary faiths, seeking to win converts from all ethnic groups and peoples across the world. While other religions might evangelize on a limited basis, only these two state that they alone are universally true.

Take the helpful recent books Mark Juergensmeyer has written, such as *Terror in the Mind of God*, together with Jessica Stern's *Terror in the Name of God* and my own works. Juergensmeyer and Stern aim to show that while most religions have extremist, terrorist wings, the consequences of this are normally manifested within the religion rather than outside it. Hindu extremists from the RSS, the group that killed Gandhi, will commit atrocities against Muslims and Christians within India, but do not take the struggle outside. The same applies, as Juergensmeyer demonstrates, with Sikh terrorist groups. This is because, although there are plenty of Hindus and Sikhs living outside of India, the real struggle is for the soul of India itself and not one for worldwide domination. Hindus and Sikhs do not want to have global jurisdiction, nor do they go out of their way to win converts from among peoples of non-South Asian origin. (There are exceptions to this, but not many.)

With Islam and Christianity it is entirely different. There is a growing number of converts to Islam in the West, and in places such as Nigeria and Indonesia Christians and Muslims are in a race for converts. This has created violent clashes among those whose idea of spreading the faith is more violent than those of the more peaceful majorities within those religions. (It should be remembered that in south-east Asia, Islam was brought peacefully, and spread through traders and merchants, rather than by the sword.) The central belts of Nigeria and areas such as Aceh in Indonesia have seen bloody fights between the two groups, with people being killed on both sides. In India, since the riots in Ayodhya in 1992, Muslims have usually been the victims of angry extremist Hindu mobs, rather than the perpetrators. (Similarly, Christians have also been victims, with both local believers and missionaries being killed.)

Some of the borders of Islam, therefore, are bloody, but it is not possible to blame the Muslim faith tout court as a result. It is the global nature of Islam coming up against an equally international faith, Christianity, with both claiming universal jurisdiction, which truly makes the clash happen. Thus radical Hindus do not kill people outside India, but extremist Muslims slaughter people from New York to London via Bali and Madrid.

As Juergensmeyer also shows – including in his book *The New Cold War? Religious Nationalism Confronts the Secular State* – many of these struggles are intra-religious. Al Qaeda is against the West, but also the Saudi regime. The extremists in Israel who murdered Rabin are as much against their own government and the peace process as they are against the Arabs.

This we see, in Islam, above all in the career of Sayyid Qutb, the Egyptian thinker who is now being written about in depth in such publications as *The Age of Sacred Terror* by Daniel Benjamin and Steven Simon, and in *Terror and Liberalism* by Paul Berman.

Benjamin and Simon rightly place Qutb, a twentieth-century thinker, in their chapter on Ibn Taymiyya, the medieval thinker we have already considered, and after their assessment of the eighteenth-century leader al-Wahhab.

What is especially interesting about Qutb is that he spent time in the USA. He was shocked by an innocent church dance in Greeley, Colorado, considering it hopelessly decadent, as he did the uniformity and neatness of the suburban lawns. But as Berman points out, what really horrified Qutb was not so much the sex or the identical appearance of the houses but the 'place accorded to religion in liberal society', and in particular the 'split between the sacred and the secular in modern liberalism'.

This confirms what was seen earlier in the Friedman/Khouri idea of the Basement and the Street. What Berman is showing is that it is not so much what the West does in the Middle East or elsewhere that matters to the Basement, but the very self-identity of the West itself.

Qutb was dismayed that much of his own part of the world was following in the footsteps of the West. He encapsulated his views in his book *Islam: Religion of the Future*. There, he wrote, the danger to the Islamic world from the West was the latter's attempt to confine Islam to the sphere of emotion and ritual, bar it from participating in the activity of life and check its complete predominance over every secular human activity, a pre-eminence it earns by virtue of its nature and function. In other words, only Islamic theocracy is legitimate, which is what Qutb and his sympathizers have wanted to restore ever since.

This is why Qutb judged Nasser's Arab socialism to be so wicked. While in prison, Qutb also wrote a massive thirty-volume commentary on the Quran. When it came to people like Nasser, he commented, there were those 'who claim to be Muslims, but perpetrate corruption', false co-religionists who 'oppose the implementation of God's law', evil rulers who 'are seriously lacking in faith and loyalty to God and Islam'.

Emmanuel Sivan, in *Radical Islam: Medieval Theology and Modern Politics*, quotes Qutb as saying about tyrants such as Nasser that in such regimes, 'man is under the domination of man rather than of Allah'. As we saw, to Qutb, 'everything around is *jahiliyya* [ignorant of Islam] . . . including a good part of what we consider Islamic culture'.

Thus Qutb rejected not just Arab socialism but Arab nationalism as well – including Nasser's brief attempt to unify with Syria in a United Arab Republic. As Qutb put it bluntly to his secret police interrogators, the 'sole collective identity Islam offers is that of the faith'. The founder of the Ba'ath Party in Syria, Michel Aflaq, was a Christian, as were numerous other Arabs around the Middle East. Unity on the basis of Arab ethnicity would include them, but that was unacceptable to a pious Muslim like Qutb.

Qutb thus rejected geographical nationalism in favour of the religious kind. As he put it:

The homeland a Muslim should cherish and defend is not a mere piece of land; the collective identity he is known by is not that of a regime . . . His *jihad* is solely geared to protect the religion of Allah and his Sharia and to save the abode of Islam and no other territory.

This is also the view of bin Laden and Al Qaeda. To extremist Muslims, there is only the *Dar al-Islam* (Realm of Islam) and the *Dar al-Harb* (Realm of War), and no other state has true legitimacy in the eyes of God. The world according to this view only has two halves – that under direct Islamic rule and the rest that is both outside it and thus in conflict with it.

(Moderate Muslims, by contrast, are active in working out how the millions of the faithful now living in the West can do so, and in a way that enables them to be both pious believers and good citizens at the same time. This is the exciting new possibility of a Realm of Peace, or *Dar al-Salaam*.)

Qutb therefore told his interrogators that 'Patriotism should consist in bonds to the faith, not to a piece of land.'

But apart from the now vanished Taliban Afghanistan, and revolutionary Iran, there has not been a fully fledged Islamic state to keep the extremist Muslims happy. If even Saudi Arabia is insufficient, then no one is truly up to the mark. What extremists want thus falls into the category of a country that once existed in a Golden Age. While Christianity and Islam are unique in their combination of universal claims and their mono-theism, radical Islam is very similar to many other faiths when it comes to internal motivations for religious terrorism. This has been pointed out very clearly by the LSE professor, Anthony Smith, in his seminal *Chosen Peoples* as well as in several of his other works. What all of these faiths look to is a heroic mythical Golden Age, when everything was as it should be, the godly members of the chosen race ruled justly and everyone followed the dictates of the faith as laid down.

In the case of Hinduism, it is nostalgia for an era before the Mughal invasions, when India was, for all intents and purposes, an overwhelmingly Hindu state. In Judaism, the extremist Zionists who wish to create a Greater Israeli state with much larger boundaries than those of the present nation, a Sanhedrin, Temple worship and besides, live in hope that this will speed the appearance of the long-awaited Messiah. Sikhs want an independent Kalistan, a country of their own as it existed before the conquests of the British.

Islamic extremists want nothing less than a full restoration of the great Caliphates. This, by definition, is considerably more than the establishment of an independent Palestinian state, because it would include restoring Islamic rule to all the former domains, Spain included, as people in Madrid found out in 2004.

(Moderate Muslims, such as Akbar Ahmed, also share a regret for the departed glories of Umayyad rule in Al-Andalus, calling it 'Andalus nostalgia'. But they accept that times have changed and that the expulsion of the Moors from Granada in 1492 became irreversible long ago.)

All this is not to deny that there are other issues involved. Many attribute much Muslim rage against Britain in 2005 to the British decision in 2003 to join America in conquering Iraq. But such things seem to be Arab Street issues – talking about Islamic terror means going to the Basement.

It is not just the Caliphates that these groups want restored. They also want a pure Islamic government, especially of the kind seen in the seventh century before the split of 680, their Golden Age of Islam when Muhammad was alive and when the Four Rightly Guided Caliphs ruled what they consider was a united all-powerful Islamic empire.

As we saw, the description given to seventh-century Muslims is *al-Salaf al-Salih*, the venerable ancestors. Followers of the return to an idyllic Golden Age are therefore called *salafiyya* or salafi, the disciples of the ancestors. While most *salafiyya* are far from being extremists, all terrorists would be very much in the *salafiyya* camp, as a *Guardian* interview with young Muslims shortly after 9/11 demonstrated. As the reporters discovered, ordinary Muslim youths despaired at the extremism of some of the radicals who had tried to turn everyone at local mosques into *salafists*.

Michael Scott Doran, of Princeton, has written in *Foreign Affairs* and in *How Did This Happen?* that Al Qaeda 'grew out of . . . [this] religious movement . . . [and that such extremists] regard the Islam that most Muslims practice today as polluted by idolatry; they seek to reform the religion by emulating the first generation of Muslims, whose pristine society they consider to have best reflected God's wishes for humans'.

Doran reminds us that by no means are all *salafiyya* Muslims violent. Nor, as he points out, do all such extremists wish to globalize their struggle: Hamas, as already noted, restricts its use of suicide bombing and mass killing to the Palestinian struggle for independence.

Sayyid Qutb, he opines, is the ideologue of the *salafiyya* movement, 'the most important Salafi thinker of the last

half-century, and a popular author in the Muslim world today,
nearly forty years after his death', which was in 1966. What he
accomplished, mainly in jail, was an update on Ibn Taymiyya
that enabled extremist Muslims to think that they could kill
apostate Muslims, especially rulers whose Islam they
considered to be compromised, or only skin deep. His disciple
Osama bin Laden has also issued many fatwas, or religious
pronouncements, either in his name or in that of whatever
front organization he was using at the time. The classic example
was the one published in early 1998, and whose significance
many did not fully grasp until over three years later, in
September 2001.

Bernard Lewis gave an excellent treatment of it in *Foreign
Affairs*, 'License to Kill', Nov./Dec. 1998. However he does
not quote from it in full, and to understand properly what is
going on with religious, *salafiyya* extremism in the early
twenty-first century, we need to have all of it. (The translation
is that given in Walter Laquer's *Voices of Terror*, Source Books,
2004.)

Praise be to Allah, who revealed the Book, controls the clouds,
defeats factionalism, and says in his Book, 'But when the forbidden
months are past, then fight and slay the pagans wherever ye find
them, seize them, beleaguer them and lie in wait for them in every
stratagem of war.' Peace be upon our Prophet, Muhammad
Bin-'Abdullah, who said, 'I have sent the sword between my hands
to ensure that no one but Allah is worshipped, Allah who put my
livelihood under the shadow of my spear and who inflicts humiliation and scorn on those who disobey my orders.'

The Arabian peninsula has never – since Allah made it flat,
created its desert and encircled it with seas – been stormed by any

forces like the crusader armies spreading in it like locusts, eating its riches, and wiping out its plantations. All this is happening at a time in which nations are attacking Muslims like people fighting over a plate of food. In the light of grave situation and the lack of support, we and you are obliged to discuss current events, and we should all agree on how to settle the matter.

No one argues today about three facts that are known to everyone. We will list them in order to remind everyone.

First, for over seven years the United States has been occupying the lands of Islam in the holiest of places, the Arabian peninsula, plundering its riches, dictating to its rulers, humiliating its people, terrorizing its neighbours, and turning its bases in the peninsula into a spearhead through which to fight the neighbouring Muslim peoples.

If some people in the past argued about the fact of the occupation, all the people of the peninsula have now acknowledged it. The best proof of this is the Americans' continued aggression against the Iraqi people using the peninsula as a staging post, even though all its rulers are against their territories being used to that end, but they are helpless.

Second, despite the great devastation inflicted on the Iraqi people by the crusader–Zionist alliance, and despite the huge numbers of those killed, which has exceeded one million, despite all this, the Americans are once again trying to repeat the horrible massacres, as though they are not content with the protracted blockade imposed after the ferocious war or the fragmentation and devastation.

So here they come to annihilate what is left of this people and to humiliate their Muslim neighbours.

Third, if the Americans' aims behind these wars are religious and economic, the aim is also to serve the Jews' petty state and to divert attention from its occupation of Jerusalem and the murder of Muslims there. The best proof of this is their eagerness to destroy Iraq, the strongest neighbouring Arab state, and their endeavour to fragment all the states of the region such as Iraq, Saudi Arabia, Egypt and Sudan into paper statelets and through their disunion and weakness to guarantee Israel's survival and the continuation of the brutal crusade occupation of the peninsula.

All these crimes and sins committed by the Americans are a clear declaration of war upon Allah, his Messenger, and Muslims, and ulema have throughout Islamic history unanimously agreed that the jihad is an individual duty if the enemy destroys Muslim countries. This was revealed by Imam Bin-Qadamah in 'Al-Mughni', Imam Al-Kisa'i in 'Al-Bada'i', Al-Qurtubi in his interpretation, and the shaykh of Al-Islam in his books, where he said, 'As for fighting to repulse [an enemy], it is aimed at defending sanctity and religion, and it is a duty as agreed [by the ulema]. Nothing is more sacred than belief except repulsing an enemy who is attacking religion and life.'

On that basis, and in compliance with Allah's order, we issue the following fatwa to all Muslims:

The ruling to kill all Americans and their allies – civilians and military – is an individual duty for every Muslim who can do it in any country where it is possible to do it, in order to liberate the al-Aqsa Mosque and the holy mosque [Mecca] from their grip, and in order for their armies to move out of all the lands of Islam, defeated and unable to threaten any Muslims. This is in accordance with the words of Almighty Allah, 'and fight the pagans all together as they fight you all together', and 'fight them until there is no more tumult or oppression, and there prevail justice and faith in Allah'.

This is in addition to the words of Almighty Allah: 'And why should ye not fight in the cause of Allah and of those who, being weak, are ill-treated (and oppressed)? – women and children –

whose cry is: "Our Lord, rescue us from this town, whose people are oppressors; and raise for us from thee one who will help!'"

We – with Allah's help – call upon every Muslim who believes in Allah and wishes to be rewarded to comply with Allah's order to kill the Americans and plunder their money wherever and whenever they find it. We also call upon Muslim ulema, leaders, youths and soldiers to launch the raid on Satan's US troops and the devil's supporters allying with them, and to displace those who are behind them so that they may learn a lesson.

Almighty Allah said: 'O, ye who believe, give your response to Allah and His Apostle, when He calleth you to that which will give you life. And know that Allah cometh between a man and his heart, and that it is He to whom ye shall all be gathered.'

Almighty Allah also says: 'O, ye who believe, what is the matter with you, that when you are asked to go forth in the cause of Allah, ye cling so heavily to the earth! Do ye prefer the life of this world to the hereafter? But little is the comfort of this life, as compared with the hereafter. Unless ye go forth, he will punish you with a grievous penalty, and put others in your place; but him ye will not harm in the least. For Allah hath power over all things.'

Almighty Allah also says: 'So lose no heart, nor fall into despair. For you must gain mastery if ye are true in faith'.

Most people will not have seen a full version, so this long quotation should be helpful. For here is as good a description of *salafiyya* doctrine as one could hope to find anywhere – the many fatwas issued by bin Laden in October 2001 and afterwards really do no more than to add to what he states here. It also demonstrates, for instance, the way he uses both the Quran and the Hadith, the latter being the authenticated sayings of Muhammad not contained in the Quran itself.

Saudi Arabia is the holiest part of Islam, because of the presence of the two special cities, Mecca and Medina. Next in holiness is Jerusalem, and then Baghdad, for so long capital of the Abbasid Caliphate, Islam's Golden Age. Note that it is the presence of Americans – infidels – on sacred Saudi soil and the need to get rid of them to restore Saudi 'purity' that so preoccupies bin Laden; pronouncements on the Palestinian issue would come later. This was underlined by the Islamic specialist Olivier Roy in the *New York Times* on 22 July 2005 – with bin Laden's ultimate aim being not to help the Palestinians, but to build a theocratic Islamic Caliphate that will restore Muslim power.

Psychologically the wording is interestingly similar to much fascist literature of the 1930s, in which Jews were described as infections in pure Aryan (or Romanian, in the case of that country) soil. Roger Griffin, a British authority on fascism, describes this phenomenon as 'palingenetics', or myth-based ultra-nationalism. Griffin argues that fascism is an 'of-this-world', secular ideology, but that the Romanian version was strongly religious. I would argue that it is legitimate to apply the palingenetics paradigm to religious nationalism as well.

It is therefore possible to say that extremist *salafiyya* Islam wants to restore an Islamic mythical nation, religiously pure and unsullied, in the same way that Nazis and Iron Guard fascists wanted to restore a Jewish-free, racially pure German or Dacian country.

In his fatwas in October and November 2001 bin Laden referred to Islam as being a nation, and the struggle as being religious. So it is not pushing an analogy too far to say that bin Laden is advocating a new kind of religious nationalism. In his case it is the whole *Dar al-Islam* (Realm of Islam), the entire Muslim umma from Morocco to Indonesia, as opposed to the more geographically limited Third Reich or Greater Romania of the 1930s. The precise words may be different, but the phenomenon is the same.

But it is Islamic rather than local nationalism that is being advocated. Bin Laden protests at the way in which the West divided the *Dar al-Islam*, a division that began with the decline and then the fall of the Ottoman Empire. While the Western powers did not intend to commit a religious act – it was Ataturk and the Turkish Parliament that abolished the post of Caliph – this is, in the view of many commentators, not believed in the Muslim world.

The same, perhaps, is true of the creation of first the Jewish mandate and then Israel itself – it was a positive move in favour of Jews rather than an attempt to deprive good Muslims of land. (This, of course, is not how the Palestinian majority saw the arrival of Jewish settlers at the time, since they were in full occupation of the territory. Nor have they seen it that way since.)

We know now that one kind of suffering – that of Jews being persecuted in Europe – led in time to another kind, that of dispossessed Palestinians. Unfortunately, those who made Jewish settlement possible in the first place, such as Winston Churchill in 1921, did not foresee that the consequences of their actions would be with us still.

In any case, at that time there were more Palestinian Christians than there are now – in many ways they are the group that has suffered the most. As the *Economist* noted in late 2001, two-thirds or more of Arab-Americans, including those from Palestine, are of Christian not Muslim origin.

Gilles Kepel and Michael Scott Doran also make the significant point that in the Middle East, it is the local rulers who are the main enemy of the jihadists rather than the West. They point out that bin Laden in attacking the USA is trying to attack an enemy of Islam – he calls the USA *Harbal*, the name for a pre-Islamic idol and false god – but in so doing is thereby hoping to destroy the one superpower that keeps the corrupt and despotic House of Saud in being. But for America, the view goes, the Saudi regime would collapse and the peninsula could return to pure Islamic rule once again.

According to such extremists, America is the far enemy, the local regimes the near one. Destroy the ability or desire of the far enemy to support the near enemy and the local apostate regimes will crumble.

As many newspaper articles in July 2005 pointed out, the radicals will use 'hot button' issues to gain support. Palestine, Iraq after 2003, the crushing of dissent in Egypt and Algeria – all these are causes that can win over the Arab Street, and maybe recruit some to the Basement. But all these are means to an end, rather than the principal goal itself.

For as Michael Scott Doran reminds us, the attempts by the Islamic revolutionaries to succeed in taking over, other than in Iran, have all proved futile. Furthermore, despotic regimes are far more ruthless than any in the West at crushing dissent, as the deaths of over 100,000 people in Algeria bear witness. (Many of these were by government forces – but thousands of ordinary Algerians also died at the hands of the Islamists, who thereby proved themselves good pupils of ibn Taymiyya and Sayyid Qutb, in that the extremists were willing to shed the blood of their fellow Muslims, whom they regarded as inadequately Islamic or compromised by secular values.) One could argue therefore that it was because the attempt to overthrow the near enemy was failing – for example after the assassination of President Sadat of Egypt when the Egyptian people failed to rise in support of the supporters of jihad – that Islamic extremists such as bin Laden shifted their attention to the far enemy, the West.

Specialists differ on what this implies for the future of Islamic terror. Gilles Kepel, for example, the author of *The War for Muslim Minds*, feels that the supporters of jihad are on the decline, whereas Malise Ruthven, in *A Fury for God*, thinks otherwise. The events in Britain in 2005 seem to suggest that the latter is right, since there is now a growing constituency among Muslims in Europe for extremist action. The majority of Muslims in the West are certainly against such atrocities, and have issued fatwas of their own to condemn them, but it only takes a very few recruits to cause completely disproportionate mayhem.

Iraq, the Palestine issue – often called the cancer at the heart of the Middle East – and the new danger of a nuclear Iran: all these add together to make the region as crucial as ever in the geopolitics of the early twenty-first century. Iran remains unpredictable. Few foresaw a moderate president being replaced by a hard-liner. Then, in Israel, the end of the Likud era, with a new, comparatively moderate party, Kadima, coming to power, was also unexpected. The same could be said for the Palestinian Authority area, when the inhabitants elected not the perennial PLO, but Hamas, a religious party, rejectionist in regard to Israel. Few brave pundits would have foretold in early 2005 what events would come later in the year, and in early 2006.

However, it is what happens in Iraq that will surely prove crucial so far as the Middle East is concerned. Much depends on whether Iraq can hold together, and on how Sunni Muslims and Kurds react to majority Shiite rule, even if there is some kind of coalition government. Certainly as the Egyptian, Jordanian and Algerian experience has shown, local governments can be far more ruthless in suppressing dissent than more liberally inclined Western regimes. An authentically Iraqi regime could thus be draconian with continued Sunni Al Qaeda-linked terrorism. But that in turn could also make the situation worse, rather than better, especially if it escalates into full-scale civil war.

We must hope for the best, for that is what the people of the Middle East so richly deserve after a century of foreign rule and internal conflict. But, as Zhou Enlai is famously supposed to have said about the long-term effects of the French Revolution, it is still too early to tell . . .

12

CASTING LEAD AND SUMMER RAINS

The politics of the Middle East are as incendiary as they have ever been. The focus of global initiatives for peace, no prospect of resolving the situation has yet proven to be sustainable.

At the end of 2006 optimism momentarily took root in the Israel–Palestine dispute, when Israel decided to withdraw its settlements from Gaza. Ehud Olmert, the then-new Israeli prime minister, had decided that since it was important for Israel to maintain its fully democratic status, to have within its state borders a potentially Arab majority was unwise. The case he made to an invited London audience not long before becoming prime minister was convincing, and left many hoping for concrete improvement. This was, however, not to be.

Iraq has suffered from major problems since 2006, but at the time of writing, civil war has not erupted, the withdrawal of most Western troops has happened without disaster and while life there cannot be described as ideal, it is certainly far better than pessimists feared it might be even a few years ago.

The Palestine-Israel-Lebanon situation is far worse, with war breaking out in 2006 and further bloodshed and conflict occurring in 2008–9. In mid–2010 the region is as tense as ever, with Gaza as much in the headlines as before, and no end to the decades–old conflict in sight.

As for Iran, which we will look at in the next chapter, the threat of nuclear escalation remains very strong, with the hard-liners appearing even more repressive than before.

The year 2006 saw two wars, both involving Israel. Casualties materialized on all sides, the extent of which are still hotly contested thanks to the waging of simultaneous propaganda wars. The Second Lebanon War (also called the July War) was a brief conflict between Israel and Hizbollah, the radical Lebanon-based Shiite group with close links to fellow Shiites in Iran. Hizbollah, led by Hassan Nasrallah, had grown increasingly powerful since the Lebanese civil war of the 1980s. The rapidly expanding Shiite population perceived Hizbollah as representing their interests and aspirations, as well as acting as a proxy for their theological and ideological allies in Iran. This perception enabled the Islamic Republic of Iran to become a major player in the Middle Eastern conflict without the Iranian state having to become directly involved.

Northern Israel had faced regular rocket attacks by Hizbollah fighters based on Lebanese soil, while the multi-faith (Christian/Sunni/Shia/Druze) government of Lebanon did all it could to stay out of the fighting. In July 2006 some of the rockets not only killed Israeli civilians but also some Israeli Defence Force (IDF) soldiers as well. Two of the IDF were also captured. Israel has a no-tolerance policy in relation to the capture of its citizens, so a massive Israeli attack on Hizbollah positions in Lebanon followed. Hizbollah retaliated by launching what they described as Operation Truthful Promise.

The fighting continued until August, with formal proceedings continuing until October 2006. This war, between Israel and Hizbollah (in which the Lebanese frequently found themselves in the way, despite the Government's neutrality) has been one of the most controversial wars fought in recent years. Unlike the Six Day War (5–10 June 1967) or that of Yom Kippur (6–26 October 1973), no side can truly be said to have won, despite what each side has declared for itself.

Cities and settlements within Israel were hit by approximately 13,000 Hizbollah rockets – mainly the Ra'ad 1 and Fajr-3 – which were clearly of Iranian derivation (it is also said that some Iranian Revolutionary Guards fought alongside Hizbollah militants). In return, Israeli bombers struck the Lebanese capital Beirut, in which the Hizbollah headquarters was a key target. Consequently there were civilian casualties on both sides, with the exact numbers, as always, being disputed.

In September 2006 Hassan Nasrallah declared that Hizbollah had won the war amid scenes of enormous rejoicing among the Shiite population. Israeli opinion polls pointed to uncertainty as to who, if anyone, had been victorious, and the former defence minister Moshe Arens proclaimed that Israel had lost. Over a quarter of a million Israeli citizens had to be evacuated temporarily from their homes in northern Israel and it was not until two years later, in 2008, that the two captured IDF soldiers were returned home.

Much discussion at the time revolved around the fact that Ehud Olmert, the prime minister (and a former Mayor of Jerusalem) was the first Israeli prime minister never to have served in the Defence Forces. The Chief of Staff, Dan Halutz was, by contrast, an airman and not a soldier. This became an important consideration given that the air force tried to achieve Israel's aims by bombing as much as by land-based strikes, with mixed results. Olmert became unpopular and subsequently had to resign in relation to possible corruption charges, and Halutz was compelled to retire in early 2007. For many the myth of Israeli invincibility had finally been punctured, and that remains the view of commentators today. However, the situation is slightly more complex than that, and a more nuanced understanding is possible to achieve.

In November 2006, Sir John Keegan, former Royal Military Academy Sandhurst lecturer and noted military historian, argued that the Israelis had not, in fact, been defeated. What had helped Hizbollah resist Israeli bombing raids was their tunnel system, which was similar to that which the Vietcong had employed to get their troops (literally) under American lines back in the 1960s and 1970s. Broadcaster Al Jazeera – notably based in Sunni-dominated Qatr – commented on another of Hizbollah's tactics, namely that many of the Hizbollah rockets were launched from civilian areas, thereby endangering inhabitants to Israeli reprisals. (According to Amnesty International, Hizbollah frequently uses civilians as human shields.) Despite these tactics, Hizbollah was hit badly, so much so that – as former Israeli general and Prime Minister Ehud Barak commented – they were unable to assist Hamas and the Gaza militants. With Hizbollah compromised, the power to launch further and even more damaging raids on Israeli territory had been severely curtailed.

In addition, the fact that Hizbollah is a Shiite organization with close ties to Iran has not made them popular in the Sunni majority states. During the 2006 conflict, the Arab League carefully supported Lebanon rather than Hizbollah. The latter were also condemned by Saudi Arabia, whose strict Wahhabi interpretation of Islam does not legitimate the Shiite version of that faith. (Though this does not prevent Shiite Iran supporting Sunni Hamas, as we shall see later.) Fear of a 'Shiite Crescent' still influences states such as Egypt, Jordan and Saudi Arabia, which in turn shapes their relationship to Hizbollah. Saudi Arabia is especially anxious about the possible development of a 'Shiite Crescent', since so much of the oil-rich territory under its sand has Shiite inhabitants.

To return to the influence of Sir John Keegan's argument, it might be better to suggest that no one won the Second Lebanon War, and that a stalemate still exists. Predictions of a new war on Lebanese soil have proved unfounded – so far.

As for Gaza, which for the last five years has continuously been in the news, no sign of peace being restored has yet materialized. The first intrusion against Gaza – after the Israelis had withdrawn their troops and settlers by the end of 2005 – was Operation Summer Rains (June–November 2006), whose last action was codenamed Autumn Clouds. The fact that Operation Summer Rains followed the Hamas victory in the elections for the Palestinian Authority area is no coincidence given Hamas' continued refusal to recognize the existence of the state of Israel.

The Hamas victory in the Palestinian Authority elections on 9 January 2006 has certainly changed the already complex situation in the Middle East. Hamas is a body that for religious reasons rejects permanently the right of Israel to exist at all. Unusually, this Sunni Muslim group is supported by Shiite

Iran, a link that – crucially – enables Iran to be a major player in the region in a way that has not before been possible.

Harakat al-Muqawama al-Islamiyya (Islamic Resistance Movement) – Hamas – is a body that is Islamic by name. This makes it by definition different from the Palestine Liberation Organization (PLO), one of whose leading representatives, Hanan Ashrawi, is, for instance, both a woman and a Christian as well as being a long-standing Palestinian nationalist. Though it is possible to be a supporter of the PLO as well as being a Christian, this is not the case with Hamas, which is entirely Islamic in its goals and outlook – a crucial distinction between the two organizations.

Hamas formally dates back to 1987. However the practice of Islamic-based opposition to any kind of non-Muslim presence in the region goes back much further. In this sense, one of Hamas' religious and ideological forbears is Sheikh Izz ad-Din al-Qassam (1882–1935), after whom the rockets propelled against Israel are named. It is significant that, in defining Hamas identity, Sheikh Izz ad-Din al-Qassam – killed in a shootout with the British in 1935 – was a Syrian and not a Palestinian. This is noteworthy because Hamas, much like the PLO, is nationalist organization. One resolution to the possible conflict posed by nationalism in defining such organizations requires reference to a particular Muslim vision of a pure Islamic state in which arcane, Western constructions such as Syrian, Palestinian and Jordanian become irrelevant, and a much larger body defined by the borders of the seventh-century Islamic Caliphate become the new focus.

As many commentators, including Beverley Milton-Edwards and Stephen Farrell in their book *Hamas: The Islamic*

Resistance Movement (2010), have written, there is more to Hamas than just extremism and violence. As one member of the Israeli security apparatus once stated, for many Palestinians the issue is simple and has little to do with extremism: would you rather be ill in a Hamas hospital or one run by the Fatah wing of the PLO? Another example, articulated by Israeli journalist Nathan Shachar, is that the choice in January 2006 for ordinary voters in Gaza and the West Bank was very straightforward: clean-living, incorruptible Hamas or deeply corrupt and factional Fatah? At the time of the elections, Hamas – thanks in large part to extensive funding from friendly devout Muslims in places such as Saudi Arabia – had an enormous welfare organization, schools, hospitals (usually free for patients and supplicants, with no bribes necessary); whereas the cost of getting anything done in Fatah-controlled areas required a great deal of corruption and even greater expense.

This domestic Palestinian point of view stood in contrast to that of the outside world, whose leadership in places like the US, along with Britain (and other European Union countries) expressed astonishment when Hamas won the election in January 2006. Surely most Palestinians wanted to be ruled by those working for peace, many journalists questioned, for a two-state solution that would guarantee an independent Palestine living in peaceful coexistence with Israel? In fact the likelihood is that most Palestinians had voted, like people the world over, for entirely domestic concerns unrelated to international affairs. The outcome did, however, pose a major problem for the West, especially for the Bush regime, given that the US had invaded Iraq in 2003 with the long-term goal of introducing democracy to the Middle East. Now here, in

2006, in the Palestinian Authority, the people had indeed voted democratically – for an organization that the international community considered to be terrorist. In 2006, the West sided with the election losers, Fatah.

This outcome is reflected upon in the work of Indian-born American thinker and writer Fareed Zakaria, whose book *The Future of Freedom: Illiberal Democracy at Home and Abroad* (2007) espouses the view that when people vote, they do not necessarily do so for liberal, democratic, pluralist parties. Voters are as capable of freely choosing profoundly illiberal and even repressive governments, if that is what they want to do.

President Abbas of the Palestinian Authority area refused to accept the election result. It took until 2007 for Saudi Arabia to broker a Fatah–Hamas government, a compromise that did not last long and soon saw the region engulfed in a virtual civil war. In effect Gaza was controlled by Hamas, the West Bank was controlled by Fatah, and what was supposed to be a two-state solution rapidly became three states: Israel, Palestine/Fatah-controlled West Bank and Palestine/Hamas-controlled Gaza. Not only was all of this unacceptable to the PLO/Fatah regime, and to the West, but also to the Israelis, who saw Hamas as a major threat to regional peace.

The trigger for Israel's attacks on Gaza was the kidnapping of Corporal Shalit of the Israeli Defence Force. At the time of writing, Corporal Shalit is still in the hands of Hamas several years after his initial capture. In addition, Qassam rockets have continued to bombard parts of southern Israel, which has also proven to be a major provocation.

As with the conflict in Lebanon, Operation Summer Rains became ferocious both in the way in which both sides fought and in the reaction of the international community. Hamas used civilians as human shields and hospitals and schools to launch attacks against the Israelis. The IDF focused their retaliation by attacking those locations that had attacked them, resulting in hospitals and schools absorbing hits from Israeli planes. Many civilians died as a consequence, and much of the blame has been allocated to Israel. Hamas' use of Qassam rockets has killed many Israeli civilians, while the IDF's use of white phosphorous has had a similar outcome on the Palestinian population. These tactics have attracted heavy criticism for both sides.

In fact Gaza suffered from not one, but two, conflicts during this time period. In June 2007 Fatah, who still controlled the West Bank and the Presidency of the Palestinian Authority, and Hamas, in Gaza, launched vicious attacks upon each other in which many were killed. Civilians once again found themselves in the middle of the fighting, with fatal results. Human Rights Watch commented on this internecine struggle (which Hamas won in terms of gaining total control of Gaza) on their website from 2007–10:

> These attacks by both Hamas and Fatah constitute brutal assaults on the most fundamental humanitarian principles. The murder of civilians not engaged in hostilities and the wilful killing of captives are war crimes, pure and simple.

What is distinct about the reading of this particular conflict is that it didn't pit Palestinians against Israelis, but against other Palestinians. In some cases it has become easy for media and public opinion to blame Israel, but this incidence of violence was committed by two groups of Palestinians against their own people, with appalling results.

The Egyptian-sponsored ceasefire, or 'lull', between Israel and Gaza lasted until December 2008. As soon as it finished, Hamas once again unleashed Qassam rockets against Israel. In this new chapter of the conflict, the Al-Quds Brigades of the Palestinian Islamic Jihad also became active in the fighting. In retaliation, the Israelis launched a new assault on Gaza, which they called Operation Cast Lead. Phase One involved bombings by the Israeli Air Force and a second attack by the IDF directly into Gaza followed early in the New Year, January 2009. Once again the fighting proved immensely controversial, made more complicated by the fact that Israel was able to ban much of the foreign media from entering Gaza. As before, the use of rockets by one side and white phosphorous by the other created international furore, and the Israeli bombing of the United Nations Relief and Works Agency office in Gaza, with resultant civilian casualties, aroused widespread condemnation.

Trying to identify precisely how many died in Cast Lead shows how hard it is to gain accurate figures, with each side exaggerating or diminishing the claims of the other. One statistic puts the Palestinian deaths at around 1,100; others put it to well over 1,600, which is quite a major discrepancy. By now it is probably impossible to verify either way. However, even the lower figure represents a high loss of life.

The United Nations asked an eminent South African judge, Richard Goldstone, to investigate the conflict, which he did in autumn 2009. Given that he was criticized by both sides and therefore did not hesitate to condemn human rights abuses by both Israel and Hamas, Goldstone's resulting research was perceived to not suffer from bias. That being said, Goldstone did comment that he had been issued a 'one-sided mandate', since his remit did not, for example, expand to cover Hamas atrocities against fellow Palestinians during the struggle with Fatah to control Gaza.

Israelis often protest in the media, when interviewed for television and radio, and in newspapers that they are held accountable to a much higher standard than those of their neighbours, which is worth noting in consideration of the frequent role of bias in reportage emerging about this conflict.

While at the time of writing there is no actual conflict in the Gaza area, that narrow strip of land continues to be in the news. In late May 2010 a flotilla of aid ships set off with supplies, aiming to break the embargo that Israel has placed on all potentially dangerous supplies entering the Gaza Strip. Most of the boats were manned by Western peace activists of various descriptions, and were certainly not armed – with the alleged exception of one of the boats. The *MV Mavi Marmora* was chartered by a Turkish organization, the IHH (Turkish Foundation for Human Rights and Freedoms and Humanitarian Relief), which some speculate has close links to violent jihadist groups in the Middle East. When Israeli commandos stormed the flotilla, most boats presented no retaliation, though the IDF gained bad publicity on YouTube and similar popular media outlets for using force against peaceful protesters. But the Turkish boat was armed, shots were exchanged, and several Turks were killed – their bodies flown home and buried ceremoniously as martyrs to the Islamic cause. The Turkish government was forthright in its condemnation of Israel, which in turn defended itself strongly in the international media.

The general consensus was that Israel had erred, especially since the country's enemies, such as Iran, were able to use the event as an excuse to portray Israel in the worst possible light. However, some commentators argued that the events played out in such as manner that suggested that Turkey supports the Islamic cause in the Middle East. This, it was suggested, could be good news for Israel, if it meant that democratic Turkey might then become a key player in regional affairs. Turkey presents a very particular role model in the context of the Middle East in that in the eyes of some, it is considered to endorse democratic, pluralist and Western-friendly values in the context of a Muslim state.

Can there be peace in the Middle East? Countless American presidents and their special emissaries have done their best to support such an outcome, in conjunction with former British Prime Minister Tony Blair. One response lies in a May 2010 publication in the influential magazine of the Carnegie Endowment for International Peace, *Foreign Policy*. The article, entitled 'The False Religion of Middle East Peace: And Why I'm no Longer a Believer', was written by Aaron Miller, who had been for three decades an American State Department Analyst and Negotiator (1978–2003). After advising six US Secretaries of State and having met all the major players in the region for over thirty years, Miller no longer believes that American intervention can secure the ever-elusive goal of peace.

Is this a counsel of despair? Certainly there have been no meaningful breakthroughs in decades. And, as we shall see in the next chapter, if nuclear war breaks out, then even the Six Day War would appear modest. It would be wonderful to think that one glorious day peace could come. But it might alas be a long way off – if it comes at all, and as experts such as Benny Morris have reminded us, the prospects, however desirable, are still tragically remote.

13

A DIFFERENT KIND OF MARTYR?

In Iran during the war with Iraq (1980–88), thousands of children died clearing minefields, blown up to prepare the way for the troops behind them. These victims were deemed martyrs for the cause of the Islamic Revolution, and are deeply revered and widely commemorated as patriots by the religious establishment, government and, to be fair, many ordinary Iranians.

20 June 2009 produced a very different kind of martyr in Iran, one for the Green Movement. The Green Movement stood in opposition to the rule of the Shiite theocracy and their nominee, President Ahmadinejad, the supposed – and hotly disputed – winner of the 2009 presidential election in Iran. Neda Agha Soltan was everything that a religious martyr is conventionally not: female, photogenic, divorced, in favour of secular rule and democracy and well educated. The twenty-six-year-old student was murdered by the *Basij* militia on 20 June 2009, and this being 2009, the event was recorded online. The mobile phone footage of her death flashed around the world and caused outrage among Iranian demonstrators and supporters of human rights and democracy.

The Internet (and YouTube in particular) transformed Neda Agha Soltan's death into a very different cult of martyrdom, one that the authorities, who have done everything possible to crush even the smallest forms of dissent ever since, disapprove of. The film about her life by British director Anthony Thomas, *For Neda*, is banned in Iran. However, her cause still recruits supporters, in much the same way that Ayatollah Khomeini's illegal tapes were listened to discreetly in the days before the overthrow of the Shah in 1979. Supporting her cause is contentious and dangerous in Iran – Neda Agha Soltan's grave has been desecrated six or more times, her boyfriend was tortured and is now exiled, as is the doctor who tried in vain to save Neda's life. By contrast, in the United Kingdom, Oxford University reacted by founding a scholarship in her name. Much scholarship has emerged as a result of Neda's death. On the first anniversary of the Green Movement demonstrations, British human rights lawyer Geoffrey Robertson pointed out in the UK's *Guardian* newspaper that the effects of Neda's death have not been straightforward. Pre-eminent American Iran expert William Polk, seen by the last Shah as one of his key opponents, echoes this thought in his book *Understanding Iran* (2009).

Advocates of democracy supported the election of Mir Hossein Mousavi as president of Iran. While some reports suggested that this outcome might have been a possibility, these reports inevitably suffered from the bias dictated by their urban, English-speaking operating basis. This reportage therefore ignored the views of those living in the countryside or in the poorer towns far from the capital. Though the educated urban elite – from which background Neda came –

may have supported Mousavi, this may not have been the case in the countryside.

There is little doubt that the Iranian elections were rigged, and that Ahmadinejad's margin of victory was thereby substantially increased; however it is possible that he would have won anyway. Given this possibility, the scale of election fraud reflects anxiety on the part of the theocracy, which engaged in ballot rigging beyond what was necessary in order to ensure that their candidate secured victory.

As Geoffrey Robertson reminds us, Mousavi is also no saint. In 1988, thousands of political prisoners were hanged or otherwise killed in Tehran's notorious Evin prison. At the time of these hangings, the president was Ayatollah Khomeini (the Supreme Leader), the commander of the Revolutionary Guard was Rafsanjani (the 'moderate' candidate in the previous presidential election against Ahmadinejad) while the prime minister in 1988 was no less than Mousavi himself. As a recent human rights investigation into the 1988 murders has demonstrated, Mousavi has never apologized for, or explained, his part in the killings.

Despite the fact that, much like Ahmadinejad, Mousavi is in favour of the development of an Iranian nuclear weapons programme, compared to his opponents, there is no question that Mousavi represents much more commonality with Western values. Mousavi's potential leadership has been the cause of much speculation: having been prime minister during the slaughter of the Iran–Iraq war, he may be less inclined to sanction this type of war again; the rights of women might be more respected; the ability to discuss contentious matters might be allowed once again; and while Iran would still be a predominantly Shiite theocracy, it would also be a country increasingly willing to implement democratic policies. This, in turn, might produce more adherences to human rights than the oppressive Sunni Muslim regimes notionally allied to the West.

All of this discussion is relevant to the key issue that keeps Iran in the international news, from Israel to Britain and from the United States to parts of the Middle East: nuclear weapons. Back in the pre-1979 days of the Shah, the United States did little to discourage the Iranians from developing nuclear power, whether for peaceful purposes only, or covertly for military reasons, since the Shah was then seen (later to his own disadvantage) to be America's policeman in the economically vital Gulf area. The advent of the Islamic Republic changed American perspective drastically. However for a long time Iran was not economically capable of undertaking nuclear research of any description, let alone launching a warhead capable of destroying Israel.

Recent research provided by Israeli writer Dr Ronen Bergman in his chilling book *The Secret War with Iran: The 30-Year Covert Struggle for Control of a 'Rogue' State* (2008) demonstrates that, astonishingly, Israel and Iran actually collaborated on many military issues in the 1980s, on the basis that 'my enemy's enemy is my friend'. Both states regarded Iraq as a major danger to their respective national security, and as a result, to use one example, Israeli jets destroyed Saddam Hussein's attempt to develop nuclear weapons capability of his own.

But as Bergman also demonstrates, when the Ayatollahs decided to launch a similar attack aimed at Israel, the situation changed yet once again. Ahmadinejad has called for the annihilation of Israel, and while leading theocrats are aware that such an attack would result in the retaliatory destruction of much of their own country, concern for a potential nuclear war motivated by religious beliefs does pose a constant threat.

Nuclear war is very much the worst-case scenario. But as we have just seen, comparatively moderate Iranians whose main motivation is patriotic rather than religious also support the existence of an Iranian nuclear programme, Mousavi among them. Would Saddam Hussein have attacked a nuclear-armed Iran? Would the US attack an Islamic Republic in possession of long-range nuclear warheads in the same way that they invaded and conquered a post-Osiris Iraq? The answer to both is surely no, and so the desire of ordinary Iranians to possess nuclear missile capability, not designed to attack Israel or any other country, but to defend Iran against outside aggression, is understandable.

Dr Bergman's sources are very close to the inner security apparatus of the Israeli state. As such, his research makes clear that his country regards the potential Iranian possession of long-range nuclear warheads capable of striking Israel as a reality that would not be tolerated. The projected Middle Eastern reply to this lack of tolerance exposes the hypocrisy of the West: Israel has not been asked to demolish its nuclear missiles, and both Pakistan and India have been forgiven for their continued possession of an even bigger and far more lethal arsenal, one that came very close to being unleashed in 2002.

But there is perhaps an even bigger danger to a nuclear-armed Iran. Iran is Shia, and Iraq's Shiite majority now wields power. The predominantly Sunni states of the Middle East, such as Saudi Arabia and Egypt, regard the emergence of what they describe as a 'Shiite Crescent' with severe alarm, especially Saudi Arabia, whose large Shiite minority are housed in some of the most oil-rich parts of the kingdom. A nuclear-weapon-capable Iran would pose a threat to Sunni dictatorships as well as to Israel. If the Islamic Republic had a nuclear capacity, they would feel obliged to follow suit, not necessarily in order to aggress, but also in order to defend. The potential for a Middle Eastern nuclear arms race has the potential to resemble the Cold War (1947–91) conflict between the capitalist West and communist East.

Given this analogy, the real danger of President Ahmadinejad and the Ayatollahs having the ability to launch nuclear weapons can be framed in relation to the Cold War. First, during the Cold War both the US and Russia were regarded as 'rational actors', in ordinary English states that had leaders who did not wish to see the destruction of their own countries as a result of nuclear war. It is with good reason that what could have developed into World War III was otherwise named 'Mutually Assured Destruction', or MAD. Armageddon never took place and the Cold War is now over, even if its repercussions are still felt today. Most ordinary Iranians would also act as rational actors, as would, for example, previous Iranian President Khatami (who served from 1997–2005), or a President Mousavi, in the unlikely event that he or someone espousing his views ever achieved power. A nuclear Iran would pose considerable threat, especially for Israel and nearby Sunni Arab countries. However, in the same way that the doctrine of MAD prevented the Cold War from becoming 'hot', it has the potential to prevent the possibility of an Israeli–Iranian nuclear exchange.

Does Ahmadinejad, and those who believe that conflict might actually assist the return of the Hidden Imam, endorse nuclear Israeli–Iranian conflict? Some experts in the West think that this is unlikely, since deep down even the theocrats are rational actors. But as Yale Divinity School Professor Lamin Sanneh (himself a convert from Islam to Roman Catholicism) reminds us in his book *Piety and Power* (1996), the secular West under-estimates the depth of religion at its peril. The West may have fought its last religious wars in the seventeenth century, but in other parts of our planet it remains a prime motivation, a helpful point Israeli historian Benny Morris has argued, as we saw earlier, along with American scholars such as Mark Juergensmeyer, whose many academic works reinforce this point.

Rational actors do not want to die. In terms of terrorism, for example, there is a conceptual difference between, say, Basque nationalist organization ETA and the Irish IRA, most of whose members wanted to inflict some casualties on the enemy without wanting to die for their cause themselves. This approach is different from the religious terrorism of the post-9/11 world, where some perpetrators actually seek death in the pursuit of as many casualties as possible. The IRA was a devoutly Catholic organization, at least in name, but unlike other religious organizations, they never endorsed the belief that to lose one's life in the pursuit of war would bring heavenly reward. By contrast, the idea of martyrdom is wired into many of the extreme forms of Islam, and features especially in the Shiite version. Martyrdom also includes a rich historical precedent – consider for example the loss of Hussein in 680 BC at the Battle of Karbala.

As the Pakistani-born writer and thinker Akbar Ahmed has frequently reminded us, millions of Muslims loathe and despise this view of martyrdom, all the more so because they regard it as discrediting their faith in the eyes of others. Many experts have warned against regarding Islamic hardliners as representative of the norm, including Georgetown Professor of Islamic Studies and International Relations, John Esposito.

To summarize, for some in the Middle East, death in combat is something that can be seen to be desirable, in that it achieves the reward of heaven. While millions throughout the Middle East contest such an interpretation, many secular Westerners find it incomprehensible. That being said, for those espousing a radically different viewpoint, the secularity of the West is precisely the problem.

The world is replete with different points of view. Attitudes about the consequences of possessing nuclear weapons are likely to be as faithful to the outlooks on life that accompany them. As such, and despite allegations that engendering such an attitude has been said to constitute scare-mongering and pandering to Western/Israeli fears, it follows that in the twenty-first century there are national leaders whose motivations are primarily loyal to histories that extend back to the seventh century, and not to the alien, contemporary demands of an international community.

This is a point also made by Middle Eastern authority Amir Taheri in his book *The Persian Night* (2009). In the West, with realist doctrine going back centuries, diplomacy is all about relations between states, which means that countries, and not the ideologies behind them, become focal points. For example, Iran both exists as a nation-state as well as an Islamic Republic that believes in the return of the Hidden Imam, and in exporting Shiite Islam well beyond the political borders of a single country. This, Taheri argues, makes Iran a 'Dr Jekyll and Mr Hyde nation', a nation-state with a powerful guiding orthodoxy that disrupts ordinary state behaviour.

However, as Taheri also goes on to say, not all Shiites would regard the Iranian interpretation of Islam as correct. Ayatollah Sistani in Iraq is equal to even Khomeini in theological authority but has a very different, much less theocratic view of Shia Islam, for example. The Ismaili sect of Shiism has further theological differences still.

But when President Ahmadinejad referred to his mystic experience when addressing the UN General Assembly in September 2006, with the Hidden Imam in the audience, bathed in a strange light, one can see that for the ruling elite in Iran it is their interpretation of Shiite Islam that actually matters. Experts may be right in hypothesizing that Iran will prove rational and act in a realist fashion in the case of war, but if they are wrong, the consequences of having irrational actors in charge of long-range nuclear weapons could be devastating.

Many are critical of what in the Middle East is perceived as Western hypocrisy, namely that Israel, India and Pakistan can all have nuclear weapons, especially the former, but Iran cannot. It is also important that the threat of Israel also extends to nations such as Egypt, Saudi Arabia and the Gulf States. A nuclear Iran would create exactly the kind of arms race that many perceived to be over, and yet which would have far-reaching implications both in the Middle East and elsewhere.

Furthermore, at the time of writing Iran is winning a major propaganda battle for the hearts and minds of street-level

Sunnis in Arab countries, as they support Hamas in Palestine, Hizbollah in Lebanon and aid those perceived as standing up most to Israel throughout the region. This makes the position of non-democratic Sunni regimes even more perilous, as the Iranians, while zealously Shia, emphasize their Islamic nature over and above any doctrinal differences, in a quest to export revolutionary values throughout the Middle East. This makes nations such as Saudi Arabia and Egypt even more nervous – they all remember the fate of the Shah and the pre-1979 Iranian elite – and thus keener still on matching any weapons that Iran comes to possess in order to defend themselves from the theocrats of Tehran.

Iranian issues are, therefore, complex, with the stability of one of the world's most volatile yet economically critical parts at stake in a starker way than ever before. Not only that, but Hiroshima and Nagasaki are the only two atomic/nuclear bombs to have been dropped, over six decades ago now. Had the 2002 Pakistan/India stand-off escalated, it is estimated that fifty-six million Pakistanis and Indians would have died in the first nuclear exchange, and that the winds could have blown radioactive material either westwards towards Iran and Central Asia or eastwards towards China and South-East Asia, with further casualties still. A similar exchange between Israel and Iran could have similar consequences for far more neighbouring countries, since radiation does not halt at national borders. It would be the first nuclear conflict in history, over twenty years after the end of the Cold War, and one of the reasons why peace in the Middle East continues to be one of the most critical issues of our time.

A SELECTIVE CHRONOLOGY OF
THE MIDDLE EAST

This is a selective chronology – had it been inclusive, it would have been far too long. Since recent events are fluid, fewer of them have been included as it is hard to know what will prove significant in the long term. I am grateful to chronologies I have seen in the works of Jacob M. Fellure, Arthur Goldschmidt Jr and Bernard Lewis. When precise dates are unknown, the c. symbol has been used, and with ancient Egyptian dates, please refer to the relevant chapter.

BC

c. 3500	Sumerians begin to use the wheel
c. 3200	Sumerian civilization starts to use the world's first written language
c. 3100	Egypt united
c. 2100	Abraham, the founder of Judaism, born in Ur
c. 2000	The Babylonian civilization emerges
c. 1700	Hammurabi promulgates his law code

c. 1440	Moses promulgates the Ten Commandments
c. 1350	Akhenaten introduces worship of the Aten in Egypt
c. 1000	Unified Kingdom of Israel, under David and then Solomon, begins
c. 930	Israel splits into Israel in the north and Judah in the south
722	Israel beaten by the Assyrians
605	Nebuchadnezzar founds a new Babylonian empire
586	Judah conquered by the Babylonians and exiled to Babylon
539	Persians conquer the Babylonian Empire and soon let the Jews return home
c. 4 BC–AD 1	Birth of Jesus Christ, the founder of Christianity

AD

c. 29–33	Ministry and crucifixion of Jesus Christ
47–49	The Apostle Paul takes Christianity beyond its roots in Palestine
63	Pompey visits the great Nabataean civilization of Petra
66–70	First Jewish revolt
70	Romans capture Jerusalem and destroy the Temple
114–117	Second Jewish Revolt
132–135	Third Jewish Revolt
224	Sassanian dynasty begins in Persia
241–244	First of many wars between the Sassanians in Persia and the Roman Empire

297	Romans gain temporary advantage over Persia
303	Persecution against Christians by the Emperor Diocletian
306	Constantine becomes Emperor
312	Constantine legalizes Christianity
325	Council of Nicaea ratifies Christian doctrine
330	Constantinople founded (now called Istanbul)
c. 337–361	Further conflicts between Rome and Persia
381	Christianity becomes the official religion of the Roman Empire
c. 503–591	More Roman/Persian conflict, with truces in some years
c. 570	Probable birth of Muhammad, the founder of Islam
610	Muhammad receives the revelations that later form the Quran
614	The Persians temporarily capture Jerusalem
622	The flight of Muhammad and his followers to Medina: Islam's calendar begins
624	Battle of Badr, in which the Islamic forces prevail
628	Truce between Muhammad and the Meccans
628	Truce between Rome and the Sassanian Empire
630	Muhammad enters Mecca
632	Muhammad dies; Abu Bakr becomes First Caliph
634	Omar becomes Second Caliph
636	Muslims win the key battle of Yarmuk over the Persians
637	Muslims win the key battle of Qadissiya over the Byzantines
638	Muslims capture Jerusalem

639–642	Islamic conquest of Egypt
644	Uthman becomes Third Caliph
656	Ali, Muhammad's cousin and son-in-law, becomes Fourth Caliph
661	Ali murdered and the Umayyads seize power
661–750	The Umayyad Caliphate, based in Damascus
680	Battle of Karbala: the Sunni Umayyads beat the Shiites, and Ali's son Hussein is killed
691	Dome of the Rock built in Jerusalem
711–1492	The Islamic occupation of Spain
720	Muslim armies temporarily seize part of southern France
732	Battle of Tours/Poitiers rescues France from invaders
750–1258	Abbasid Caliphate, based in Baghdad after 762
786–809	Reign of the Caliph Harun al-Rashid
909	Beginnings of Fatimid rule in northern Africa, starting in Tunis
969–1171	Fatimid Caliphate based in Egypt
1071	Seljuk Turks defeat Byzantine forces at the Battle of Manzikert
1096	Crusaders from the West enter the region
1099	Crusaders capture Jerusalem
1171–1193	Reign of Saladin based in Cairo
1187	Saladin recaptures Jerusalem
1250–1517	Mamluk rule over Egypt
1258	Mongols sack Baghdad and massacre its inhabitants
1260	Mamluks beat the Mongols at the Battle of Ayn Jalut

1326	Ottomans capture Bursa in Anatolia
1354	First Ottoman incursion into Europe, in the Balkans
1389	Serbs lose the Battle of Kosovo
1451–1481	Reign of Ottoman Sultan Mehmed II (the Conqueror)
1453	Ottomans capture Constantinople, which becomes their new capital Istanbul
1492	Last Moors expelled from Spain
1517	Ottoman capture of Egypt (and also of the Holy Places, Mecca and Medina)
1520–1566	Reign of Ottoman Sultan, Suleiman the Magnificent
1529	First unsuccessful Ottoman siege of Vienna
1571	Ottoman navy beaten by Don John of Austria at Battle of Lepanto
1683	Second and final unsuccessful Ottoman siege of Vienna
1699	Treaty of Carlowitz – first major Ottoman territorial reverse
1774	Further Ottoman humiliation at the Treaty of Kuchuk Kainarji with Russia
1798–1801	French occupation of Egypt under Napoleon
1803	First Wahhabi occupation of Mecca and Medina
1805–1849	Mehmet Ali the effective ruler of Egypt, his dynasty lasting until 1952
1826	Sultan Mahmud II destroys the Janissaries
1829	Greece the first Balkan state to gain independence from the Ottomans
1830	Algeria seized by the French

1853–1856	Crimean War
1869	Suez Canal opened
1878	Ottoman Empire humiliated by Russia then rescued by Britain at the Congress of Berlin
1881	France seizes Tunis
1882	Britain takes effective control of Egypt
1901	Ibn Saud begins his long rule, beginning in Najd
1908	The Young Turk revolution
1912	Ottoman Empire loses Libya to Italy and territory in the First Balkan War
1913	Ottomans regain some territory in the Second Balkan War; CUP seizes power
1914	The Ottoman Empire sides with Germany in the First World War
1915–1916	Ottoman forces win against Britain and Australia at Gallipoli
1916	The Sykes–Picot agreement, which the British soon regret
1916–1918	The Arab Revolt led by the Hashemite clan, with T. E. Lawrence helping
1917	British and Australian forces capture Jerusalem and Baghdad
1918	Ottoman Empire defeated
1920	At San Remo, the Western allies carve up the Ottoman Empire into Mandates
1920–1922	Turkish war against Greece, won by the Turks under Mustapha Kemal
1921	Churchill creates Iraq and Transjordan at the Cairo Conference

1923	Victorious Turks sign new Treaty of Lausanne, expelling the Greeks
1923	Mustapha Kemal becomes Kemal Ataturk; the Ottoman Empire abolished
1924	Ataturk also abolishes the Caliphate; Ibn Saud conquers the Hijaz
1932	Notional Iraqi independence; Ibn Saud creates Saudi Arabia
1945	Syria and Lebanon gain independence from France
1948	Britain gives Israel independence, but the first Arab–Israeli war then follows
1949	Abdullah of Jordan seizes the West Bank and absorbs it into his country
1952	Coup in Egypt overthrows the monarchy
1954–1970	Nasser the ruler of Egypt
1956	The Suez debacle; Britain and France have to withdraw under American pressure
1958	Iraqi monarchy overthrown in bloodthirsty coup
1962	Slavery finally abolished in Saudi Arabia
1964	The PLO founded
1967	The Six Day War, won by Israel
1970	Nasser dies and succeeded as president by Sadat (until latter's murder in 1981)
1973	The Yom Kippur War: Israel wins but Egypt regains face
1973–1975	Initial phase of the Lebanese Civil War
1977–1983	Menachem Begin Prime Minister of Israel
1978	Camp David talks between Begin, Sadat and US President Jimmy Carter

1979	Overthrow of the Shah of Iran and the beginning of the Islamic Republic
1979	Egypt–Israel Peace Treaty (still in force); Saddam Hussein president of Iraq
1979–1981	American hostage crisis with US diplomats held in Tehran
1980–1988	Iran–Iraq war, with nearly a million casualties
1981	Sadat assassinated by Islamic extremists, some of whom later help form Al Qaeda
1982	Israelis invade Lebanon, Phalangists massacre civilians in Sabra and Chatilla
1987–1993	First Palestinian uprising, or Intifada
1989	Death of Ayatollah Khomeini; Ayatollah Khameini becomes Supreme Leader
1990	Iraq invades Kuwait
1991	US-led coalition expels Iraq from Kuwait: the Gulf War
1992	Palestinians and Israel start secret talks in Oslo
1993	Palestine/Israel accord signed in Washington DC
1994	Jordan/Israel Peace Treaty (still in force)
1995	Murder of Israeli Prime Minister Rabin by Jewish extremist
1998	First major fatwa by Osama bin Laden and Al Qaeda attack on US embassies
2000	Abortive Camp David discussions between PLO and Israel
2000	Second Palestinian Intifada begins (and still in progress)
2001–2006	Ariel Sharon Prime Minister of Israel
2001	September 11 attack by Al Qaeda on the USA

2003	US–led invasion of Iraq; Saddam Hussein overthrown
2005	Hardliner Mahmoud Ahmadinejad elected president of Iran
2006	New Kadima Party becomes main partner in new Israeli government
2006	Hamas, the Islamist and rejectionist party, wins the Palestinian elections

GLOSSARY

al–Fatah: conquest.

al–Jabr: restoration, the origin of the word 'algebra'.

al–Salaf al–Salih: the venerable ancestors.

ayatollah: a Shiite Muslim term for a senior legal interpreter of the Quran, not a clergyman in the Western sense but a religious authority with similar stature. There is no equivalent in Sunni Islam.

Bayt al–Hikmah: the House of Wisdom – the place of learning established in Baghdad by the Abbasid Caliphs.

colons **(French):** the French settlers in Algeria.

cuneiform: an early form of alphabet created by the Sumerians.

Dar al–Harb: the realm or abode of war used to refer to areas not ruled by Islamic law.

Dar al–Islam: the realm of Islam – the lands under the rule of Islam, past as well as present.

Dar al–Salaam: the realm of Peace – a newer concept, a realm where there is neither war nor Islamic control.

dervishme: the unpopular Ottoman practice of kidnapping Christian boys, converting them to Islam, and training them as administrators.

dhimmis: non-Islamic protected peoples.

Faqih: Supreme Leader, or interpreter of the Quran.

fatwa: a religious pronouncement; a ruling on a point of Islamic law given by a recognized authority.

ferengi: Franks – the word used for all Crusaders.

fiqh: man-made justice.

Hadith: the recorded non-Quranic sayings of the Prophet.

Haj: the pilgrimage to Mecca, which all Muslims should make at least once.

haraka: the Islamic movement. The word is often used as a political term.

Harakat al-Tahrir al-Filistani: The Movement for the Liberation of Palestine.

hijra or (in Latin) **hegira:** the flight of Muhammad from Mecca to Medina in AD 622.

IDF: the Israeli Defence Force.

ijtihad: exercising individual interpretation as regards Muslim doctrine.

Intifada: literally means 'uprising' and refers to the Palestinian rebellion against Israeli rule since the late 1990s.

jahili: un-Islamic.

jahiliyya: ignorance of Islam.

jihad: a personal or military struggle. The term is often used to describe an Islamic holy war against unbelievers.

millet: the Ottoman system, in which everyone was classified by their religion, rather than by their ethnicity (except Jews, since theirs was a dual category).

mujadid: an interpreter of Islam.

outremer: means 'beyond the sea' and is the name given by the Crusaders to their territories in the Holy Land.

PLO: the Palestinian Liberation Organization, the main nationalist vehicle for Palestinian independence until Hamas won the elections of 2006. The PLO is essentially secular though most of its members are Muslims.

Rashidun: the 'Rightly Guided Caliphs', successors of Muhammad.

RSS: an extremist Hindu organization in India said to be responsible for the murder of Mahatma Gandhi.

salaf: the revered ancestors of the first Islamic century.

salafiyya or salafi: the disciples of the ancestors and the followers of the Golden Age of Islam.

SAVAK: the name for the secret police during the reign of the last Shah of Iran.

sharia: God-given Islamic law based on the Quran. In Saudi Arabia, it is part of the constitution. As it is God-given, it cannot be disputed.

Sharifs: bona fide descendants of the Prophet.

Shia't Ali: now known as the Shia, and its adherents as Shiites. About 15 per cent of Muslims worldwide are Shiites, mainly in Iran and southern Iraq.

Shiism: the practice of Shia Islam, those Muslims awaiting the return of the Hidden Imam.

sunna: the example of the life of Muhammad. The term is not to be confused with Sunni, the 85 per cent of Muslims who agree with the authority of the first four Caliphs.

sura: a section of the Quran.

Tanakh **(Hebrew):** the Scriptures, also known as the Old Testament.

UAR: the United Arab Republic – the temporary union of Egypt and Syria in 1958, which lasted until the withdrawal of Syria in 1961.

ulema: the Muslim name for collective legal experts.

umma: the new Islamic community.

untermenschen **(German):** a Nazi term meaning 'under men' used to describe Slavs, Jews and other races the Nazis persecuted.

vilayet **(Turkish):** an administrative province in the Ottoman Empire.

Wafd: Egyptian Arab nationalists. The term literally means 'delegation'.

BIBLIOGRAPHY

Note

Inclusion in this bibliography means that I used the book – given the controversial and highly polemical nature of Middle East studies, inclusion does not therefore imply agreement. What follows is a selection of the numerous books read – and if I had included all the articles, the bibliography would have been three or four times as long.

Abdullah, Thabit, *A Short History of Iraq*, London and Harlow: Pearson Longman, 2003

Adelson, Roger, *London and the Invention of the Middle East*, New Haven CT: Yale University Press, 1996

Ahmed, Akbar, *Discovering Islam*, London: Routledge and Kegan Paul, 1988

———*Islam Today: A Short Introduction to the Muslim World*, London: IB Tauris, 1999

———*Islam Under Siege*, Cambridge: Polity Press, 2003

Ahmed, Akbar and Brian Forst, eds, *After Terror*, Cambridge: Polity Press, 2005

Akbar, M.J., *Shade of Swords: Jihad and the Conflict between Islam and Christianity*, London: Routledge, 2002

Allen, Charles, *God's Terrorists: The Wahhabi Cult and the Hidden Roots of Modern Jihad*, London: Little, Brown, 2006

Allen, Sir Richard, *Imperialism and Nationalism in the Fertile Crescent*, New York: Oxford University Press, 1974

Anderson, Benedict, *Imagined Communities*, London: Verso, 1991

Arab World Human Development Report, UN sponsored (152)

Armstrong, Karen, *A History of God*, New York: Ballantine, 1993

———*Islam: A Short History*, London: Weidenfeld and Nicolson, 2000

———*Muhammad: A Biography of the Prophet*, London: Phoenix, 2001

Asher, Michael, *Lawrence: The Uncrowned King of Arabia*, London: Viking, 1998

Assayas, Michka, *Bono: In Conversation with Michka Assayas*, New York: Riverhead Books, 2005

Ayoub, Mahmoud, *The Crisis of Muslim History: Religion and Politics in Early Islam*, Oxford: One World Publications, 2003

———*Islam: Faith and History*, Oxford: One World Publications, 2004

Balakian, Peter, *The Burning Tigris*, London: HarperCollins, 2003

Bard, Mitchell, *The Complete Idiot's Guide to the Middle East Conflict* (2nd edition), New York: Pearson Education, 2003

Benjamin, Daniel and Steven Simon, *The Age of Sacred Terror*, New York: Random House, 2002

Bergen, Peter, *Holy War Inc.*, London: Weidenfeld and Nicolson, 2001

Berger, Peter, ed., *The Desecularization of the World: Resurgent Religion and World Politics*, Grand Rapids MI: William B Erdmans, 1999

Berman, Paul, *Terror and Liberalism*, New York: Norton, 2003

Bloom, Jonathan and Sheila Blair, *Islam: A Thousand Years of Faith and Power*, New Haven CT: Yale University Press, 2002

Bonney, Richard, *Jihad: From Qur'an to bin Laden*, Basingstoke: Palgrave, 2004

Bregman, Ahron and Jihan El-Tahri, *The Fifty Years War: Israel and the Arabs*, London: BBC Books and Penguin, 1998

Brotton, Jeremy, *The Renaissance Bazaar: From the Silk Road to Michelangelo*, Oxford: Oxford University Press, 2002

Burke, Jason, *Al Qaeda: Casting a Shadow of Terror*, London: IB Tauris, 2003

Buruma, Ian, *Occidentalism: The West in the Eyes of Its Enemies*, London: Penguin, 2004

Busch, Briton Cooper, *Britain, India and the Arabs 1914–1921*, Berkeley and Los Angeles CA: University of California Press, 1971

Cambridge Medieval History, Volume IV: *The Eastern Roman Empire*, planned by J. B. Bury, Cambridge: Cambridge University Press, 1923

Carson, D.A., ed., et al., *The New Bible Commentary: 21st Century Edition*, Downers Grove IL: InterVarsity Press, 1994

Carter, Jimmy, *Our Endangered Values*, New York: Simon and Schuster, 2004

Catherwood, Christopher, *A Crash Course on Church History*, London: Hodder and Stoughton, 1998

——*Why the Nations Rage: Killing in the Name of God*, Lanham MD: Rowman and Littlefield, 2002

——*Christians Muslims and Islamic Rage*, Grand Rapids MI: Zondervan, 2003

——*Winston's Folly*, London: Constable & Robinson, 2004

Cook, M.A., *Muhammad (Past Masters)*, Oxford: Oxford University Press, 1996

——*The Koran: A Very Short Introduction*, Oxford: Oxford University Press, 2000

Corbin, Jane, *The Base: In Search of Al Qaeda*, London: Simon & Schuster, 2002

Crone, Patricia, and M.A. Cook, *Hagarism: The Making of the Islamic World*, London: Macmillan, 1997

Dawood, N.J., ed., *The Koran*, London: Penguin Classics, 2003

Doran, Michael Scott, 'Someone Else's Civil War' in *Foreign Affairs*, January/February 2002, and in *How Did This Happen?* ed. Gideon Rose, London: HarperCollins, 2001, pp. 31–52

Esposito, John, ed., *The Oxford History of Islam*, Oxford: Oxford University Press, 1999

——*The Islamic Threat: Myth or Reality?* (2nd edition) Oxford: Oxford University Press, 1995

——*Islam: The Straight Path* (3rd edition), Oxford: Oxford University Press, 1998

——*Unholy War: Terror in the Name of Islam*, Oxford: Oxford University Press, 2002

——*What Everyone Needs to Know About Islam*, Oxford: Oxford University Press, 2002

Fellure, Jacob, *The Everything Middle East Book*, Avon MA: Adams Media, 2004

Firestone, Reuven, *Jihad: The Origin of Holy War in Islam*, Oxford and New York: Oxford University Press, 1999

Fitzsimmons, M. A., *Empire by Treaty: Britain and the Middle East in the Twentieth Century*, London: Ernest Benn, 1965

Fletcher, Richard, *The Cross and the Crescent: Christianity and Islam from Muhammad to the Reformation*, London: Allen Lane, 2003

Friedman, Thomas, *From Beirut to Jerusalem* (rev. edition), New York: Anchor Books, 1995

Fromkin, David, *A Peace to End All Peace*, New York: Henry Holt, 1989

Fukuyama, Francis, *The End of History*, London: Hamish Hamilton, 1992

Geisler, Norman, *When Critics Ask*, Grand Rapids MI: Baker Book House, 1992

Gelvin, James L., *The Modern Middle East: A History*, New York: Oxford University Press, 2005

Glain, Stephen, *Dreaming of Damascus*, London: John Murray, 2003

Goldhagen, Daniel, *Hitler's Willing Executioners*, London: Little, Brown, 1996

Goldschmidt Jr, Arthur, *A Concise History of the Middle East*, (5th edition) Boulder CO: Westview Press, 1996

Goody, Jack, *Islam in Europe*, Cambridge: Polity Press, 2004

Gorenberg, Gershom, *The End of Days: Fundamentalism and the Struggle for the Temple Mount* (2nd edition), New York: Oxford University Press, 2002

Gunaratna, Rohan, *Inside Al Qaeda*, London: C. Hurst & Co., 2002

Hamilton, Jill, Duchess of, *God, Guns and Israel*, Stroud: Sutton Publishing, 2004

Hastings, Adrian, *The Construction of Nationhood: Ethnicity, Religion and Nationalism*, Cambridge: Cambridge University Press, 1997

Hodgson, Marshall, *The Venture of Islam* (3 vols), Chicago IL: University of Chicago Press, 1974

Hoge, James, and Gideon Rose, eds, *How Did This Happen: Terrorism and the New War*, New York: Public Affairs, 2001

Holt, P.M., Bernard Lewis and A. Lambton, eds, *The Cambridge History of Islam* (two volume version), Cambridge: Cambridge University Press, 1970

Hornung, Eric, *Akhenhaten and the Religion of Light*, Ithica NY: Cornell University Press, 2001

Hourani, Albert, *Emergence of the Modern Middle East*, London: Macmillan, 1981

——*A History of the Arab Peoples*, Cambridge MA: Belknap Press, 1991

Huntington, Samuel, *The Clash of Civilizations*, London: Simon and Schuster, 1996

IVP Bible Dictionary, Leicester: InterVarsity Press, 1980

James, Peter, *Centuries of Darkness*, London: Jonathan Cape, 1991

Janowski, James, *Egypt: A Short History*, Oxford: Oneworld Publications, 2000

Jenkins, Philip, *The Next Christendom*, Oxford and New York: Oxford University Press, 2002

Johnson, Paul, *A History of the Jews*, London: Weidenfeld and Nicolson, 1987

Juergensmeyer, Mark, *The New Cold War? Religious Nationalism Confronts the Secular State*, Berkeley and London: University of California Press, 1993

————*Terror in the Mind of God*, Berkeley and Los Angeles: University of California Press, 2000

Karsh, Efraim, *Islamic Imperialism*, New Haven CT and London: Yale University Press, 2006

Karsh, Efraim, and Inari Karsh, *Empires of the Sand: The Struggle for Mastery in the Middle East 1789–1923*, Cambridge MA: Harvard University Press, 1999

Keay, John, *Sowing the Wind: The Seeds of Conflict in the Middle East*, London: John Murray, 2003

Kedourie, Elie, *The Chatham House Version*, London: Weidenfeld and Nicolson, 1970

————*Arabic Political Memoirs and Other Studies*, London: Frank Cass, 1974

Kennedy, Hugh, *The Early Abbasid Caliphate*, London: Croom Helm, 1981

————*The Prophet and the Age of the Caliphates*, Harlow: Longman, 1986

————*The Court of the Caliphs*, London: Weidenfeld and Nicolson, 2005

Kepel, Gilles, *The Revenge of God*, Cambridge: Polity Press, 1994

————*Jihad: The Trail of Political Islam*, Cambridge MA: Belknap Press, 2002

————*The War for Muslim Minds: Islam and the West*, Cambridge MA: Belknap Press, 2004

Klieman, Aaron, *Foundations of British Policy in the Middle East*, Baltimore MD: Johns Hopkins Press, 1970

Laquer, Walter, ed., *Voices of Terror*, New York: Source Books, 2004

Latourette, K. S., *A History of the Expansion of Christianity* (7 vols), London: Eyre and Spotiswoode, 1938–1945

Lawrence, T. E., *Seven Pillars of Wisdom*, privately printed, 1926 (in Cambridge University Library) and London: Jonathan Cape, 1935

Lewis, Bernard, *The Muslim Discovery of Europe*, New York: Norton, 1982

———*Islam and the West*, Oxford: Oxford University Press, 1993

———*Islam in History*, Chicago IL: Open Court Press, 1993

———*The Arabs in History* (6th edition), Oxford: Oxford University Press, 1993

———*Cultures in Conflict: Christians, Muslims and Jews in the Age of Discovery*, New York: Oxford University Press, 1995

———*The Middle East*, London: Weidenfeld and Nicolson, 1995

———*The Future of the Middle East*, London: Weidenfeld and Nicolson, 1997

———*What Went Wrong? Western Impact and Middle Eastern Response*, Oxford: Oxford University Press, 2002

———*The Crisis of Islam: Holy War and Unholy Terror*, London: Weidenfeld and Nicolson, 2003

———*The Assassins: A Radical Sect in Islam*, London: Phoenix, 2003

———*From Babel to Dragomans: Interpreting the Middle East*, London: Weidenfeld and Nicolson, 2004

Lippman, Thomas, *Understanding Islam* (2nd rev. edition), New York: Meridian, 1995

MacCulloch, Diarmaid, *Tudor Church Militant*, London: Allen Lane, 1999

Mack, Rosamond, *Bazaar to Piazza: Islamic Trade and Italian Art 1300–1600*, Berkeley and Los Angeles: University of California Press, 2002

Macmillan, Margaret, *Peacemakers*, London: John Murray, 2001

Manji, Irshad, *The Trouble with Islam*, Edinburgh: Mainstream Publishing, 2004

Mansfield, Peter and Nicholas Pelham, *A History of the Middle East*, Harmondsworth: Penguin, 2003

Mazower, Mark, *Salonica: City of Ghosts*, London: HarperCollins, 2004

McCarthy, Justin, *The Ottoman Peoples and the End of Empire*, London: Arnold, 2001

McDougall, Walter, *Promised Land, Crusader State*, Boston MA: Houghton Mifflin, 1997

Miller, Judith, *God Has Ninety-Nine Names*, London: Simon and Schuster, 1999

Montgomery, Robert L., *The Lopsided Spread of Christianity: Towards an Understanding of the Diffusion of Religions*, Westport CT: Praeger, 2002

Napoleoni, Loretta, *Modern Jihad*, London: Pluto Press, 2003

Ostler, Nicholas, *Empires of the Word: A Language History of the World*, London: HarperCollins, 2005

Ovendale, Ritchie, *The Longman Companion to the Middle East since 1914* (2nd edition), London: Longman, 1998

Palmer, Alan, *The Decline and Fall of the Ottoman Empire*, New York: Barnes and Noble Books, 1994

Pape, Robert, *Dying to Win: The Strategic Logic of Suicide Terrorism*, New York: Random House, 2005

Qutb, Sayyid, Arabic title trans. as *Signposts Along the Road* (sometimes translated as *Milestones*) and *Islam: Religion of the Future*, distributed by the Islamic Book Service, Texas

Rashid, Ahmed, *The Arabs in History* (6th edition), Oxford: Oxford University Press, 1993

——*Taliban*, New Haven CT: Yale University Press, 2000

——*Jihad: The Rise of Militant Islam in Central Asia*, New Haven CT: Yale University Press, 2002

Renfrew, Colin, *Archaeology and Language*, London: Jonathan Cape, 1987

Renfrew, Colin and Peter Bellwood, eds, *Examining the Farming/Language Dispersal Hypothesis* (selected papers from 2001 symposium), Cambridge: McDonald Institute, 2002

Riddell, Peter and Peter Cotterell, *Islam in Conflict: Past, Present, Future*, Leicester: InterVarsity Press, 2003

Riley-Smith, Jonathan, *What were the Crusades?*, Basingstoke: Macmillan, 1992

Robinson, Francis, ed., *The Cambridge Illustrated History of the Islamic World*, Cambridge: Cambridge University Press, 1996

Robinson, Ronald and John Gallagher, *Africa and the Victorians*, London: Macmillan, 1961

Rohl, David, *Test of Time*, London: Century, 1995

Rushdie, Salman, *The Satanic Verses*, London: Viking, 1998

Ruthven, Malise, *Islam in the World* (2nd edition), Oxford: Oxford University Press, 2000

————*A Fury for God: The Islamist Attack on America*, London: Granta, 2002

————*Fundamentalism: The Search for Meaning*, Oxford: Oxford University Press, 2004

Sachar, Howard, *The Emergence of the Middle East, 1914–1924*, New York: Knopf, 1969

Said, Edward, *Orientalism*, London: Penguin, 2003

————*Covering Islam*, Pantheon Books, 2003

Saikal, Amin, *Islam and the West*, Basingstoke: Palgrave, 2003

Sanneh, Lamin, *Piety and Power*, Maryknoll NY: Orbis, 1996

Sawar, Muhammad and Brandon Toporov, *The Complete Idiot's Guide to the Koran*, New York: Pearson Education, 2003

Scheuer, Michael, *Through Our Enemies' Eyes and Imperial Hubris: Why the West is Losing the War on Terror*, Washington DC: Potomac Books, 2006 and 2005

Schulze, Reinhard, *A Modern History of the Islamic World*, London: IB Tauris, 2000

Scruton, Roger, *The West vs. the Rest*, London: Continuum, 2002

Shadid, Anthony, *The Legacy of the Prophet*, Boulder CO: Westview Press, 2001

Sicker, Martin, *The Arabs in History* (6th edition), Oxford: Oxford University Press, 1993

————*The Islamic World in Ascendancy*, Westport CT: Praeger, 2000

————*The Pre-Islamic Middle East*, Westport CT: Praeger, 2000

————*The Islamic World in Decline*, Westport CT: Praeger, 2001

————*The Middle East in the Twentieth Century*, Westport CT: Greenwood, 2001

Simons, Geoff, *Iraq: From Sumer to Post-Saddam*, Basingstoke: Palgrave, 2004

Smith, Anthony, *Chosen Peoples*, Oxford: Oxford University Press, 2003

Spencer, Robert, *The Politically Incorrect Guide to Islam (and the Crusades)*, Washington DC: Regnery, 2005

Stern, Jessica, *Terror in the Name of God: Why Religious Militants Kill*, New York: Ecco, 2003

Stott, John, *The Christian Counter-Culture*, Leicester: InterVarsity Press, 1978

Taymiyya, Ibn, *The Goodly Word* (translated and abridged by Ezzedin Ibrahim and Denys Johnson-Davies), Cambridge: Islamic Texts Society, 2003

Tibi, Bassam, *The Challenge of Fundamentalism: Political Islam and the New World Disorder*, Berkeley and Los Angeles: University of California Press, 1998

————*Islam between Culture and Politics*, Basingstoke: Palgrave, 2001

Tripp, Charles, *A History of Iraq*, Cambridge: Cambridge University Press, 2000

Viorst, Milton, *In the Shadow of the Prophet: The Struggle for the Soul of Islam*, Boulder CO: Westview Press, 2001

Waines, David, *An Introduction to Islam*, Cambridge: Cambridge University Press, 1995

Wallis, Jim, *God's Politics*, Oxford: Lion Hudson, 2006

Walls, Andrew, *The Cross-Cultural Process in Christian History*, Edinburgh: T&T Clark, 2002

Watterson, Barbara, *The Egyptians*, Oxford: Blackwell, 1997

Wells, Colin, *The Complete Idiot's Guide to Understanding Saudi Arabia*, New York: Pearson Education, 2003

Wheatcroft, Andrew, *Infidels: The Conflict between Christendom and Islam 638–2002*, London: Viking Press, 2003

Wright, Melanie, *Moses in America: The Cultural Uses of Biblical Narrative*, New York: Oxford University Press, 2002

Yapp, Malcolm, *The Making of the Modern Middle East 1792–1923*, Harlow: Longman, 1998

Ye'or, Bat, *The Decline of Eastern Christianity under Islam: From Jihad to Dhimmitude*, Cranbury NJ: Associated University Presses, 1996

——*Islam and Dhimmitude: Where Civilizations Collide*, Cranbury NJ: Associated University Presses, 2002

Zadeh, Firooz, *Islam versus Terrorism*, Twin Lakes: Twin Lakes CO, 2003

ACKNOWLEDGEMENTS

While most authors end their acknowledgements with thanks to their patient spouse, I always begin mine with warmest possible thanks to my wife. Let me therefore give profoundest thanks to Paulette. She is my constant inspirer, soulmate, muse, moral support and much more besides.

Editors often get thanked rather late in the traditional acknowledgements as well. So let me express warmest gratitude to my splendid editor at Constable, Becky Hardie. Her patience, along with her excellent comments on the text, is something for which I am most grateful. I must also thank her predecessor, Nicola Chalton, who commissioned this book and who now runs her own company. She was vital in putting together the synopsis that formed the basis of what you have just read.

Warmest thanks also go to Becky's equally helpful editorial colleague, Hannah Boursnell, who did a splendid job wrestling with the original manuscript. The same is true of my wonderful copy-editor Andrew Maxwell-Hyslop, to whom I am very grateful. Any remaining errors are my responsibility, not his.

The genesis of this book was a conversation at the Constable & Robinson booth at the London International Book Fair with Andy Hayward of Constable and Richard Reynolds, an award-winning buyer at Heffers in Cambridge. I am greatly obliged to them both.

This book was written in two most congenial settings. The first was the fifteenth-century attic of my parents' mainly early-nineteenth-century house in Balsham, just outside Cambridge. The other is the Douglas Freeman Office for visiting professors in the History Department of the University of Richmond in Richmond, Virginia.

My warm gratitude to my parents, Fred and Elizabeth Catherwood, is naturally profound and lifelong.

But over the past ten years I have also become indebted to the faculty and staff of the University of Richmond, where I have been a Writer in Residence each summer in the History Department. Special thanks therefore go to Hugh West (the current Department Chair), his predecessor John Gordon, and to the legendary John Treadway, who has created a splendid office and bedroom in his house that operates as a home from home for me and for my wife every summer. Thanks in the History Department also go to Bob Kenzer, Kathy Fugett and Debbie Govoruhk.

I am also most grateful for the opportunity to teach students each year at the University of Richmond's Summer School through their School of Continuing Studies. Warmest thanks as always go to Pat Brown, David Kitchen, Jim Narduzzi and Cheryl Genovese, and to Michele Cox and Krittika Onsanit of the International Department. Thanks also at Richmond to Ellis Billups Jr and to Cindy Lloyd.

I have also benefited substantially from the assistance given to me by the staff firstly at the Boatwright Library, in particular Noreen Ann Cullen and Chris Kemp, and secondly at the excellent university bookshop, including Roger Brooks, Victoria Halman, Douglass Young, Sharon Crumley and Marina Scheidt.

In Cambridge I am as always grateful to St Edmund's College, in particular to the former Master, Sir Brian Heap, and his successor Professor Luzio, and to my colleagues Simon Mitton, Douglas Paul, Stephen Lynch, Geoffrey Cook, Brian Stanley and Moira Gardiner. I also teach for an American course based in Cambridge, INSTEP, which is linked to Wake Forest University, Tulane University, Rice University and several other institutions. Special thanks as well to Geoffrey Williams, the distinguished authority on geopolitical and strategic issues, and his wife Janice.

Many thanks this year also go to the distinguished former Director of the University's Centre of International Studies, Philip Towle. I am also pleased to acknowledge the many insights of my Oxford contemporary, Professor John Charmley, of the five-star ranked University of East Anglia's History Department. Final thanks among others to Mark Ashton, James and Camilla Ward, Rusty and Cynthia Booker, Lewis and Nancy Booker, Richard and Sally Reynolds, John and Susan Gordon, Sujit and Caroline Sivasundaram, Professor Larry and Beth Adams, Claude and Leigh Marshall, Professor A. E. Dick and Mary Howard, Professors Bill and Stephanie Black, Brock and Bodie Thoene, Professor Maggie Bailey, Drs Andrew Kearsley and Jonquil Drinkwater, Andrew and Clare Whittaker, and Lamar and Betsy Weaver.

My father-in-law John Moore was, like my parents and his daughter, Paulette, the very model of warmth, kindness, and encouragement. Many of the books used were read in his welcoming apartment, and his scholarly eye has been invaluable. I am sad that he died just as I was finishing the manuscript of this book, about which he knew and was most supportive.

Christopher Catherwood
Summer 2006

Further Acknowledgements

When I first started writing the original of this book, Colonel Simon Tustin was at CENTCOM in Baghdad, as part of the coalition forces. He is now Colonel Dr Simon Tustin, and a schoolteacher in Sharnbrook Upper School in Bedfordshire. He very kindly incorporated my book into his curriculum, and has had me to speak to his pupils: I am most grateful to him and to them for making this possible. I have also taught Middle Eastern history for the Cambridge Education Group's Pre-Masters programme at Cambridge Arts and Sciences: I am most grateful to Howard Warren, Dorothy Hawkins and Claire Stanfield for making this such an enjoyable experience. Finally, I have taught this subject at the University of Richmond, and my gratitude to those thanked elsewhere in these acknowledgements continues to be profound.

I also have a new editor for this edition at Constable & Robinson in Leo Hollis. I am most grateful to him for commissioning this update, and to say that working on a history title with someone who is a trained historian and author in his own right has been a rare privilege and pleasure: an eagle-eyed editor who knows what he is talking about. Warmest thanks must also go to Jo Stansall, and to copy-editor Jenny Doubt, for their careful work on the text: a wise author always accepts their copy-editor's wisdom!

My earlier acknowledgements paid proper tribute to the wonderful staff of the University of Richmond, in Richmond VA. I have now had the additional pleasure of teaching this book as a course there, and my gratitude to that great place continues to be profound. I have also taught this as an INSTEP course in Cambridge, to pupils from Tulane University and Hampden Sydney College, and my thanks to the splendid couple that run INSTEP, Geoffrey and Janice Williams, is as full as ever.

Sadly since the original edition Mark Ashton has died: my gratefulness to him runs deep. My parents sold their home eleven miles outside Cambridge, and I now write most of my books in the magnificent setting of the Churchill Archives Centre at Churchill College, the institution that was established as the Commonwealth's thank offering to Sir Winston Churchill in 1960. I was elected an Archive By-Fellow for 2008, and have been an Associate of their Senior Combination Room since that term expired.

So I am, as always, profoundly grateful to all the wonderfully kind, patient and ever friendly Archives staff, from the Director Allen Packwood on through to all the full-time employees here: Andrew Riley, Natalie Adams, Katherine Thompson and Sophie Bridges – whom I have been glad to get to know along with her equally delightful partner Patrick

– Dr Lynsey Robertson and especially Caroline Herbert, who will have moved to London with her husband Peter by the time this new edition is published. Thank you also to the less-often seen staff: the conservator, Sarah Lewery, her assistant Bridget Warrington and, last but not least, Julie Sanderson, the administrator.

Christopher Catherwood
Cambridge, June 2010

INDEX

A Brief History of the Crimean War
Alexis Troubetzkoy

In September 1854, the armies of Britain, France and Turkey invaded Russia, ostensibly over disputed access to the holy sites of Jerusalem. But few wars in history reveal greater confusion of purpose than this 'notoriously incompetent international butchery' (Hobsbawm). In the months that followed over half a million soldiers died from wounds, disease, starvation and sheer cold. We all know of the heroic folly of the Charge of the Light Brigade.

The Crimean War was a medieval conflict fought in a modern age. This new account by a Russian historian shows that the extraordinary struggle was fought not only in the Crimea, but also along the Danube, in the Arctic Ocean, in the Baltic and Pacific.

Much has been written about the war itself and Troubetzkoy does not aim to cover old ground, but traces its true causes and sketches a vivid picture of the age up to the Allies' departure for the Crimea. Woven with developments in diplomacy, trade and nationalistic expression are descriptions of the Russian, Turkish and British armies and the principal players – Napoleon III, Marshal St Arnaud, Lord Raglan, the great Russian engineer Todleban, Florence Nightingale and Nicholas I.

A Brief History of Globalization
Alexander MacGillivray

Our planet is shrinking – what does that mean for us?

Globalization is one of the most over-used and least understood words in the world today. To deny it, says Nelson Mandela, is 'like saying I do not recognize winter'. The accelerating political, economic, cultural and environmental interconnections that it describes are powerful and controversial. But what does it really mean?

Ever since Pythagoras first imagined the world as a sphere revolving around the sun, our planet has been shrinking. This book covers all angles, from fifteenth-century exploration to the rise of the multi-national corporation; from the Great Wall of China to the birth of the football World Cup. Offering a clear guide to the complex economics behind the controversies, Alex MacGillivray gives equal play to technology and culture, politics and war.

A Brief History of Hitmen and Assassinations
Richard Belfied

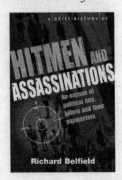

'This chilling account of political murder is a must-have.'
John Hughes-Wilson, author of *The Puppet Masters*

We live in a new age of political assassination; in the last fifty years all the senior members of the UN Security Council have used it as an extension of political policy in every corner of the globe. In each case, the orders came from the very top. Today, while leading governments use covert operations, drones and laser-guided missiles, terrorist car bombs and suicide bombers make the game increasingly dangerous.

In this compelling exposé of hitmen, assassinations and the men who contract them, Richard Belfield uncovers a hidden world of killers and cover-ups, from Julius Caesar to the present day, and how they changed the course of history.

Here are the true stories behind some of the most shocking assassinations in recent history.

- How the assassination of President Sadat of Egypt launched Al Qaeda
- Why JFK ordered the death of President Diem of Vietnam
- Revealing excerpts from CIA and Al Qaeda manuals

A Brief History of the Holy Grail
Giles Morgan

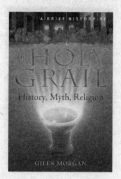

The myths and history of the Holy Grail revealed

A Brief History of the Holy Grail charts the origins of this story from early Christian gospels through to Eastern mysticism and the rise of medieval romances and Arthurian legends. The Grail reappears once more in the story of the Crusades and in particular the rise and dramatic fall of the Knights Templar, who it is said were the guardians of the cup, newly discovered in Jerusalem.

The myths have been more powerful than the facts and the allure of the Grail has attracted the attention of modern writers and artists in search of an ancient symbol of purity. Psychologist Carl Jung, composer Richard Wagner, poets William Blake and T. S. Eliot, and the Pre-Raphaelite painters have all been seduced by the legend. Today the Grail quest can be found in films such as *Lord of the Rings*, *Star Wars*, *Indiana Jones* and *Excalibur*, as well as Dan Brown's *Da Vinci Code*, which revived a radical reinterpretation of the myth. Giles Morgan's fascinating exploration on the myth and history of the Grail is an essential read.

A Brief History of the War of the Roses
Desmond Seward

'A brilliant study of the period. Rich in historical detail, yet passionately written, the smell of battle seems to linger on the page.' *Yorkshire Post*

During the fifteenth century (c.1455-85) England was riven in bloody conflict between the houses of York and Lancaster over who should claim the crown. Out of this bitter war between the white rose and the red, the Tudor dynasty eventually came to power. In this thrilling account, acclaimed historian Desmond Seward maps the trials of five men and women who experienced the upheaval first-hand, interwoven with the key events of a great turning point in British history.

'It is hard to imagine a historian more in command of his subject, or better able to bring it howling and thundering to life.' *Independent*

'This [is a] splendidly and vividly written book.' *Evening Standard*

A Brief History of Mankind
Cyril Aydon

The history of us – humanity's great moments of civilization and discovery

From the moment our ancestors took their first tentative steps out of Africa, to the day human beings set foot on the moon; from the building of the pyramids to the designing of the world wide web, Aydon's entertaining and informative account takes us through the key periods of our history.

Informed by the latest historical and archaeological research, the focus is not on conventional kings and queens, battles and politics, but developments that have shaped our lives around the globe: the Neolithic revolution in agriculture, the invention of writing, the rise and fall of empires, the birth of great religions, the industrial revolution. Now, as the world shows signs of damage from our actions, Aydon considers whether Homo sapiens have changed, or if we remain Stone Age people living in a Techno Age.

'Full of good sense and written with an engaging lucidity and wit.' *BBC History Magazine*

'Marvellous and immensely readable.' *Good Book Guide*